GOD

|CENTERED|

BIBLICAL
INTERPRETATION

VERN S. POYTHRESS

GOD

~⊶~

|CENTERED|

BIBLICAL
INTERPRETATION

P&R PUBLISHING

P.O. BOX 817 • PHILLIPSBURG • NEW JERSEY 08865-0817

Composition by Colophon Typesetting

Printed in the United States of America

Library of Congress Cataloging-in-Publication Data

Poythress, Vern S.
    God-centered biblical interpretation / Vern Sheridan Poythress.
        p.   cm.
    Includes bibliographical references and index.
    ISBN 0-87552-376-5 (pbk.)
    1. Bible—Hermeneutics.   I. Title.
BS476.P68   1999
    220.6′01—dc21   98-53148

To my parents,
God's greatest blessing to me during the earliest
times when he was at work in my life

CONTENTS

Contents

Contents

.

CHAPTER I

THE CHALLENGE OF UNDERSTANDING THE BIBLE

On the campus of Commoner College, Libbie Liberal has invited her friends together for a discussion of the Bible.

Libbie Liberal: *I'm glad to see you here. The Bible is really a stimulating book for me. I hope you will experience the same thing as we look at it together. My favorite character is Jesus, and today we will be discussing a passage that talks about him. He is such an inspiring person because he reminds me of how God loves everyone and accepts everyone as his child. He encourages me to believe in the preciousness of humanity and the ultimate goodness underneath even the most forbidding exterior. I hope you feel the same way.*

Is everyone here? Let's see. Where is Heidi Hedonist?

Natalie Naturalist: *She's gone to the beach with her latest boyfriend.*

Liberal: *What about Ivan Indifferent?*

Roland Relativist: *He's hanging out in the game room.*

Liberal: *Well, we'd better begin. The passage for today is Luke 4:31–37. Norma, would you read it for us?*

Norma Narratologist: *Sure. It says, "Then he went down to Capernaum, a town in Galilee, and on the Sabbath began to teach the people. They were amazed at his teaching, because his message had authority.*

"In the synagogue there was a man possessed by a demon, an evil spirit. He cried out at the top of his voice, 'Ha! What do you want with us, Jesus of Nazareth? Have you come to destroy us? I know who you are—the Holy One of God!'

" 'Be quiet!' Jesus said sternly. 'Come out of him!' Then the demon threw the man down before them all and came out without injuring him.

"All the people were amazed and said to each other, 'What is this teaching? With authority and power he gives orders to evil spirits and they come out!' And the news about him spread throughout the surrounding area."

Liberal: *Now let's discuss it. What's your reaction?*

Naturalist: *It shows what I've always suspected: the Bible comes from primitive, superstitious times. People attributed natural phenomena like mental illness to demons and occult forces. They used God and the supernatural to allay their fears. Then science came along and gave us the true explanation of how the world works. I would guess that Jesus had some kind of personal influence that helped those who were mentally ill, and then people exaggerated it into a story about an evil spirit.*

Liberal: *Isn't Jesus' concern for the mentally ill inspiring!*

Naturalist: *Well, at least he tried to help them. But he was a person of his own times, and probably believed a lot of that superstitious stuff himself. I really don't see what's so exciting, Libbie. Everything of significance can be found in a much more enlightened form in modern scientific thinking.*

Carol Critical-Method: *It is still illuminating to apply modern historical methods to ancient documents. I've been doing some research. We can establish that this story was once transmitted as an oral tale during the period of the early church. It belongs to the category "miracle story" and the subcategory "exorcism." The early church used it to reinforce its claim that Jesus had divine power and to confirm the authority of its teaching, which it claimed was derived from the Master. But as people passed on the story, they introduced changes and embellishments over time. There is probably some historical core to this story. But it is so typical of the genre that it would be impossible to be dogmatic. We really don't know what happened.*

Naturalist: *So why should we bother to discuss this story?*

Danny Demythologizer: *Wait a minute. Don't dismiss the story out of hand. Martin Heidegger and Rudolf Bultmann, two of our outstanding modern thinkers, showed us that mythical stories like this one can still have a hidden message for us today. The man possessed by a demon is a picture of every individual who is alienated from God and therefore alienated from his fellow human beings. He lives a confused, inauthentic life, in bondage to hidden psychic powers that he does not acknowledge. Then he meets Jesus. Jesus shows that authentic, free living can be achieved by communion with God. Jesus calls him out from the alienation that fears death and hidden powers. He moves him into the joy of* loving and respecting others. Through this call of Jesus, people can still have an existential encounter with God today. People in the ancient world expressed these truths in mythical form, because that was part of their culture. Our culture is different, but the fundamental human struggles are still the same.

Theo Therapist: I feel that Danny is onto something. But he is still too caught up with the religion thing. Sure, the culture back then was different. But what is the same is the need for self-esteem. This guy described as demon possessed must have had low self-esteem. He was kind of weird, and so everybody despised him and called him names. They began to say that he was demon possessed. This accusation only made him worse. Because of the power of suggestion, he began to believe it himself, and acted more and more in the way that other people expected a demon-possessed man to act. Jesus broke the power of his psychic dysfunction by affirming him. Jesus distinguished between the man himself and the picture of low self-esteem that others had imposed (symbolized by the demonic voice).

Newton New-Ager: Theo, you're right. In a sense, it all has to do with self-esteem. But what is this self that we are supposed to esteem? Do most people really know? We rush around with trivial kinds of busyness. We never stop to meditate and discover who we really are. Psychotherapy can help people part of the way. But in my experience it does not touch the deepest recesses of the self. Those deepest recesses are spiritual.

When I started exploring my spiritual self, I began to see that mysterious spiritual forces are at work in a lot of areas. I've started trying to get into contact with spiritual forces. I grew in self-esteem only when I really began to discover my inner divine self. I think Jesus knew something about this secret. Doesn't the Bible say somewhere that Jesus was God? Well, we all have that divine spark within us. He manifested it much more fully. That gave him spiritual power. So I'm not so surprised that he had a deep spiritual influence on someone whose spiritual self was tangled up.

You know, if I studied the Bible some more, maybe Jesus could give me some tips about how to manifest my divine self.

Relativist: This discussion is a perfect illustration of the need for everyone to react to ideas in his or her own way. Each one of us has different ideas about this text. Each person sees the text against a different background of previous views and experiences. So the ideas are inevitably different. Sometimes our ideas are even opposite to each other's. How *much richer we are for appreciating everyone's point of view! We can all benefit from the Bible, or from any other book, by letting it stimulate our ideas. Each of you must discover what is true for you. Whatever works for you is true for you.*

Dick Deconstructionist: *Roland, people's reactions differ because language is always fluid, flexible, and inherently ambiguous. No one can affix a meaning once and for all to this passage. And no meaning, even if it could be fixed, could be passed on to someone else without changing it.*

Marvin Marxist: *But most of it is propaganda and power plays. Luke probably wrote this piece to buttress his authority and the authority of the church leaders of his day. The church offered deliverance for the disenfranchised classes, as symbolized by the demonized man. But once people were in the church, they had to submit to the authority of the leaders, as symbolized by Jesus.*

Liberal: *Oh, my! Our time is already up. And we haven't heard yet from Olivia Occultist, Norma Narratologist, Fay Feminist, or Susan Sociologist. Let's continue this discussion next week.*

Susan Sociologist: *I'd like to hear from Chris Christian, too. Can we get him to come?*

Liberal: *Well, to tell you the truth, I didn't invite him. He's so, uh, narrow, you know. He actually believes that the Bible is literally God's word and is completely true.*

(Laughter)

God is who he is, in all his power and mercy and majesty. He is supremely good and desirable (Pss. 16:11; 27:4; 34:8; 84:10–12). So why do we not see everyone eagerly seeking him and honoring him? In the West, many people are interested in spiritual things. The Bible is available in bookstores and hotel rooms. But people are largely bent on fleeing from him.

Why? In a sense, hostile responses are not new. Ever since sin entered the human race, people have been fleeing and hiding from God (Gen. 3:8!). They can do so even in religious practices (Judg. 2:11–13; Ezek. 8:9–18; Matt. 23). They can do so even when they are studying the Bible (Matt. 22:29).

But what is happening now in the West? What makes it possible for people to discuss the Bible as Libbie Liberal's group did?

Christianity has been practiced in the West for hundreds of years. In the course of that long history, Christians have committed plenty of horrendous sins and made ghastly mistakes that discredit the faith. Moreover, those antagonistic to the God of the Bible have, over a period of several centuries, produced a whole marketplace of culturally fashionable stratagems for evading God. Some are incredibly sophisticated and awesomely complex.[1] They include ways of immunizing ourselves from the Bible and its message. So we have plenty of ways to hide our spiritual nakedness.

Christians Reading the Bible

Within this atmosphere, we who are Christians can also be seduced. Like the naturalists, we can begin to read the Bible as a merely human book. Or, with secular psychotherapists, we can read it merely as one more source for advice: we can use it on our own terms to promote our self-esteem. Or, with New Age religion, we can search the Bible for stimulating thoughts about angels, demons, and altered states of consciousness. Or, with the hedonists, we can simply go on our pleasure-seeking way, without taking time to meditate on the word of God.

Maybe we have escaped these blatant distortions. But we may still carry more subtle distortions into our study of the Bible. As an illustration, let us break into another Bible discussion, this time among Christians.

In another room on the campus of Commoner College, Chris Christian is meeting with a group. The discussion happens to be focusing on the same passage, Luke 4:31–37.

Peter Pietist: *The central purpose of the Bible, and of Christianity as a whole, is to promote a life of intimate personal devotion to the Lord. In Luke 4:31–37, the Lord speaks with authority to the sinful tendencies in my heart. I react to him by acknowledging him, but also fearing him. He says to my sin, "Be quiet," and "Come out of him!" The passage promises that, as a result, I will be delivered. It tells me that I should be amazed at Jesus' work in my life, and that I should be zealous to tell others about my deliverance.*

Dottie Doctrinalist: *No, you are missing the point. The central purpose of the Bible, and of Christianity as a whole, is to promote sound doctrine. This passage teaches the deity of Christ by calling him "the Holy One of God" and by demonstrating his divine authority and power. It teaches that there is a realm of evil spirits, and that these spirits can take control of a person. But it also shows the sovereignty and the grace of God in delivering people from these spirits.*

Curt Cultural-Transformationist: *You are both missing the point. The central purpose of the Bible is to promote the transformation of the* world. This passage shows Christ transforming the world, so that we ourselves may engage in active transformation under the authority of Christ. The passage shows us the authority of Christ, not as a doctrinal abstraction, but as an active, powerful authority engaging in world transformation. The overthrow of the demonic realm and the entry of the Holy One with his power imply a reordering of political, social, aesthetic, and linguistic structures. The passage illustrates this reordering by speaking of the utter destruction of evil, the total change in the formerly demonized man, and the obvious social consequences in the reaction of the crowd and the people in the surrounding region. It energizes us to attack the demonized structures of evil in the institutions of our day.[2]

Laura Liturgist: The central purpose of the Bible is to restore true worship. Out of worship will flow healing that affects all of life. The passage sets forth a pattern for an order of worship: first, proclamation of the authority of God; then, awe and fear at the holiness of God; next, reception of the saving word of God; next, response of amazement and gratitude; finally, dismissal to go out to tell others.

Missy Missiologist: The story ends with the news spreading "throughout the surrounding area." That reminds us that our task is to spread the news of the gospel throughout the world. In some areas of the world, Christians have to engage in spiritual warfare against evil spirits and against demon-possessed people. This passage provides a basis for casting out demons when the missionary church comes up against the powers of darkness. We in the West tend to have a horizon that is too narrow. If we don't see demons in our own situation, we imagine that they don't exist. We imagine that our problems with personal piety or with corrupt institutions are the only ones out there. We have to hear what's going on in other parts of the world and in other cultures in order to see the full force of this passage.

Fatima Factualist: I think that we are letting our imaginations run away with us. The message is simple and obvious. The passage is just saying that these things happened when Jesus was on earth. The evidence of miracles shows that Jesus is who he claimed to be, and that the Bible is what it claims to be. It furnishes us with historical evidence with which to confront unbelievers.

Amy Affirmationist: You are all saying such wonderful things! I think everyone is right. The Holy Spirit can bring different messages to different people. Maybe the Spirit intends to minister in different ways to each person's need. He is speaking to each of us according to our needs. We don't need to be upset when people see different ideas in the same passage.

Oliver Objectivist: Amy, affirming everything is no solution at all. Look, we're in a pickle because we haven't got a clear objective when we read. Everybody is being swept along by his own prejudices. To have a clear objective, and for agreement even to be possible, there must be only one meaning to the passage. That meaning is the intention of Luke, the author. It is there objectively, for all time, before we start our discussion. Our task is to determine that meaning. Everything else belongs to what E. D. Hirsch calls "significances," that is, the relationships between the one meaning and our outside interests. These outside interests naturally differ from individual to individual. So there are many possible significances, but only one meaning. We have had a problem up to now because all of us have gone and looked for significances instead of the meaning. We have brought in our own personal agenda prematurely. First, we must look at the one meaning.[3]

Herman Hermeneut: Oliver, you want all of us to use your theory of meaning. But how do we know that your theory is right? Maybe it is only one more instance of the "prejudices" that you abhor.

Objectivist: My theory is right. It has to be right. It is the only way that we can hope to move beyond the prejudices that personal interests introduce.

Hermeneut: Your theory advocates focusing on the single, objective meaning. Peter Pietist would object that your theory intrinsically distorts interpretation by ignoring the essence of the matter, namely, personal fellowship with God. Curt Cultural-Transformationist would object that you distort interpretation by exalting theoretical knowledge over cultural action. Laura Liturgist would object that you wrongly prefer theoretical knowledge to worship. Missy Missiologist would object that your approach is monocultural. Amy Affirmationist would object that you have misjudged the work of the Spirit.

You have a preference for theoretical, objective meaning. They have preferences for various other things. So how is your preference any less "subjective" than theirs? What gives it any special claim to be free from all "prejudice"?

Objectivist: We must first study the Bible objectively. Only after that, as a second step, can we decide whether the Bible primarily promotes piety, doctrine, worship, or whatever. Whichever way the Bible points, we will follow. We will then adopt a life in conformity with its direction.

Hermeneut: I don't think that you understand deeply enough the others' viewpoints. From their viewpoints, the theory you propose involves not minor errors, but fundamental misjudgments that are bound to corrupt the entire process of interpretation. You think of your theory as a reliable vehicle for arriving at any destination to which the text may steer us. But we see your theory as a preprogrammed, computerized vehicle. It will frustrate anybody who tries to steer it over terrain that it does not recognize.

You want your theory to be a neutral arbiter among opinions. But to us, it represents one more opinion, one more point of view about the manner in which we understand the Bible. It seems to me to be just one more view alongside the others. So why should we adopt your point of view?

Objectivist: Because I am right and the rest are wrong!

Hermeneut: But can you show us so in an objective manner?

Objectivist: My approach is necessary if we are to decide among competing interpretations and attain the truth. If we pursue ten or a hundred different goals, we obviously get chaos. How do we get unity? We must accept that the author provides our control. He has one meaning that he has expressed. Determining his meaning is then the goal that we can all pursue. We argue methodically from the textual data in order to test our ideas of what this one meaning is.

Missiologist: People from non-Western cultures often do not agree with you. Not all cultures prize methodological control. They may not even see why you treasure a theory of objective meaning. For example, Asian cultures are more concerned with practice and life, not merely theoretical agreement.

Affirmationist: Objectivist, why not just trust that the Spirit will lead us all? Is your method superior to the Spirit? I will admit that your method may be something into which the Spirit has led you. But he may lead others in other ways.

Objectivist: Scholars agree that we must have objective control.

Hermeneut: Do they, now, all of them?

Objectivist: Well, scholarship these days is degenerating seriously around the edges. But scholars used to know that interpretation should be objective.

Hermeneut: Yes, the historical-critical school desired scientific objectivity. Did they achieve it?

Objectivist: No, they had a prejudice against miracles and the supernatural. We certainly have to free ourselves from that prejudice. We do so precisely in order to be objective. Many conservative scholars, and not just antisupernaturalist critics, agree that objective meaning and objective methods are necessary.

Hermeneut: Maybe scholars like your theory because it fits the inclinations of their profession. Scholars are occupied with issues of intellectual content and intellectual control. So they are occupationally comfortable with a theory that promotes their class interests.

Objectivist: I admit that the full-blown theory originates primarily from the scholarly world. But it is designed to describe in principle what everyone should be doing.

Hermeneut: But perhaps your theory of meaning has hidden prejudices against the nonscholarly origins of the views of Pietist and Affirmationist. Or are you prejudiced against Missiologist's non-Western cultures?

Objectivist: No, no, it's not prejudice; it's the truth.

Hermeneut: But according to your own desire to be objective, you must ground your claim in something deeper than your own preferences or the preferences of a select group of scholars.

Objectivist: (desperate): I will show you from the Bible.

Hermeneut: Very well. You will show us how your theory of meaning derives from the Bible?

Objectivist: Yes.

Hermeneut: And what principles of interpretation should we use as we proceed to study the Bible?

Objectivist: My objective principles, of course.

Hermeneut: But we do not yet agree to yours.

Objectivist: Well, I admit that is a problem.

Hermeneut: It's called the hermeneutical circle. We all have assumptions before we start. We must critically examine those assumptions. In order to appreciate our problem, let's read some advanced twentieth-century hermeneutical literature together.

Doctrinalist: Wait, Herman. I admit that you have given Objectivist a lot to think about. In fact, you have given us all something to think about. Much of what you have said applies not only to Objectivist, but to all of us, including you. We are all making assumptions, and we do not agree about what assumptions are most fitting. We do not agree about how to interpret the Bible. But neither could we agree about how to interpret the hermeneutical writings that you are so keen on. So how could those writings resolve our problem?

Pietist: Aren't unbelievers producing most of the "advanced hermeneutical literature"? If we read that stuff, we will probably fall victim to the spirit of false philosophies, as Hermeneut suspects Objectivist has done already. If we cut loose from the Bible in order to do *hermeneutical self-examination, we are just staring at our navels. We are no better than the Hindu gurus. I agree with Objectivist that we had better go to the Bible.*

Hermeneut: *But we don't agree on how to interpret it!*

Doctrinalist: *So what? The Bible will make itself clear. The Bible is self-interpreting. God has put within it sufficient directions to guide us in its interpretation, even if our first attempts are biased.*

Affirmationist: *And the Spirit will be with us.*

Strengthening the Foundations

People can do all kinds of crazy things with the Bible. But if we would profit spiritually, we must reckon with what God himself requires. Some ways of reading are right, and other ways are wrong. God himself speaks to us to indicate the difference: "Teach me, O LORD, to follow your decrees; then I will keep them to the end. Give me understanding, and I will keep your law and obey it with all my heart" (Ps. 119:33–34).

The Bible itself is our primary resource. But we also receive some help through other channels. We use our own previous experience in interpretation. Our fellowship in the church nourishes us spiritually. Those around us with gifts of teaching set an example. Any number of books give guidance on improving our practical skills.[4] But these secondary channels are all fallible. To some extent, they rely on an unsure foundation, namely, various popular theories and unexamined assumptions about language, meaning, history, and human nature. These assumptions may or may not be fully in accord with biblical truth. In fact, as we shall see in the course of this book, present-day thinking on the Bible needs radical reform.

It is thus worthwhile to reexamine foundational questions. Who is God? What is his relation to the Bible? What sort of things are the human languages in which the Bible is written? What is meaning? How does God expect us to respond to the Bible? What interpretive procedures do justice to the character of the Bible and our responsibility? In this book we reevaluate these foundations.

We leave it to other books to focus more on the step-by-step development of detailed skills. Those skills are important. But it is equally important that practical skills should operate within a framework and with a controlling direction set by the word of God. Otherwise, we may find ourselves like the foolish man in Jesus' parable, the man who built his house without a foundation on rock (Matt. 7:24–27).

ENDNOTES

1. For a popularized account of the process, see the works of Francis A. Schaeffer, especially *Escape from Reason* (Downers Grove, Ill.: InterVarsity, 1968) and *The God Who Is There* (Chicago: InterVarsity, 1968).

2. The idea for these three types of approach came from Nicholas Wolterstorff, "The AACS in the CRC," *Reformed Journal* 24, no. 10 (December 1974), 9–16.

3. E. D. Hirsch, *Validity in Interpretation* (New Haven: Yale University Press, 1967).

4. One of the best elementary guides is Oletta Wald, *The Joy of Discovery in Bible Study*, rev. ed. (Minneapolis: Augsburg, 1975). For group study, see James F. Nyquist and Jack Kuhatschek, *Leading Bible Discussions*, rev. ed. (Downers Grove: Inter-Varsity, 1985). Slightly more advanced is T. Norton Sterrett, *How to Understand Your Bible*, rev. ed. (Downers Grove: InterVarsity, 1974). Then there are fuller and more elaborate expositions: Dan McCartney and Charles Clayton, *Let the Reader Understand: A Guide to Interpreting and Applying the Bible* (Wheaton, Ill.: Victor Books, 1994); Louis Berkhof, *Principles of Biblical Interpretation* (Grand Rapids: Baker, 1950); and many more.

CHAPTER 2

.

GOD AND BIBLICAL
INTERPRETATION

Chris Christian's Bible discussion group has decided to learn more about interpreting the Bible by studying the gospel of John.

Chris Christian: *We're beginning with John 1: "In the beginning was the Word, and the Word was with God, and the Word was God. He was with God in the beginning.*

"Through him all things were made; without him nothing was made that has been made. In him was life, and that life was the light of men."

This passage sounds pretty foundational in character. What do you think are the implications of beginning the gospel in this way?

Peter Pietist: *God is showing me how important Jesus is, and how fellowship with him should be central in my life. My devotion to him is of utmost importance. My fellowship with Jesus means communion with God himself, the Creator.*

Dottie Doctrinalist: *I agree with what you say, Peter. But that is not the main point. The passage indicates that God is bigger than your devotional life or mine. God is who he is forever. He was always there, before we were born, before the world was made. He isn't just there to serve our devotional needs. Rather, we are here to serve him.*

This passage is a passage of doctrine. It makes a propositional statement to teach us about the doctrine of the Trinity. It asserts that Jesus is the eternal God, with the Father. From other passages we learn about the Spirit as the Third Person of the Trinity.

Curt Cultural-Transformationist: *Yes, this passage has teaching. But it presents God as someone who is not just a teacher. God made the world. He acted. He is the source of life and of our empowerment to change the world.*

13

Missy Missiologist: *Yes, Jesus brings life to the whole world, not just to our circle. So we should take the message to everyone all over the world.*

Laura Liturgist: *The passage does not just talk about action, but about God. God does not exist only when he acts in the world. He exists eternally. The passage speaks of his eternal existence as the Father and as the Word. Here is the mystery of the Trinity. None of us really fathoms this mystery. God's greatness is more than we can imagine. We are to stand in awe of him, not just analyze him. We worship. The passage has propositional content, what Doctrinalist calls "doctrine." But it goes deeper than that. It introduces the Word. The Second Person of the Trinity is not just a proposition, but a person whom we worship and adore.*

Doctrinalist: *Well, I will admit I hadn't thought of things that way. I believe that the doctrine of the Trinity is important. But it is also sound doctrine to insist that God is incomprehensible—he is infinitely greater than my propositional summary.*

Missiologist: *Yes. Maybe there is more to this passage in the Bible than what I thought. I can see that the picture includes reckoning with who God is, and not just with the process of missionary growth. Maybe the gospel of John is going to expand my horizons, just as interaction with Christians from another culture would.*

Fatima Factualist: *I thought that the Bible was a book of rock-hard facts. And here are the hardest facts of all: the Word is God, and he is with God. But somehow this is not what I expected. These are facts unlike anything else I have examined. Clearly, they are the most basic facts of all. But I can't just manipulate them. Liturgist is right. I don't fathom God. I can't manipulate him. And God made everything. Maybe, then, I don't fully comprehend the facts about what he is doing in this world he made. That thought is rather upsetting. If God is like that, maybe he has other ideas in the Bible that don't simply match my expectations.*

Amy Affirmationist: *Maybe we can all learn something. I admit that this passage does not exactly fit my expectations, either. I am beginning to realize that the eternal Word is the ultimate measuring rod or standard for our words. And, looking ahead, I can see that pretty soon the gospel of John is going to point out that there is darkness in human understanding. Maybe I have been a little too optimistic in thinking that everyone's ideas are spiritual.*

Oliver Objectivist: *We can all gain insight as we approach more and more to the one meaning of the human author.*

Herman Hermeneut: *Doesn't this passage locate ultimate meaning in the Word? Doesn't John point beyond himself to the Word? So how* *could we stop with John's comprehension? Don't we have to reckon with God's comprehension?*

Objectivist: *God understands perfectly what John means.*

Hermeneut: *Undoubtedly. My point is that both God and the human author seem to push us beyond the finiteness of the human author, to reflect on the infinitude of the Word. The term "Word" identifies the Second Person of the Trinity as in some way the transcendent source of meaning that is embodied in the text.*

Objectivist: *But we must stick with what the text says.*

Hermeneut: *Would you be willing to add, "And with what God, the author, means by it?"*

From this conversation we may learn a simple but basic lesson: knowing God can shake up what we think we know about the Bible. Let us then consider the implications of knowing God.

Knowing the Father and knowing Jesus Christ are at the heart of salvation: "Now this is eternal life: that they may know you, the only true God, and Jesus Christ, whom you have sent" (John 17:3). As a summary of his work, Jesus declared, "I have made you [God the Father] known to them, and will continue to make you known" (John 17:26). The Bible gives us not merely information, but a knowledge of God. This knowledge, in turn, influences how we read and understand the Bible. How can we expect to understand the Bible without understanding its author?

If we reckon with who God is, we can immediately exclude certain kinds of interpretation. Natalie Naturalist is wrong in her naturalistic worldview. Carol Critical-Method is wrong to exclude the possibility of miracles. Roland Relativist also comes to grief. He wants everyone's opinion to be equally right. But in doing so, he does not reckon with the fact that God, too, might have an "opinion." God's "opinion"—that is, what he knows—is the standard that measures all human opinions. Moreover, salvation comes not in whatever way we invent in our minds, but by the one way that God endorses: salvation comes only through Jesus, the Son of God.

We can avoid other misunderstandings on the basis of what the Bible says about God. He is able to speak to people. Hence, the Bible can indeed be God's word. Libbie Liberal's friends are mistaken in thinking that they are dealing with merely human words that they may accept or reject as they please.

God, the Creator, is distinct from human beings, the creatures of God. Thus, unlike the New Age religion of Newton New Ager, we do not simply look deep within ourselves to hear our own inmost being and treat that as if it were divine.

God is the ultimate authority, not human beings. Hence, proper interpretation does not involve imposing our own ideas on a text, as Danny Demythologizer and Theo Therapist might. We are listening to God. We ought to be willing to be surprised or have our minds changed.

Human beings are made in the image of God, with the capacity to have fellowship with him. Hence, it is possible for us, with God's help, to understand. We do not give way to skepticism or despair, as Dick Deconstructionist might.

God demands our worship. Hence, our goal is not merely to fill our minds with correct information from the Bible, but to worship and obey God.

Such implications as these are elementary. But in our day they are worth saying. They exclude the approaches to interpretation taken in Libbie Liberal's Bible discussion group. Further reflection on the character of God would suggest ways in which each of the people in Chris Christian's group has limitations. Sometimes, because of limited vision, they make claims that are false or only partially true. Even when they are at their best, they represent a one-sided, partial approach.

The Trinity and the Word of God

To move beyond the limited insight expressed in Chris's group, let us consider another passage, John 17. This is an important passage for us to reckon with, because it brings together several key topics: God, the word of God, and the accomplishment of salvation. It explicitly includes two persons of the Trinity conversing with one another, and so it is important for our understanding of language and communication.

In John 17, Jesus presents himself in both his human and his divine nature. The opening verse presupposes the human nature of Jesus: "After Jesus said this, he looked toward heaven and prayed." The words "He looked toward heaven" describe Jesus as he was physically present before his disciples. The man Jesus, whom his disciples could see and handle, speaks the entirety of John 17. This chapter is frequently called Jesus' "high-priestly prayer," and rightly so. Just before sacrificing himself on the cross, Jesus prays for his disciples (v. 11) and for all believers (v. 20). He is our human representative and intercessor before God, just as the high priest of Israel interceded for the Israelites whom he represented (Heb. 7:23–28; Num. 17:1–18:7; Ex. 28:29–30).

But Jesus' speech proceeds also from his divine nature. In John 17:5, he speaks of "the glory I had with you before the world began." Who is the

"I" who speaks here? The Son of God became man at the moment of his incarnation. But, as this verse insists, this "I" had glory before the world began. The verse speaks of an eternal existence in the past. Such existence applies only to Jesus' divine nature. We must conclude that Jesus is here speaking not merely from his human nature, but from his divine nature also. Such speaking continues throughout the chapter. It contains repeated references to "glory," alluding back to verse 5. And near the conclusion it contains another reference to eternal existence: "to see my glory, the glory you have given me because you loved me before the creation of the world" (v. 24). It says, "You loved me." Here again, "me" refers to one who existed "before the creation of the world." It thus affirms Christ's divine nature.

Verses 5 and 24 stand like two bookends, enclosing almost the entire passage. Together they indicate that the whole passage is a conversation between the Word (the Second Person of the Trinity) and the Father (the First Person).[1]

How shall we understand Jesus' relationship to the Father in this passage? Clearly, we are confronted with the mystery of the Trinity. God is Three in One. The Father and the Son are eternal persons, distinct from one another, who converse meaningfully with one another. They also indwell one another, so that they are in unity (17:21). The Father is God, and the Son also is God (John 1:1; 20:28). Yet there is only one God (Deut. 6:4). The Holy Spirit is "another Counselor," distinct from the Father and the Son (John 14:16). Yet in the Spirit's action of indwelling, the Father and the Son are also present (John 14:23).

John 17 does not explicitly mention the Holy Spirit. But elsewhere the Bible shows a close correlation between the Spirit and the glory of God.[2] First Peter 4:14 says that "the Spirit of glory and of God rests on you," by analogy with the cloud of glory that rested on the Old Testament tabernacle.[3] Romans 6:4 and 8:11 assign parallel functions to "glory" and "Spirit." "Glory" is closely related to the Spirit. Apparently, it is a manifestation of the Spirit or an effect of the Spirit. Hence, we may infer that the Spirit is indirectly represented in John 17 through the mention of "glory."

The Word of God

What is the word of God?

John 17 ties the knowledge of God to the word of God. Words pass between the Father and the Son. John 17 exhibits the Son speaking to the Father. But in this speech he also refers to the "word" or "words" that the

Father has given him (17:8, 14, 17). Jesus, in turn, has "words" that he has given to the disciples (v. 8), "these things" that he is speaking (v. 13). His words to the disciples are the very "words you gave me" (v. 8; cf. v. 14).

We can distinguish several levels of speech in John 17. First, the Father speaks to the Son. He gives him his "word" or "words." Second, the Son speaks to the Father in the whole chapter. In particular, he acknowledges having received the Father's words. Third, the Son speaks to the disciples during his earthly life. When the Son speaks, the Father also speaks: "The words I say to you are not just my own. Rather, it is the Father, living in me, who is doing his work" (John 14:10).

In these statements about God's words, the New Testament, as a collection of written documents, is not directly in view. But there are hints. Jesus' concern extends to "those who will believe in me" (17:20). They will believe "through their message [word]" (v. 20). In this process, the divine word is present. Jesus says, "Sanctify them by the truth; your word is truth" (v. 17). His request clearly hints that the word of the Father, as delivered through the Son, remains accessible among the disciples, in order to sanctify them. Moreover, the Holy Spirit is present as the divine teacher (John 14:26–27; 15:26–27; 16:12–15, 25–28). The Father, the Son, and the Spirit, by virtue of mutual indwelling, have a deep unity in their speech. Jesus says,

> He [the Spirit] will not speak on his own; he will speak only what he hears, and he will tell you what is yet to come. He will bring glory to me by taking from what is mine and making it known to you. All that belongs to the Father is mine. That is why I said the Spirit will take from what is mine and make it known to you. (John 16:13–15)

John 17 by itself is not explicit about the role of the Bible. But elsewhere Jesus confirms the divine truthfulness of the Old Testament (John 10:35; Matt. 5:17–20; John 5:45–47). And he commissions the apostles with his authority (John 20:21–23). It only remains for the New Testament in various ways to confirm that it has the same divine origin and authority as the Old (e.g., 1 Cor. 14:37; 15:2–3; 1 Thess. 2:13; 2 Peter 3:16; Rev. 1:1; 22:18–20).[4] John 17 itself is an example of the inspiration of the New Testament. The Beloved Disciple, under the inspiration of the Spirit, writes the words of Jesus for the benefit of "those who will believe in me through their message" (John 17:20).

Thus, through the text of the gospel of John, we modern readers also become recipients of the word of Christ. Our final list, therefore, includes six kinds of speech.

1. The Father speaks to the Son (John 17:8).
2. The Son speaks to the Father (17:1–26).
3. The Son speaks to the disciples while on earth (17:13).
4. The Spirit hears from the Father and the Son (16:13).
5. The Spirit speaks to the apostles and other inspired writers (16:14–15).
6. The Spirit speaks to us through the inspired writings (20:31).

Communication Within the Trinity

The first, second, and fourth levels are particularly significant, because they all involve communication among the persons of the Trinity. As we have already seen, the Son's words to the Father, recorded in John 17, involve Christ's divine nature. God the Son speaks to God the Father. In like manner, the words of the Father to the Son are divine words to a divine person. For example, "the words you gave me" in John 17:8 are those to which God the Son responds in the rest of the passage. God the Son must first have heard the Father in order to respond. Moreover, the "me" in 17:8, like the "I," "me," and "mine" throughout the chapter, is most naturally understood as referring to the whole person, divine and human. Only with great artificiality could we extract a purely human "me" from a context filled with indications of exalted knowledge and unprecedented intimacy with the Father. The whole person of Christ, divine and human, is involved in the speech in John 17.

We must still deal with one possible objection. John 17 focuses on redemption. So someone might argue that it is wholly limited to redemption in time. Does the passage have implications for divine action, as we have argued? Let us reflect again on "the words you gave me" (John 17:8). The language of "giving" is closely associated with the language of "sending," as in verse 18, "You sent me into the world." The chief purpose of the giving and the sending is for Christ to come into the world with the message of salvation and the presence of salvation. The giving and the sending are oriented to the specific task of redemption. This redemption takes place at a specific time and place in history. It involves the Incarnation and the appearance of Christ in his human nature. But sending into the world already presupposes existence before he is sent. In the case of Christ, this existence is eternal preexistence, as John 1:1 declares explicitly. The specific redemptive task, far from excluding thoughts of Christ's deity, presupposes it. Likewise, any "giving" of instruction to Christ's human nature presupposes a giving of the entirety of knowledge to the divine Son (Matt. 11:27).

The Father's and the Son's communication to the Spirit is also fully divine. The Spirit's hearing, as mentioned in John 16:13, involves hearing from God the Father and God the Son. In the neighboring verse 15, "all that belongs to the Father," which Jesus says is "mine," is comprehensive. God the Father and God the Son speak to the Spirit.

Theologians immersed in the atmosphere of modernity have often supposed that language about God speaking must be an oblique and inadequate way of talking about something that in reality is beyond all speech, a "Wholly Other."[5] Speech, according to this view, would be a garbled manifestation of a wordless Beyond. But John 17 clearly has something quite definite in view. These specific utterances, recorded in John 17, are utterances spoken by God to God. They are divine discourse.

Infinite Meaning

When both the speaker and the hearer are divine, their discourse has a most extraordinary depth. How can we, as finite creatures, understand speech and communication with such depth?

A husband and a wife, after years of marriage, may have developed certain "code phrases" that evoke rich memories of shared knowledge. "The pink rose" may allude to a long period of working through forgiveness and healing. "The upside-down diaper" may evoke sweet laughter of common memories.

Or consider a humorous story. A new inmate came to a grim prison with few amenities. He joined the group of prisoners sitting together. One said, "Fourteen," and the group responded with chuckles. Another said, "Twenty-nine," and the group burst out with uproarious laughter. "Fifty-five," added another, and there were guffaws.

The new inmate asked, "What's going on?" His companion explained, "In the whole prison we have only one book of jokes. Everyone has heard the jokes so many times that we know them by heart. So all we need to do is mention the number of the joke, and everyone knows what it is."

The inmate, eager to experiment, said, "Seventeen." There was utter silence. "Why didn't they laugh?"

"That one isn't funny at all."

Thus, human beings who share in common knowledge may communicate richly even with few words. How is it when God communicates?

Jesus says, "And now, Father, glorify me in your presence with the glory I had with you before the world began" (John 17:5). Every phrase in this request, as well as the statement taken together, evokes depths of common knowledge shared by the Father and the Son. "The glory" points toward the eternal richness of divine splendor and majesty. "I had with you" speaks of the indwelling and sharing among the persons of the Trinity. "I" and "you," of course, refer to the fullness of the divine persons, known fully only to one another. "Father" evokes the intimacy of love between Father and Son. "Glorify me" encapsulates the crowning action of the entire plan of redemption, as played out in the Crucifixion, the Resurrection, the Ascension, Christ's sitting at God's right hand, and even the Second Coming (John 17:24–26). Although some aspects may be more in focus than others, the whole must be included. "In your presence" bears the freight of the distinct experience of presence with the Father that only the Son has (John 1:1).

Their communication, then, has infinite content. But this conclusion may seem paradoxical to some. How can words belonging to human language carry infinite content? One possible response is to say that the content communicated to human readers of John 17 is still finite. But that still leaves infinite content in the communication from divine person to divine person. So the paradox is still there.

Should we say that the sense, the meaning, is finite while the referent is infinite? The sense remains confined to the finite function of the words, while the reality to which the words refer has infinite content. We might produce an analogy to this situation in human communication. Suppose I tell you, "Wellington defeated a French general at the battle of Waterloo in 1815." My statement provides only limited information about Napoleon, whereas much more information could come from an encyclopedia article on Napoleon. We can then distinguish linguistic meaning from encyclopedic information. By analogy, God has complete encyclopedic knowledge of all facts. But he does not necessarily put that knowledge into words when he speaks to someone else.

Things are not quite so simple, however. The expression "glorify me" in John 17:5 evokes the complete plan of God concerning the climax of salvation—all events and all their significance, in general and in detail. We are still dealing with an infinitude. Can we escape by using the analogy of Napoleon? Let us see. My limited statement about Napoleon evokes in an expert a host of memories pertaining to Napoleon. But those memories are not actually implied by what I say. Indeed, I probably do not know what the expert knows. The evoking of his memories is a secondary effect that I did not even intend.

Is John 17:5 operating in the same way? I do not think so. Jesus' request to the Father is not merely a statement that evokes the Father's memories. It relies on the knowledge shared between the Father and the Son. The Son requests the Father to act, to do everything within the scope of the plan. The Son requests the Father to do A, B, C, D, and so on, all in their relations to one another and in their total significance. He requests an infinitude of actions and purposes. Or, if you will, in the one overall request he includes by implication an infinite number of subordinate requests. The Son does not simply allude to an infinity that resides elsewhere. He includes the infinity in his act of requesting. The Son intends to convey that infinitude of implications to the Father, and the Father understands this infinitude. As finite human beings, we do not possess this infinitude, but in the context of the mutual knowledge of the Father and the Son, the Son requests an infinite content through a single sentence.

Similarly, consider the statement in John 17:4, "I have brought you glory on earth by completing the work you gave me to do." "The work you gave me to do" encompasses an infinite number of implications. The Son declares, by implication, that he has accomplished A, B, C, D, and so on—everything that belongs to "the work."

In conclusion, then, at least some of the divine speech in John 17 has infinitely rich content, infinite meaning. What about the rest of John 17? Much of the time, the Son speaks to the Father concerning events and facts that we might say are "within the world." Aren't these merely finite? The world, the created things, are finite. But the key redemptive events within the world take place through the providential actions of the Trinity of persons in their interaction with one another. Events and facts within the world imply that certain divine acts undergird them. God plans, ordains, and powerfully orders whatever happens (Lam. 3:37–38; Eph. 1:11). God's acts are infinitely rich and incomprehensible to us. Hence, it seems reasonable to conclude that the other utterances in John 17, in their context of divine knowledge, imply an infinitude of meaning within the divine, interpersonal, mutual commitment, as request, assertion, and compliance take place.

But how can this be? The words, we may tell ourselves, are words belonging to human language. They are simply finite and creaturely, nothing more. There is a permanent mystery here. And we would wander too far from the main point if we undertook here an extensive analysis of language. We must be content with several observations.

First, God fits together the words of John 17 into sentences and discourse.

He says something new, something different, although he uses words that occur also in other contexts. The speech in John 17 is something quite different from mechanically mashing together a heap of words, without regard to order. The meaning of the whole does not consist merely in the sum of the meanings of the individual words. It has its own unique character.

Second, discourses make sense only within a context of speaker, addressee, and situation. The speech in John 17 is loaded with infinite meaning because it is a particular speech by the Son to the Father, within the context of the knowledge that the Father and the Son have of one another. Similarly, a husband and a wife can share rich knowledge using a few words. The human declaration "Guilty!" pronounced by a judge in the context of a trial has momentous consequences.[6]

Third, words themselves do not have a merely human origin. It is customary in our materialistic Western culture to think that they do. But that is because the West is in flight from God, trying to escape from the presence of God. The Bible reminds us, precisely in John 17, that what we call "human" languages are not merely human, but shared with God, who speaks and listens.

So it was from the beginning. Even before human beings existed, God spoke to create the world and what is in it. "Let there be light," he said, and there was light (Gen. 1:3). Before creating man, he discoursed with himself, "Let us make man in our image, in our likeness" (Gen. 1:26). "Us" and "our" indicate a plurality. God confirms that this plurality is genuine by saying in Genesis 3:22, "The man has now become like one of us." Interpreters debate whether the immediate reference is exclusively to God or also to the court of angels that minister to him (as in Job 1:6; 2:1; 1 Kings 22:19–22; Ps. 89:5–7; and other passages). But the court of angels is a created shadow or reflection of God's self-consultation with his wisdom (cf. Prov. 8:22–31). Thus, the deepest root of God's speech in creation is his speaking with himself.

The speaking between the Son and the Father in John 17 is thus not an isolated peculiarity. It is an instance of the same kind of divine speaking that has gone on from the beginning.

Now let us look again at the speech at the beginning of Genesis. The speech in Genesis 1:26 is a foundation for the speech that God will conduct with the human beings that he has created. Right after the act of creating man, God speaks to him, "Be fruitful and increase in number; fill the earth and subdue it" (Gen. 1:28). As God gave names to created things, so Adam names the animals (Gen. 2:19–20). Human speech is possible because God made man in his image, in his likeness. Human speech imitates divine speech and is analogous to it. Not only so, but speech in human language can be used and actually is used by both God and man to speak to one another (note the interchanges in Genesis 3:9–19). In fact, language is a principal mode through which God and human beings bring to expression and promote the personal, spiritual, and responsible relationship that they enjoy with one another.

The phrase "human language" is thus a one-sided and potentially misleading label. God "is not far from each one of us" (Acts 17:27). "In him we live and move and have our being" (Acts 17:28). Every human language on the face of the earth is also divine language, superintended and fashioned by God's providence and wisdom to be an instrument through which he speaks.

"But," someone may still object, "it is all impossible. Human language involves human vocal chords, human ears, human brains, and airwaves. These elements are creaturely, not divine."

So they are. So is the human nature of Jesus Christ. In his incarnate state, Christ has vocal chords, ears, a brain, and all. God uses these created means to speak. The created means are not thereby made divine. But neither does divine speech lose its divinity.

It may help us to realize that the medium of speech can be transformed without depriving speech of its meaning. Among human beings, substantially the same speech can be delivered through airwaves alone, or aided by a microphone, or delivered over the radio, or through a tape recording. Or we may develop written media, CD-ROMs, sign language, and so on. The speech may remain in human memories even when all other physical copies have disappeared.

Jesus says, "Heaven and earth will pass away, but my words will never pass away" (Matt. 24:35). What does he mean? He is not claiming that copies of the Bible will not burn up or wear out. But the message and the speech remain in other copies. If, hypothetically, all copies were destroyed, the whole could still be reproduced from God's mind (cf. Jer. 36:28–32).

Even human words do not simply evaporate or vanish into nothingness over time: "But I tell you that men will have to give account on the day of judgment for every careless word they have spoken. For by your words you will be acquitted, and by your words you will be condemned" (Matt. 12:36–37). A particular human speech is not merely a dumb created thing, like a rock, that unconsciously sits there. Human speech is personal action before the face of God. A human being speaks the truth of God, truth that remains forever—or perhaps he fails so to speak, and violates that truth. A human being issues commands in a manner attuned to the authority of divine commands—or he fails to do so, and issues unrighteous commands that violate divine norms. Thus, human speech sits, as it were, within the web of context formed by divine speech, divine knowledge, and divine norms. The idea that its context is purely human is an artifact of modern spiritual blindness.

We conclude that God *can* speak to human beings in language. But does he? Genesis 1:28 and subsequent passages indicate that he does. God spoke to the disciples when Jesus spoke to them while he was on earth. God spoke the Ten Commandments to the Israelites in a loud voice at Mount Sinai (Ex. 20:1–19; Deut. 5:22).

We hear in the Bible that God speaks. But is the Bible only a later report, a merely human report, of these speeches? Or is it also the word of God?

ENDNOTES

1. The NIV is not completely adequate as a translation of the passage. Several times the NIV includes the words "pray" or "prayer" to describe Jesus' conversation. These words could tempt us to restrict the entire passage to Jesus' humanity, and not include his deity. We might think that a human being prays, but not God. The original Greek, however, contains only general words like "ask" and "say," not the specific words for prayer. The passage surely is a prayer with respect to Jesus' human nature. But it is also an "asking" and a "saying" that proceeds from his divine nature.

2. See Meredith M. Kline, "The Holy Spirit as Covenant Witness," Th.M. thesis, Westminster Theological Seminary, 1972.

3. See Edward G. Selwyn, *The First Epistle of St. Peter,* 2d ed. (London: Macmillan, 1947), 222–24.

4. For further argumentation on the doctrine of inspiration, one may consult many works by evangelical scholars. The classic work is Benjamin B. Warfield, *The Inspiration and Authority of the Bible* (reprint, Philadelphia: Presbyterian and Reformed, 1967). See also Ned B. Stonehouse and Paul Woolley, eds., *The Infallible Word* (reprint, Grand Rapids: Eerdmans, 1953); John W. Montgomery, ed., *God's Inerrant Word* (Minneapolis: Bethany Fellowship, 1974); D. A. Carson and John D. Woodbridge, eds., *Hermeneutics, Authority, and Canon* (Grand Rapids: Zondervan, 1986).

The question of the extent of the canon—Why these sixty-six books?—is an important one. But we cannot devote space to it here. On the New Testament canon, see especially Herman N. Ridderbos, *Redemptive History and the New Testament Scriptures,* rev. ed. (Phillipsburg, N.J.: Presbyterian and Reformed, 1988). On the Old Testament canon, see Roger T. Beckwith, *The Old Testament Canon of the New Testament Church and Its Background in Early Judaism* (Grand Rapids: Eerdmans, 1985). 5. See Nicholas Wolterstorff, *Divine Discourse: Philosophical Reflections on the Claim That God Speaks* (Cambridge: Cambridge University Press, 1995), 1–74.

6. Ibid., 85–89.

■

CHAPTER 3

WHAT IS THE BIBLE?

Let us consider the nature of the Bible. Chris Christian's Bible study confronts the subject.

> **Herman Hermeneut:** *Before getting into the text any further, shouldn't we first determine what sort of object and what sort of communication the Bible is?*
>
> **Dottie Doctrinalist:** *That's easy, Herman. The Bible is the word of God.*
>
> **Hermeneut:** *But nowadays lots of people don't accept that.*
>
> **Doctrinalist:** *You're right. Non-Christians and liberals don't. But if we accept Jesus' teaching and other teachings in the Bible itself, we become convinced. We can study the texts on inspiration and biblical authority.*
>
> **Peter Pietist:** *No, let's not. Among ourselves, at least, I think that we are all convinced that the Bible is God's word. So all we have to do is to listen to what God says.*
>
> **Oliver Objectivist:** *Not so fast. You should have said that we have to listen to the human authors. If we try to go around the human authors, we get subjective. We attribute to God whatever we think he should say, or whatever nice thoughts come into our heads.*
>
> **Curt Cultural-Transformationist:** *But wait. Doesn't the Bible itself say that God's word governs the whole creation? How could his word be sewed up within the confines of a book?*
>
> **Doctrinalist:** *Maybe we do need to study what the Bible teaches about the word of God.*
>
> **Fatima Factualist:** *Maybe we should find out the facts about how*

the Bible came to be. Won't these facts give us an understanding of what sort of book the Bible is?

The Word of God

The Bible teaches that it is the very word of God addressed to human beings. What the Bible says, God says. Various human beings participated in producing the Bible. But God bore them along and controlled them in such a way that the written product is not only the production of human beings, but a communication breathed out by God.

The classic texts putting forth this claim are 2 Peter 1:21 and 2 Timothy 3:16. Second Peter 1:21 is particularly pointed: "For prophecy never had its origin in the will of man, but men spoke from God as they were carried along by the Holy Spirit." Second Timothy 3:16 reinforces the point by using the key word "God-breathed" ("inspired," *theopneustos*). It thereby indicates that the Scripture is breathed out by God. We need not rehearse here the details of these passages, which are discussed at length in classic works on inspiration.[1]

Jesus also confirmed the authority of the Bible. He lived his whole earthly life with the understanding that in his actions the Scriptures were being fulfilled (e.g., Matt. 26:54; Luke 24:24–27, 44–49). He explicitly affirmed the authority of the Old Testament (Matt. 5:17–20; John 10:35). He quoted Genesis 2:24, an ordinary part of Old Testament narrative, as what *God* said (Matt. 19:5).

If the Bible is what God says, it has God's own truthfulness, righteousness, and purity. We are to believe its assertions, trust its promises, obey its commands, and respond to its entreaties in the way that we respond to God himself. In particular, since God does not lie (Num. 23:19), neither does the Bible. It is completely true in what it affirms. It is without error (inerrant).[2]

The Bible as Covenantal

Key communications from God to human beings have taken the form of covenants. For example:

> Then God said to Noah and to his sons with him: "I now establish my *covenant* with you and with your descendants after you." (Gen. 9:8)

The LORD made a *covenant* with Abram and said, "To your descendants I give this land, from the river of Egypt to the great river, the Euphrates." (Gen. 15:18)

Then he took the Book of the *Covenant* and read it to the people. They responded, "We will do everything the LORD has said; we will obey." (Ex. 24:7)

This is my blood of the *covenant,* which is poured out for many for the forgiveness of sins. (Matt. 26:28)

He has made us competent as ministers of a new *covenant*—not of the letter but of the Spirit. (2 Cor. 3:6)

For this reason Christ is the mediator of a new *covenant,* that those who are called may receive the promised eternal inheritance. (Heb. 9:15)[3]

The covenant established through Moses at Mount Sinai is particularly significant, because it takes the form of a written document, "the Book of the Covenant" (Ex. 24:7). This "Book" probably contained the material in Exodus 20–23. The Ten Commandments are the core of this covenant. They are called "the words of the covenant" (Ex. 34:27–28) or simply "his covenant" (Deut. 4:13; see 5:2). God instructs Moses to put "the tablets of the covenant" (Deut. 9:9–11), containing the Ten Commandments (Deut. 5:22), into "the ark of the covenant" (Deut. 10:2, 5, 8). To this core of Ten Commandments, other words are added from time to time. For example, "These [words in Deuteronomy] are the terms of the covenant the LORD commanded Moses to make with the Israelites in Moab, in addition to the covenant he had made with them at Horeb [Sinai]" (Deut. 29:1). Moses tells the Levites to deposit the later material beside the ark (Deut. 31:24–26).

The procedures of depositing the words are most significant. Meredith G. Kline rightly sees here the first steps in the formation of a canon, a body of holy writings that God produces, sets aside, and consecrates as "a witness against you" (Deut. 29:26).[4] We cannot go into the details of Kline's extended argument. It is enough for us to observe the covenantal structure of the canon. Earlier in history God had spoken orally to human beings. But now the Bible draws attention for the first time to a written word, namely, the tablets of stone containing the Ten Commandments. This written word is a covenant. Later words are added in the form of "this Book of the Law"

(Deut. 31:25–26), and they too form a "covenant" (Deut. 29:1). All this material is placed in the Most Holy Place in the tabernacle, because it is itself holy. God also indicates that further words are coming through prophets (Deut. 18:15–22). These later words will be "my words" (18:18), as indeed the later prophets claim with the expression "thus says the LORD." In effect, this arrangement instructs Israel to see the later words as supplements to and reinforcements of the earlier covenantal words. The whole canon, as it grows through the addition of later words, is firmly covenantal in character.

Hence, the particular covenants that God makes with human beings offer a window or perspective on what God is doing with the Bible as a whole.

What then is a covenant? God's covenants with human beings are agreements between two parties, the Lord God and the people who are his servants. God makes commitments to us in the form of promises. We have obligations to him in the form of his commandments. In the ancient Near East, covenant treaties typically had other elements as well. A covenant included (1) identification of the covenant Lord or suzerain, (2) a history of his past benefits, (3) the "stipulations" concerning the people's obligations, (4) blessings and curses for obedience and disobedience, and (5) provisions for passing on the covenant, such as storage, public reading, or provision for the next generation.[5] One can see these elements illustrated in Exodus 20 and the book of Deuteronomy.[6] But, more broadly, the picture in Deuteronomy 31 invites us to see the entire Bible from the same perspective. The whole Bible is about God—it identifies the suzerain. The Bible records the history of God's past dealings for our benefit. It states God's promises and our obligations. It blesses and curses. It looks forward to all generations.

In addition, through covenants God establishes a relationship of personal intimacy with his people: "I will . . . be your God, and you will be my people" (Lev. 26:12; cf. Ex. 6:7).

A similar combination of speech, intimacy, and action appears in John 17. The Father gives words to the Son (v. 8). He is in personal intimacy with the Son in their mutual indwelling (vv. 21–22). They give glory to one another (vv. 4–5, 24). They share possessions (v. 10).

In Chris Christian's Bible discussion, Peter Pietist had an eye only for personal intimacy. Doctrinalist had an eye only for verbal content (teaching). Cultural-Transformationist had an eye only for pragmatic action that transforms the world. Liturgist had an eye for the ceremonies in making and renewing covenant with God. Factualist had an eye only for the record of past events. In fact, all these aspects form a unity in a covenantal relationship.

What are the implications for interpreting the Bible? We need the combined insights of Pietist, Doctrinalist, Cultural-Transformationist, Liturgist, and Factualist. Understanding the Bible involves understanding God's covenant with us. And that understanding is inexhaustible. To begin with, there are many important particular covenants: covenants with Noah, Abraham, Isaac, Jacob, Moses, and David. But because of its centrality, covenant is also a way by which we can view the entirety of God's relationship with human beings.[7]

Thus, the entire record of God's relationships with human beings colors our understanding of the covenant, and this understanding, in turn, controls our use of the Bible. Or, to put it another way, we must enter into a relationship with God and his word with our entire being. Our response as a whole influences the individualities of interpretation, since our covenantal relationship to God affects everything. The individual passages, in turn, teach about God and his covenants, and these then influence the total character of our covenantal response.

Moreover, when we are in covenant with God, we either receive blessing for obedience or curse for disobedience. Since our obedience is inadequate and imperfect, we always need Christ for atonement and substitution. The atoning work of Christ must operate in order that we may be blessed and not cursed in responding to the Bible.[8]

God's Speaking in Other Ways

We have seen that divine speaking can take different forms. God addressed people in oral speech at Mount Sinai. He gave written speech in the Ten Commandments recorded on stone. We need to consider how the Bible in particular is related to other forms of God's speech.

God spoke the words that brought the universe into being. "And God said, 'Let there be light,' and there was light'" (Gen. 1:3). The word "said" indicates that God used genuine speech, though he was not at that point speaking to human beings. Subsequent to creation, God has continued to rule the world by speaking. He rules all things by the power of his word: "Is it not from the mouth of the Most High that both calamities and good things come?" (Lam. 3:38). The Son sustains "all things by his powerful word" (Heb. 1:3).

God has also addressed human beings. He spoke orally to the patriarchs, Abraham, Isaac, and Jacob (Gen. 12:1–3; 15:1, 4–5, 7; etc.). He spoke audibly to the people of Israel at Mount Sinai (Ex. 20:1, 19, 22; Deut. 4:33; 5:22–27). He spoke at the Mount of Transfiguration (Matt. 17:5).[9]

At other times, instead of addressing people directly from heaven, God used human beings, such as the prophets and apostles, as his spokesmen. They spoke his word orally, in preaching and teaching, as well as in the writings that make up the books of the Bible.[10] God spoke through the words of Jesus Christ while he was on earth, including some words that have not been included in the Bible (John 21:25).

Finally, Jesus Christ himself, as the Second Person of the Trinity, is called the Word in John 1 and Revelation 19:13.[11]

In sum, God speaks in a variety of ways, through a variety of media. Within the Bible, he speaks about a variety of subjects through a variety of types of literature, such as history, song, teaching, and prophecy.

How do we understand this variety? How is the diversity compatible with the fact that all these varieties can be equally described as God's word or God speaking? In order to answer this question at a fundamental level, we must first reflect on the divine character of all God's words.

The Divinity of the Word of God

In each form taken by the word of God, God is speaking. What God says has his own authority, power, righteousness, and truth. For example, his words of creation, such as "Let there be light" (Gen. 1:3), resulted in creative acts. Only God's power can bring about such acts. Hence, the word that he speaks has divine power. Likewise, since he is righteous, all his utterances and judgments are righteous: "Righteous are you, O LORD, and your laws are right" (Ps. 119:137). Because God is true, his word is true (Num. 23:19; John 17:17).

The same conclusions that hold for God's creative words in Genesis 1 hold also for his address to human beings. Note first the close relationship between God's creative words and his words to human beings. In the Psalms, people revere, praise, and honor the covenantal word given through Moses, right alongside words pertaining to the creation and providential sustaining of the universe (Pss. 19:1–11; 119:48, 89–96, 120, 129, 137, 144, 152, 160). Just as God's creative words have divine power and righteousness, so do his words to human beings. The law is perfect, eternal, and life-giving (Pss. 19:7; 119:50, 89; 1 Peter 1:25; Luke 21:33). To God's word Jesus ascribes divine authority to judge (John 12:48). If God's word did not display the attributes of God, it would not in fact be God's word, but something else.

We may therefore make the same fundamental affirmations concerning all forms of God's word. In particular, the word of God is eternal; it endures forever (Ps. 119:89; Matt. 24:35). The word of God endures forever into the future, in the sense that it never passes away and its truth never changes. It endures forever into the past, in the sense that even before it was first uttered to human beings, it was hidden in God's wisdom from the very foundation of the world (Matt. 13:35).

When God first utters a particular word to a human being, his act is no more incredible than that most incredible act, the Incarnation. Let us consider the Incarnation for a moment. In the Incarnation, God the Son, the Word, became man. He remains God forever. In becoming man, he became what he was not at any earlier time. This incarnation is ultimately mysterious. We believe that Christ became incarnate, not because we can fathom it, but because God says so in the Bible.

Now consider the analogous events with respect to God writing the Bible. The eternal Word is the Truth. He is forever God and is with God. This Truth, remaining an expression of God's inscrutable wisdom from all eternity, becomes what it was not, a particular utterance in a particular human language to particular human beings.

Let us return to the point. All of God's words have divine attributes. Therefore, God's words are themselves divine.

Many people think that since the Bible consists of human words, it quite obviously cannot be divine. But, as we have seen from John 17, this argument is fallacious. Since the time of his incarnation, Jesus has been fully human (Heb. 2:14). The words that Jesus spoke on earth are obviously human. But Jesus is also divine, and the words that he spoke are therefore divine. If Jesus Christ is God, as the Bible teaches, then he must be obeyed absolutely. We cannot separate obeying him from obeying his words (John 12:48–50). His words have the authority of the speaker, that is, divine authority. The same divine authority attaches to the words of the Bible.

Since twentieth-century pride resists this truth, it is worthwhile to underscore it. According to Deuteronomy 5:27–33, the mediation of Moses was "good." The people were obligated to obey the word delivered through Moses, just as they were to obey the voice of God speaking directly from Mount Sinai (v. 22). Moses' writings had the same authority as the tablets written by the finger of God (Deut. 31:24–29). There is no suggestion of diminution, but rather faithful continuation, of the same fundamental character of divine speaking. Now Moses is the model for the later prophets (Deut. 18:16–22), and the Ten Commandments are the model for later Scripture (Deut. 31:24–29). Hence, the same truths hold for the later inspired speakers and inspired writings.

An objector may say, "To worship a book would be idolatry." But one must avoid the fallacy of equating the word of God with paper and ink. We have already noted that the message remains even when the media change or copies are destroyed.

The analogy with the incarnation of Christ also shows that there is no contradiction between the eternity of the word of God and its inscripturation. The Second Person of the Trinity exists as God for all eternity. In his deity, he does not change (Mal. 3:6). In accordance with the unchanging eternity of his plan, he becomes man. He speaks, acts, and accomplishes miracles at particular moments of time. Analogously, the word of God, remaining divine, becomes human words communicated to particular people at particular times.[12]

The Bible endorses the analogy in another way, through the language of the covenant. The entire Bible is covenantal, as we have seen. But at the heart of the covenants is God's saving commitment to his people, and the final expression of this commitment is Christ himself. "For no matter how many promises God has made, they are 'Yes' in Christ" (2 Cor. 1:20). He is the "one mediator between God and men" (1 Tim. 2:5). Only through Christ are we fit for fellowship with God (Acts 4:12; Heb. 10:14). Since all of God's covenantal words establish at least some degree of fellowship, they all tacitly presuppose the undergirding work of Christ. Through him alone can we draw near to God. The covenants unite God with human beings in a way that prefigures the final unity of God and man in the divine-human person of Christ. In Isaiah 42:6 and 49:8, Christ as the coming Servant of the Lord is actually identified as the covenant.

John 1 underlines the analogy between the Second Person of the Trinity and the particular words of God spoken at particular times. To begin with, John uses the term *word* to designate God the Son, already suggesting a connection. But there is more.

John 1:1–3 alludes to Genesis 1.[13] In Genesis 1, God creates by speaking. The verbal utterance "Let there be light" inaugurates the first specific act of creation (v. 3). Creation continues with the repeated command, "Let there be . . ." (vv. 6, 9, 11, etc.). The narrative includes instances where God names created things: "God called the light 'day,' and the darkness he called 'night'" (v. 5). Psalm 33:6 sums it up by saying, "By the word of the LORD were the heavens made, their starry host by the breath of his mouth." John says in a parallel manner, "Through him all things were made; without him nothing was made that has been made" (John 1:3).

At the very least, these connections may mean that the words spoken in Genesis 1 are analogous to the eternal Word, the Second Person of the Trinity. But closer reflection shows that John makes a much more startling claim. The utterances of God spoken in Genesis are themselves the manifestation and expression of God in his triunity. John 1:3 implies as much by asserting that the Second Person of the Trinity, in his capacity as the Word, was the means through which creation came to be. The Word is the means, whereas in Genesis 1 the particular words are the means. Clearly, the particular words are expressions of the one Word. They are the manifestation and action of the Second Person of the Trinity. None of the utterances in its particularity and specificity exhausts the eternal Word, since other utterances occur besides. But each utterance is an operation of the eternal Word, through whom all things came to be (John 1:3; Col. 1:16; 1 Cor. 8:6; Heb. 1:2). According to the analogy, God the Father is the speaker in both cases. From all eternity, God speaks the eternal Word. In creating the world, God the Father spoke the particular words recorded in Genesis 1.

We must include here not only the utterances directed to the subhuman world, but also the verbal communications with human beings in Genesis 1:28–30. For one thing, these verbal communications, no less than all the rest, are what God speaks. In addition, they function specifically to light the path of human service and endeavor. They are thus an aspect of the life that "was the light of men" (John 1:4). Jesus speaks similarly of his own words: "The words I have spoken to you are spirit and they are life" (John 6:63).

Moreover, the word of God is closely correlated with the name of God. Both involve the use of language. In John 17, Jesus speaks of "the name you gave me" (vv. 11–12) in close relation to "the words you gave me" (v. 8). The name of God is an expression of his very character, as in Exodus 34:5–7. The presence of God's name involves the presence of God himself (Ex. 23:21; Deut. 12:5; 1 Kings 8:29). The name of God is thus undoubtedly divine. The phrase "word of God" is not synonymous with "name of God," but designates God's speech about any subject whatsoever. God's speech about himself, including his utterance of his name, is in one sense only one part of the totality of his speech. Yet, in a broader sense, all of God's speech shows something about who he is, and is thus an expression of his character. It is only a short step from acknowledging the divinity of the name of God to acknowledging the divinity of the word more broadly.[14]

How can we possibly understand this situation? If there is only one God, and if the incarnate Word of God is God, how can there yet be a great diversity of distinct and different divine words? If the Word of God is divine, if he is himself God, how can he speak of the particulars of history? After all, these particulars are not themselves a necessary aspect of God's being. God existed before creation began. The Second Person of the Trinity exists eternally. God exists necessarily with his Word, the Second Person of the

Trinity. But it was not necessary for God to create in time, nor was it necessary that he speak the words calling light into being.

We will never be able to exhaust this mystery. But we obtain help in understanding it through the starting point provided in John 1. John 1 presents us with the reality of eternal divine speaking in the being of the Trinity. This eternal speaking is the original. Our own language and speech are derivative. Man was made in the image of God (Gen. 1:26–30). But, as Colossians 1:15 indicates, Christ, the Second Person of the Trinity, is the original image on whom all of creation depends. We are images by analogy with his original imaging. The Second Person is the original Word. He is the *archetype,* the original model on which all else is based. All other words are analogous and derivative. They are *ectypes;* that is, they are copies imitating the original, the archetype.

This Trinitarian original provides the ultimate basis for the fact that the word of God is both one and many. First, there is unity. The Word is the Word of the Father. As such, he presents the plan, the will, the mind, and the attributes of the Father. He is one with the Father (John 10:30). But there is also diversity. The Word is eternally distinct from the Father. The Father utters the Word that is distinct from himself.

The unity and diversity in the Trinity is the archetype or original. The unity and diversity in God's speaking to us is analogous to this original. We may speak of the ontological unity and diversity in the Trinity as the archetype, while the unity and diversity in God's word to us is an ectype. But we must note that God's words to us are still divine. As we noted above, they have divine power, authority, and purity. His words to us, as ectype, are still divine, along with the archetype. Thus, in addition to the created ectypes, such as man made in the image of God, there are divine ectypes—particular words that imitate the archetypal unity and diversity in the Trinity. Everything that God says is divine, a manifestation of the one Word who is one with God. Everything God says has distinctness, analogous to the distinctness of the Son from the Father.

Coinherence: God's Dwelling in His Word

We can understand God's presence in his word still better by considering the role of the Holy Spirit.

John 3:34 provides one way of understanding the role of the Spirit: "God gives the Spirit without limit" to the Son. That is, the Spirit is the Father's gift to the Son. As such, he is the expression of the Father's love: "The Father loves the Son and has placed everything in his hands" (3:35). We know that the Spirit is given to us to express the Father's love for us (14:23–27). Through the Spirit, both the Father and the Son dwell in us (14:23). The Son's dwelling in us is analogous to the Father's dwelling in the Son (17:21–23). In other words, God's dwelling in us is an ectype, an image, of God's dwelling in God. The Father dwells in the Son, and the Son in the Father. This indwelling takes place through their mutual love, which is the gift of the Spirit. Indwelling does not confuse the persons of the Godhead, however. Each person remains distinct from the others, while they dwell in one another.

Through the Spirit, then, the persons of the Godhead dwell in one another. Each is present in the works of the others. Each shares the attributes of the others. This relation of persons is termed *coinherence,* because each person "inheres" in the other persons; each belongs to the others and is in the others.[15]

The coinherence of the persons of the Trinity provides a background for understanding the character of God's word. The persons of the Trinity are present to one another. The Word is "with God," according to John 1:1. He is "at the Father's side" (NIV) or "in the bosom of the Father" (RSV, KJV), according to John 1:18. This coinherence provides the archetype. In an ectypal way, God is present in all his words with respect to creation. The Father is "in" the Son (14:10) without being identical with the Son (the two are distinct persons). Similarly, the Father is present in his words without being identical with those words. Since the Son is in the Father, the Son is also present in all the words of God. The eternal Word of John 1:1 is present in all the particular words. Thus, there is a unity of being to all the words. All the words of God are not only words from God as speaker, but also words that manifest the presence of the eternal Word. They are expressions and manifestations of that one Word.

Now we can see the significance of the speaking and hearing of different persons in John 14–17. We have seen many different instances of speaking from one person to another. The differences cohere in a unity guaranteed by the fact that the persons dwell in their words and in one another. For example, the words that the Son receives from the Father he gives in turn to the disciples (John 8). As a result, the disciples hear the Father and the Son. The Father dwells in the Son and so is speaking when the Son speaks. "The words I say to you are not just my own. Rather, it is the Father, living in me, who is doing his work" (14:10). The Spirit speaks what he hears (16:13). This speaking is then also the speaking of the Father and the Son.

Figure 3.1. Triad of imaging

We can summarize our results in terms of three aspects or perspectives on the word of God, namely, the originary, the manifestational, and the concurrent aspects. First, we have an *originary* aspect. God speaks in accordance with who he is, and in accordance with the permanent truths of his original plan. In the originary perspective, we look at how God's word makes known the Father's plan.

Second, God speaks in particular ways in particular manifestations. In the *manifestational* perspective, we look at the particular expression of the word in its particular form. For example, Jesus speaks the particular words of John 15:7 to his disciples, indicating the consequences of abiding in him.

Third, God is present through all the manifestations. He dwells in the manifestations, so that any one of them is a manifestation of who he is. We can grasp the original plan of God through its manifestation. The original dwells in the manifestation, and the manifestation dwells in the original. The two are concurrent with one another. In the *concurrent* perspective, we focus on the relation of the other two aspects. The originary aspect is concurrent with the manifestational aspect, in that the two are present in one another. The original plan is in the particular manifestation and is expressed in the manifestation. For example, God the Father makes known his plan for the disciples through the words of John 15:7. Thus, the Father's plan is concurrent with the particular expression in the words of John 15:7.

Let us consider another illustration. The words that the Father gives to the Son are originary. As John 17:8 says, "For I gave them the words you gave me and they accepted them." What Jesus calls "the words you gave me," that is, the words of the Father, are *originary*. The words that the Son gives to the disciples are *manifestational*. Since the Father dwells in the Son, the disciples hear not only the Son speaking, but also the Father speaking. Here the speaking of the Father and of the Son are *concurrent*. The two speakers are concurrent in the bond of the Holy Spirit. Hence, three aspects—originary, manifestational, and concurrent—correspond respectively to the interactive roles of the Father, the Son, and the Holy Spirit.

Each of the three aspects coheres with the others, because the three are ultimately derived from the triunity of the coinherence of the persons of the Trinity. Because of coinherence, any one aspect provides a perspective on knowing God. Through hearing the Son, in the manifestational aspect, the disciples know God the Son. Through hearing the Son, they hear the words of the Father, and thereby know the Father. They hear the Father speaking. This speaking gives the originary perspective. They also know the coinherence of the Father in the Son, thereby knowing the Spirit who provides the bond of this coinherence.

Each of these perspectives presupposes the others. The manifestational aspect, the Son speaking, presupposes something that he makes known, namely, the originary aspect, the words of the Father. The originary aspect comes to the disciples only by being made known in concrete and specific form, thus presupposing the work of the Son. The concurrent aspect has to do with the relationship between the Father's speech and the Son's speech. The two are concurrent in that each is in harmony with the other. The concurrent aspect must be presupposed so that the manifestational is truly a manifestation of the originary. Conversely, the concurrent aspect presupposes the existence of the other two aspects. Concurrence can occur only if there are other aspects on which it can operate. There must be two items that can be concurrent with one another. Thus, concurrence presupposes the originary and the manifestational.

Since we will use the idea of perspectives in our later reflections, let us illustrate it now. Through Jesus Christ, we know the Father as well as the Son (John 14:7, 9; Matt. 11:27). There is no other way to know the Father (John 14:6). Thus, we may say that knowing Christ provides the *perspective* or window on knowing the Father. In fact, each of the persons of the Trinity is indispensable in knowing God. Only through the Father do we know the Son: "No one knows the Son except the Father" (Matt. 11:27), and "No one can come to me unless the Father who sent me draws him" (John 6:44). Only through the Spirit do we know the Father and the Son: "The man without the Spirit does not accept the things that come from the Spirit of God, for they are foolishness to him, and he cannot understand them" (1 Cor. 2:14). Each person of the Trinity has a distinct role. The Father is the source of knowledge, the Son is the channel, and the Holy Spirit is the one changing our hearts to be receptive to the truth.

At the same time, each person points to the work of the others and presupposes the work of the others. The Son is the bearer of knowledge because of the commission of the Father who sent him. The Son's work is explicable only if we see him not merely as a human being, but as the unique Son. Thus, the Son presupposes the Father. Conversely, the Father's revelation presupposes the Son. Since he is holy, the Father makes himself known savingly to sinners only through the Son, the mediator (1 Tim. 2:5). And finally, the Holy Spirit works only as one sent by the Father and the Son. He presupposes their activity. At the same time, God becomes savingly known to us only if we have a change of heart, and this change takes place only through the Holy Spirit: "I tell you the truth, no one can enter the kingdom of God unless he is born of water and the Spirit" (John 3:5). Thus, knowing the Father and the Son presupposes the work of the Spirit.

In sum, the three persons of the Trinity coinhere in the work of making God known. This is only one instance of coinherence, which God expresses in all his works. He manifests coinherence in each particular kind of work, because he is himself eternally coinherent in the being of the Trinity. He acts toward us in a way that manifests who he is in himself.

The most fundamental coinherence is that of the persons of the Trinity. But we see derivative coinherence in the perspectives in which God manifests himself. One such triad consists in the originary, manifestational, and concurrent perspectives explained above.

We would do well to note that the three perspectives are always involved in one another and cannot be neatly separated. We can illustrate this fact by looking more closely at the work of the Holy Spirit in John 16:13–14. The Holy Spirit "will speak only what he hears, and he will tell you what is yet to come." The Holy Spirit, as hearer, receives words from the Father and the Son. His own speech is manifestational in relation to the originary word of the Father. The Spirit himself can thus be viewed from the manifestational aspect. And in relation to human words about him, the Spirit is originary. The Spirit's relation to the Father who speaks is a relation in harmony. Thus, the Spirit has a concurrent relationship to the Father. Depending on our point of view, we can view the Spirit as originary, manifestational, or concurrent.

Earlier, we correlated each of the three aspects with only one person of the Trinity. The originary aspect was linked to the Father, the manifestational aspect to the Son, and the concurrent aspect to the Holy Spirit. But we oversimplify if we say that each aspect correlates exclusively with only one person. The aspects are inseparable, and in fact each belongs to all three persons of the Trinity. Precisely because the persons dwell in one another, we cannot penetrate this ultimate mystery.

Imaging

We may reexpress these truths using the language of imaging. The Son is the exact image of the Father, according to Colossians 1:15 and Hebrews 1:3. So he is able to present the Father to the world: "Anyone who has seen me has seen the Father" (John 14:9). Jesus then explains that the Father is present through indwelling: "Don't you believe that I am in the Father, and that the Father is in me?" (v. 10). The Son images the Father and presents him to the disciples because the two persons dwell in one another. As we have seen, the dwelling of the Father in the Son and of the Son in the Father is closely associated with the Holy Spirit. The Holy Spirit is their bond of union. The Son is the image of the Father through the Spirit. The Spirit represents the concurrent aspect, the relation between the Father and the Son. Because of the close relation of the three aspects to imaging, let us then call the triad consisting in originary, manifestational, and concurrent perspectives *the triad of imaging.*

In a unique sense, the Son is the exact image of the Father. But the Bible also uses the language of imaging with respect to man. "God created man in his own image, in the image of God he created him" (Gen. 1:27). Man is the image of God (1 Cor. 11:7). Moreover, the idea of imaging does not simply stop with the creation of the first man. Genesis 5:1–3 goes on to say,

> When God created man, he made him in the likeness of God. He created them male and female and blessed them. And when they were created, he called them "man."
>
> When Adam had lived 130 years, he had a son in his own likeness, in his own image; and he named him Seth.

God made man in his image and named them "man." Adam had a son in his image and named him Seth. Adam imitated God in these actions. He was "imaging" God in the process of producing another image. Seth was the image of Adam. Adam was the image of God. And God has an imaging relation within himself, in the relation of the Father to the Son. Each derivative imaging relation is itself an image of a higher imaging relation.

Imaging, apparently, is all over the place in the description of man. And no wonder! If the Father loves the Son (John 3:34!), it is fitting for him to act out of his love when he creates, and to celebrate that love by producing pictures of it within creation.

We can reexpress this situation using the triad of terms that we already introduced: the originary, manifestational, and concurrent aspects or perspectives. Start with the Son imaging the Father. The Father is originary; the Son is manifestational; the Spirit, who represents the relation between them, is concurrent. When God made man, God was originary, man was manifestational, and the permanent relation of imaging, brought about through breathing into him (Gen. 2:7), was concurrent.

Now consider further the concurrent aspect, that is, the imaging relation between God and man. The imaging relation is the model for Adam having a son in his image. In this context given by Genesis 5:1–3, the relation between God and man is originary, whereas the relation between Adam and Seth is manifestational. The imitating relation between the two is concurrent.

Similarly, the imaging relation between the Father and the Son is originary in comparison to the manifestational imaging relation between God and man. The presence of the Spirit is the bond, by which these two kinds of imaging are concurrent. Note how a renewed imaging relation between God and man is expressed in John 17:21–23 in terms of indwelling:

> . . . that all of them may be one, Father, just as you are in me and I am in you. May they also be in us so that the world may believe that you have sent me. I have given them the glory that you gave me, that they may be one as we are one: I in them and you in me. May they be brought to complete unity to let the world know that you sent me and have loved them even as you have loved me.

Consider the three terms—*originary, manifestational,* and *concurrent.* As we have already seen, these three terms describe aspects that derive originally from the distinct roles of the Father, the Son, and the Spirit in revelatory actions. Since revelatory actions reveal something of who God actually is, the three terms are an image or mirror of the Trinitarian relations. They tell us something of who God is in his Trinitarian being. In every case, what is permanently true about who God really is (that is, the originary aspect) is manifested in a particular way in revealed form. The manifestation relates to the originary aspect by way of concurrence: each dwells in the other. God is the Trinity. And his manifestations are necessarily Trinitarian in character.

The Ontological and the Economic Trinity

Much of the Bible focuses on God's relations to us and the historical out-working of redemption. God's Trinitarian character stands forth most fully and eloquently in the redemptive events where each of the persons of the Trinity has a distinct role (e.g., Matt. 3:16–17; Acts 2:33; Rom. 8:11; 1:4; John 16:13–15). God reveals himself to us through his activity in the world. We observe the interrelations of the persons of the Trinity as they function in creation, redemption, and consummation. The manifestation of the Trinity in God's activity in the world is traditionally called the "economic" Trinity. (*Economic* here bears the older sense, having to do with managing household affairs; it does not refer to the production and distribution of goods and services.)

The Bible does sometimes, as in John 1:1, focus more directly on aspects of the "ontological" Trinity, that is, on God as he is in his own being, before creation and independent of creation. But even here we recognize that the language of the Bible is crafted for the purposes of nourishing our faith, enlarging our understanding, and promoting our redemption. Hence, even these statements are tied in with "functional" purposes.

Since God is our standard and his word is our standard, there is nothing more ultimate than this revelation of himself. We believe that God is true. He truly reveals himself, not a substitute or a mirage. We believe it because God says so. Hence, we believe that God is in conformity with what he reveals. Moreover, in John 17 what God says is said to himself and not merely to us. What he says is then in full conformity with who he is. The Trinity in functional activity reveals the ontological Trinity. Hence, we cannot make strictly or exhaustively functional (economic) or ontological statements about the Trinity. For a creature to attempt to do so would be a repudiation of creaturehood.

Awe in the Study of the Bible

What do we conclude concerning the study of the Bible? When we study the Bible, we study the word of God. We also know that God speaks words to the creation (Ps. 147:15, 18). The Second Person of the Trinity is the Word. The word of God occurs in all these forms. The Bible, as one form, coinheres with other forms. Christ himself dwells in the biblical word. Thus, the particular word always comes in a context, the context of coinherence in God. That context is inexhaustible, and so there is an inexhaustibility to God's word. Because we are focusing on the Bible, we shall, through the rest of this book, have the Bible in view when we speak of God's word. But the larger picture remains an indispensable background.[16]

Since the word of God is divine, it is, in the technical sense of the term, incomprehensible. We do not mean by this that the word is unintelligible or meaningless to us. Rather, the word of God is accessible—"near you" (Rom. 10:8), as Paul says. But it is near you in the same way that God is near you. We know God truly and know many truths about him. But God remains mysterious, unfathomable in the depth of his wisdom. Similarly, we know what the word of God says, yet simultaneously it remains mysterious to us; we do not fully fathom it.

Let us consider a particular example. John 2:16 says, "And he told those who sold the pigeons, 'Take these things away; you shall not make my Father's house a house of trade'" (RSV). We claim that this verse is incomprehensible. But its meaning is intelligible. Jesus told the pigeon sellers to remove their goods from the temple area. Jesus gave a direct instruction and expected a direct response. We can easily understand the verse to this extent. But we have not yet exhausted its import.

On the surface, the meaning may seem to be straightforward. But Jesus' explicit instruction also points indirectly to depths of meaning. Behind the explicit instruction lie motives. The instruction reveals Jesus' zeal, as the next verse notes: "Zeal for your house will consume me." The verse itself includes a reason, "You shall not make my Father's house a house of trade." With this negative statement Jesus indicates that the temple is not for "trade." But he hints thereby that it has a positive purpose, a purpose indicated by the whole Old Testament. It is a house for honoring God. It is the place where God has put his name (1 Kings 8:29). It displays God's majesty and provides access to God for sinful people. In the last days, as Isaiah says, "My house will be called a house of prayer for all nations" (Isa. 56:7; cf. Mark 11:17).

Through this statement, in fact, Jesus points to the full meaning of the temple, as that meaning is developed extensively throughout the Old Testament. The text in John 2:16 thus invites us to look not only at what it says on its surface, but also at what it implies as it calls to mind the teaching of the Old Testament.

Now some people may say at this point that we are dealing no longer with John 2:16 but with other passages, all of which have meanings of their own. They may argue that John 2:16 in and of itself does not have all these implications. And there is some truth in their position. Certainly we have to be aware of the difference between what a passages says and what related passages say. Yet do we really know what we mean when we talk about John 2:16 "in and of itself"? At a fundamental level, there is no such thing as a passage in and of itself. John 2:16 is part of the Bible, and God intends that we read it and understand it in relation to all the other parts of the Bible. When he caused these words to be written in the gospel of John, he already intended that they should be seen as we are seeing them, namely, in connection with other passages that together unfold the purpose of God.

Moreover, in John 2:16 Jesus calls the temple "my Father's house." Jesus claims a special relationship with God, who is his Father. Because of his relationship with the Father, he has a special concern and zeal for the temple. And, in spite of the Jews' demands and objections in John 2:18–20, Jesus has authority over the temple, as the Son. Jesus' statements and demands with respect to the temple arise out of his zeal for it and for the honor of his Father. This zeal, in turn, arises from Jesus' special understanding of, and love for, his Father. Out of this understanding and love, Jesus knows the Father's purposes. He knows that they are violated by trading in the temple. He acts confidently against that violation because he is confident in his knowledge of the Father. His statement in John 2:16, then, presupposes the Son's knowledge of, and communion with, the Father. That communion is even explicitly expressed when Jesus calls God his Father. The passage invokes the infinitely deep communion between the Father and the Son. Thus, the passage reveals depths that we cannot fathom.

In addition, we should have learned something from John 17. God, as well as human beings, can hear what Jesus says. The Son addresses the Father in John 17. Similarly, the utterance in 2:16, "You shall not make my Father's house a house of trade," means something not only to us, but also to God. God the Father hears the Son speaking. God the Father knows the intimacy that the Son expresses with the words "my Father's house." He also knows the zeal that the Son expresses with the words "Take these things away." The Father, knowing the Son, knows depths of nuance and shared knowledge that we cannot fully see. In hearing these words which Jesus speaks, he understands in depth, because he brings to them his prior understanding of the Son, and this prior understanding enriches the understanding of the words themselves. The Father sees implications that we do not see. There is an infinite fullness of meaning here, just as we began to find in John 17.

The name of God, as a concentrated form of the word of God, shows similar features. First of all, the name of God genuinely reveals God. It describes his character. Thus,

> [God] proclaimed his name, the LORD. And he passed in front of Moses, proclaiming, "The LORD, the LORD, the compassionate and

gracious God, slow to anger, abounding in love and faithfulness, maintaining love to thousands, and forgiving wickedness, rebellion and sin. Yet he does not leave the guilty unpunished; he punishes the children and their children for the sin of the fathers to the third and fourth generation." (Ex. 34:5–7)

To "proclaim [God's] name" is expounded by a description of God's character, including such attributes as "compassionate" and "gracious."

The name of God says something definite about God. It makes it clear who God really is and what our responsibilities to him are. The name of God brings God near to us, as is clear from the dwelling of God's "name" in Jerusalem (Deut. 12:5; 1 Kings 8:29). But God's name is simultaneously mysterious, awesome, and transcendent. It indicates all that God is, and we cannot exhaustively comprehend what that involves. For instance, the messenger of the Lord who wrestles with Jacob brings him face-to-face with God (Gen. 32:28, 30). The messenger refuses to reveal a name (v. 29). Similarly, the messenger who comes to Manoah is later recognized as divine (Judg. 13:22). He indicates only that his name is "wonderful," or, as the NIV has it, "beyond understanding" (v. 18). The Psalms praise the name of God and celebrate its excellence (e.g., Pss. 8:1, 9; 9:2; 34:3; 44:8; 54:6; 72:19; 86:12). His name is glorious, exalted, holy, and awesome (Pss. 72:19; 103:1; 148:13; 145:21; 99:3; 111:9). God's name transcends human analysis and knowledge. Similarly, the word of God, which is exalted together with God's name (Ps. 138:2), transcends human knowledge.

The transcendence of the word of God has implications for our manner of approach to it. Humility is necessary. We should be suspicious of any supposedly simple solution to the profundities of interpretation, or any claim to have mastered language and communication.

Let us state the matter another way. The Second Person of the Trinity has been incomprehensible from the beginning of time. He remained incomprehensible when he became incarnate. The Incarnation makes Jesus Christ accessible to us, and we understand him in a sense through his humanity. But instead of overcoming mystery, the Incarnation adds still another mystery to those already existing: how can God become man and still remain God?

John 17 shows that the words of the incarnate Christ are incomprehensible. His words have infinitely rich meaning. We can generalize to the entirety of Scripture. The word of God remains incomprehensible when it becomes Scripture. The fixity, accessibility, specificity, and clarity of Scripture do not in the least diminish its incomprehensibility, but rather add a further mystery: How can God's eternal, omnipotent word become human speech and still remain divine?

ENDNOTES

1. Benjamin B. Warfield, *The Inspiration and Authority of the Bible* (reprint, Philadelphia: Presbyterian and Reformed, 1967); Louis Gaussen, *Theopneustia: The Bible, Its Divine Origin and Entire Inspiration* (reprint [as *The Divine Inspiration of the Bible*], Grand Rapids: Kregel, 1971); more recently, Ned B. Stonehouse and Paul Woolley, eds., *The Infallible Word* (reprint, Grand Rapids: Eerdmans, 1953); John W. Montgomery, ed., *God's Inerrant Word* (Minneapolis: Bethany Fellowship, 1974); D. A. Carson and John Woodbridge, eds., *Scripture and Truth* (Grand Rapids: Zondervan, 1983); D. A. Carson and John D. Woodbridge, eds., *Hermeneutics, Authority, and Canon* (Grand Rapids: Zondervan, 1986).

2. Such conclusions have been disputed by many, notably by Jack Rogers and Donald McKim, *The Authority and Interpretation of the Bible: An Historical Approach* (New York: Harper & Row, 1979); Donald K. McKim, ed., *The Authoritative Word: Essays on the Nature of Scripture* (Grand Rapids: Eerdmans, 1983). But see the reply in John D. Woodbridge, *Biblical Authority: A Critique of the Rogers/McKim Proposal* (Grand Rapids: Zondervan, 1982). Affirming inerrancy (no errors) does not imply taking a wooden approach to interpreting the Bible: see Moisés Silva, "Ned B. Stonehouse and Redaction Criticism," *Westminster Theological Journal* 40 (1977–78): 77–88, 281–303.

3. When citing these and other texts, I am certainly aware of scholarly debates concerning their interpretation. But it would clutter the exposition to interact with all the various opinions, especially those in mainstream historical-critical scholarship. It should be apparent later in this book that the presuppositions of mainstream scholarship are seriously flawed. Hence, "accepted" opinion must be critically rethought from the beginning. Scholarship, not the Bible, is in need of revision.

4. Meredith G. Kline, *The Structure of Biblical Authority* (Grand Rapids: Eerdmans, 1972).

5. Ibid.

6. Meredith G. Kline, *Treaty of the Great King: The Covenant Structure of Deuteronomy: Studies and Commentary* (Grand Rapids: Eerdmans, 1963).

7. One may receive instruction here from the many works on aspects of covenant theology. Books on Reformed systematic theology contain extensive discussion. See

Louis Berkhof, *Systematic Theology*, 4th ed. (Grand Rapids: Eerdmans, 1968); Charles Hodge, *Systematic Theology* (reprint, Grand Rapids: Eerdmans, 1970). We also have more recent treatments from a redemptive-historical point of view: Kline, *The Structure of Biblical Authority;* O. Palmer Robertson, *The Christ of the Covenants* (Grand Rapids: Baker, 1980); Geerhardus Vos, *Biblical Theology* (Grand Rapids: Eerdmans, 1966).

8. See Vern S. Poythress, "Christ the Only Savior of Interpretation," *Westminster Theological Journal* 50 (1988): 305–21.

9. See John M. Frame, *Perspectives on the Word of God: An Introduction to Christian Ethics* (Phillipsburg, N.J.: Presbyterian and Reformed, 1990), 23–24.

10. Ibid., 24.

11. For more wide-ranging reflections, see ibid., 3–35.

12. One may compare my view with G. C. Berkouwer, *Holy Scripture* (Grand Rapids: Eerdmans, 1975), 195–212. Berkouwer usefully reflects on a long history in which theologians have spoken of an analogy between the Incarnation and inscripturation. He rightly points to nuances and sensitivities that ought to be maintained. But I am uncomfortable with the excessive caution and negation he exhibits at some points.

For example, according to Warfield and Berkouwer, in Scripture there is no question of "personal union," that is, the union of two natures in one person. The analogy between the Incarnation and inscripturation is therefore "remote" (pp. 201–2). The statement about "personal union" is technically correct. But it seems to me that the uniqueness of Christ's being, far from implying that the analogy is "remote," makes Christ indispensable to understanding Scripture!

Consider: We are sinful. God is holy. How can God speak to us without our dying (cf. Ex. 20:19)? Ultimately, he does so only through Christ, the one mediator between God and men (1 Tim. 2:5). The union of natures in the person of Christ must form an ontological and redemptive ground for the speaking of God to sinful human beings at all times. It is then the exemplar for understanding scriptural speech. Such speech is not impersonal. In Scripture, it is God who speaks through Christ. Even in Old Testament times, God's speaking looked forward to Christ's incarnation and redemptive work. There is then no way of adequately understanding scriptural speaking except in a way that links it with the prime exemplar, Jesus' speaking in his incarnation. Moreover, people are likely to take offense at the doctrine of the Incarnation unless the Old Testament prepares them for it by its repeated covenantal structures, which involve divine-human words.

Berkouwer says, "Scripture was not given to us in the climate of a stupendous miracle" (p. 204)—as if the voice from Mount Sinai and the Ten Commandments graven on stone by the "finger of God" did not involve a miracle! Perhaps Berkouwer wants us to think of the fact that at times Scripture came less spectacularly, as in the gospel of Luke. So also Jesus' teaching on earth was sometimes given less spectacularly, without the fanfare of a spectacular visible miracle. But is his incarnate speech less weighty, less awesome, less inexhaustible, just because we are not dazzled by a magician's fanfare? It is not clear what point Berkouwer expects to make.

Berkouwer also believes that the analogy breaks down because we reject bibliolatry, the adoration of Scripture (p. 204). But he does not explore the distinction that I made above between the media (stone tablets, or paper and ink) and the message (the word of God).

Berkouwer rightly sees that we ought to avoid a "docetic" view of Scripture, in which its human form is suppressed (pp. 198, 202n). But where is there an analogous discussion of the "adoptionist" views surrounding us today?

It seems to me that Berkouwer's discussion has overlooked an important point. When Jesus spoke with a human voice on earth, his speech offered a bridge between the fact of the Incarnation and the issue of divine-human speaking as it occurs in the Bible.

13. Speculations abound as to the possible sources and allusions behind John 1:1–3 and the use of the term "the Word" *(ho logos)*. But we must not miss the obvious allusion to Genesis 1. The gospel of John invites Christian readers to understand it primarily in the light of its Old Testament background. As Jesus says later in John, "If you believed Moses, you would believe me, for he wrote about me" (John 5:46). Elsewhere in John, allusions abound to the Mosaic festivals and other symbolic materials from the books of Moses.

14. For a fuller discussion of the doctrine of the word, I must refer readers to the forthcoming book by John M. Frame on the doctrine of the word of God. Unfortunately, the material is available at present in its fullest form only in a classroom syllabus, "Doctrine of the Word of God," for a course at Westminster Theological Seminary in California. But for a condensation, see Frame, *Perspectives on the Word of God.*

15. Systematic theology has also used the terms *circumcession, circumincession, perichoresis,* and *emperichoresis* to express this relationship.

16. Modernist theology in all its forms denies these crucial conclusions. Some forms of modernism rebel against biblical teaching in obvious ways. But neoorthodoxy looks more attractive. It has many fine-sounding things to say about the word of God, but one seldom knows what is meant by "the word of God." Is such theology referring to Jesus Christ incarnate, subsequent to the Incarnation, or to the Second Person of the Trinity both before and after the Incarnation, or both to Jesus Christ and to the speech of God in Scripture, or to Scripture ? If neoorthodoxy calls Scripture the word of God, it does so only obliquely: Scripture supposedly "becomes" the word of God only at those times when it rises to become a dynamic pointer to Jesus Christ, who alone is the word of God in the proper sense. Neoorthodoxy pretends to appeal to the Bible, but, in the end, directly contrary to the Bible (see John 12:47–50), it simply smuggles in the idea that one can honor Jesus Christ and simultaneously not

honor his words. See the critique of neoorthodoxy in John Frame, "Scripture Speaks for Itself," in *God's Inerrant Word,* ed. Montgomery, 178–200; and J. I. Packer, *"Fundamentalism" and the Word of God* (Grand Rapids: Eerdmans, 1958).

Neoorthodoxy uses immense learning, profundity, and cleverness to conceal from itself the fact that it has smuggled in a mere autonomous supposition, the Kantian idea that God cannot manifest himself in the phenomenal world, and particularly in the world of human language. Not the Bible, but human philosophy in rebellion against God (emboldened by the "assured results" of modern criticism) has told them that the Bible is not actually the word of God, but only "conveys" the word from time to time into noumenal contact with the human soul.

■

CHAPTER 4

THE PURPOSE OF THE BIBLE

What is the purpose of the Bible? Understanding purpose is crucial to interpretation. People may, if they wish, use Milton's *Paradise Lost* to teach English, to practice counting letters, or to study poetic rhythms. But none of these is the main purpose for which Milton composed the poem. People may miss the main point if they use the poem for other purposes.

Indeed, this is part of the problem with the Bible discussion group that Libbie Liberal organized. The participants play with fascinating ideas that they spin off from their reading of the Bible. But they do not adequately reckon with God's purpose in it. Even in the Bible discussion that Chris Christian organized, people disagree. Peter Pietist thinks that the purpose of the Bible is devotion. Dottie Doctrinalist thinks that its purpose is to teach doctrine. Curt Cultural-Transformationist thinks that it is to set transforming human action in motion. Missy Missiologist thinks that the purpose is to bring the message of God to all cultures.

Let us again listen in on the conversation in Chris Christian's Bible discussion group. We join in the middle of a discussion of biblical purpose.

> **Oliver Objectivist:** *The purpose of any passage in the Bible is exactly the purpose that the human author expressed in the passage.*
>
> **Fatima Factualist:** *Unless there is explicit indication to the contrary, we should assume that the purpose is to tell what happened or what someone believes.*
>
> **Herman Hermeneut:** *But can't we see a larger purpose in a whole work, such as in the prophecy of Isaiah? Isaiah has a larger purpose in mind than stating each sentence, one at a time. If he does, doesn't God*

have a larger purpose in giving us the entire canon of Scripture, a purpose perhaps larger than that of any one book of the Bible?

Amy Affirmationist: *The Holy Spirit could have different purposes for each person who reads the Bible.*

Many Purposes

According to Scripture, the Bible does have many purposes. It is "useful for teaching, rebuking, correcting and training in righteousness, so that the man of God may be thoroughly equipped for every good work" (2 Tim. 3:16–17). Paul tells Timothy to "preach the Word; be prepared in season and out of season; correct, rebuke and encourage—with great patience and careful instruction" (2 Tim. 4:2). There are many different functions for various parts of the Bible, in teaching and instructing, rebuking and encouraging. At the same time, since God is one, there is naturally a unity of purpose to all his word. All his words manifest his glory (cf. John 17:1). In all his words to us, God enjoins us to "be holy, because I am holy" (1 Peter 1:16; Lev. 19:2; 20:7). Or, as James says, "Do not merely listen to the word, and so deceive yourselves. Do what it says" (James 1:22). All of the Bible leads to Christ (Luke 24:44–49).

We may misconstrue the Bible either by paying attention only to one purpose, or by reducing all the purposes to one, or by artificially isolating the purposes, as if we could adequately accomplish one in isolation from the rest. To avoid the extremes of isolation and reduction, we can once again use the model provided by the Trinity. We have already seen a unity in diversity and a diversity in unity in considering the forms of the word of God. The archetype for unity and diversity is found in God himself. Hence, we may conveniently begin with God's Trinitarian character.

Triune Purpose

In John 17, the Son reflects on his work by speaking of the "word" that the Father has spoken and that he has delivered. He also speaks of mutual indwelling (vv. 21–23) and of manifesting glory (vv. 4–5, 24). He speaks of communicating "the love you have for me" (v. 26), of having made and continuing to "make you known" (v. 26), and of the disciples' work in the world in imitation of his work (v. 18). We have many purposes here. But it is rather easy to see that they are all perspectives or ways of talking about one purpose, a comprehensive purpose involving the entire redemptive plan of the Father. The Son can express that one purpose in more than one way, and can describe it from more than one angle.

The angles of expression reflect in certain ways the distinctions and the unities among the persons of the Trinity. The statements about "work" focus preeminently on the work of the Son on earth. The Son has completed "the work you gave me to do" (v. 4). On the basis of this work, the disciples are sent out to work (v. 18).

The Son uses many expressions in speaking about his work. But since they all point to the same work, even one expression would in principle include the whole. For convenience, and to remind ourselves of the diversity as well as the unity in the work, we may sum up the expressions under three headings, corresponding respectively to the prominence of the Father, the Son, and the Spirit.

First, the Son asks that the Father equip, protect, and sanctify the disciples. The work of God involves action, power, and control from the Father. We may view the entire work from the perspective of *control*. (We associate *control* with the Father.)

Second, the work of God involves giving and receiving the truth, primarily through the Son: "I have made you known to them, and will continue to make you known" (v. 26); "I gave them the words you gave me, and they accepted them. They knew with certainty that I came from you" (v. 8). Truth is manifested in the Son (cf. John 14:6). We may view God's entire work, then, from the perspective of *meaning,* truth, and knowing. (We associate *meaning* with the Son.)

Third, God is personally present with the disciples through the process

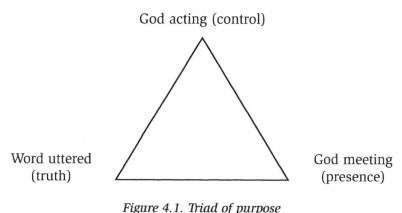

God acting (control)

Word uttered
(truth)

God meeting
(presence)

Figure 4.1. Triad of purpose

of indwelling, mediated by the Holy Spirit (vv. 21–23). Thus, we may view God's entire work from the perspective of personal *presence*. (We associate *presence* with the Spirit.)

In sum, we have three perspectives: control, meaning, and presence.[1] These are three ways of looking at the work of God in the world. We look at God controlling events; we look at the meaning and the truth that God makes known; we look at God's presence in the world and among his people. Through any one of these, as through a window, we can examine any particular work of God, or all the works comprehensively, just as Jesus did in John 17. Each is then a perspective on the whole.

We may apply this triad of perspectives specifically to God's word. The communication of words is one aspect to which Jesus refers (John 17:8, 14, 17). Since it coheres with the other aspects, we should expect that it manifests them all—and it does. The word of God controls people and events in the world. The word of God expresses and asserts meaningful truth. The word of God makes God himself present with us. God brings himself into contact with those addressed by his word.

Let us confirm these points one at a time. First, the word of God controls the sanctification of the disciples (John 17:17). Similarly, through the name of God (closely related to the word of God), the disciples are "kept" (vv. 11–12). Second, the words that Jesus speaks in John 17 are themselves representative of the "word" about which he speaks; they have infinite meaning. Third, through the words that Jesus speaks, the Father, as well as the Son, is personally present (John 14:9–10). The words "my words remain in you" in John 15:7 are parallel to "I in them" in John 17:23. The author is present in the words that he speaks. As the words remain in the disciples, they bear fruit through union with him.[2] Let us call this triad of terms (*control, meaning,* and *presence*) the triad of purpose, because each term represents one aspect of the way in which God expresses his purposes.

We saw that control, meaning, and presence can, in John 17, be correlated respectively with the Father, the Son, and the Holy Spirit. But the correlation is mysterious. And we must not think that it is the whole story. Because of the coinherence of the persons of the Trinity, they share in acts of control, meaning, and presence. For example, through the presence of the Holy Spirit (John 14:16–17), the Son also will come and be present (v. 18). Both the Father and the Son dwell in the believer (v. 23). Thus, all three persons participate in God's personal presence with believers. Similarly, all three persons exercise control in God's works, and all three express meaning in the word of God. All three persons share in the one purpose of God.

Remember now the triad of imaging, mentioned earlier, consisting of the originary, manifestational, and concurrent perspectives. How does this earlier triad relate to the present triad of purpose, consisting of control, meaning, and presence? When we compare triads like these, we may expect coinherence without mere mathematical identity. The two triads are not merely two names for exactly the same thing. Rather, the triad of imaging focuses on God's representation of himself, while the triad of purpose focuses on God's carrying out of his purposes. So the two triads speak in two different ways about the unity and diversity in God. Each term in one triad therefore involves features relating to all three terms in the other triad.

For example, God's control involves an originary aspect, consisting in God's attribute of omnipotence. God's control involves a manifestational aspect, consisting of actual acts of control over what he has made. God's control involves a concurrent aspect, in that the acts of control are in harmony with who God is in his omnipotence. Similarly, God's meaning involves originary, manifestational, and concurrent aspects. God's truth as it is eternally known to himself is originary. God's truth as it is made known to us is manifestational. And the harmony between our knowledge and God's originary knowledge is concurrent.

Although all these aspects involve one another, we may also sometimes notice a tantalizing relationship between the two triads. One triad, in some fashion, "mirrors" the second triad. For example, God's meaning exists even before it is manifested, which is closely related to the originary perspective. Thus, in some sense, meaning mirrors the originary perspective. God's control involves his action, which is closely related to his manifestation of himself. Control mirrors manifestation. God is present with us through indwelling, which is the concurrent aspect. Presence mirrors concurrence. (But note that we have reversed the normal order of control and meaning. Such rearrangements of order can occur when we try to compare two triads.)

The triad of control, meaning, and presence exists archetypally in the eternal relations of the persons of the Trinity. It applies ectypally in God's communication to the world and to us. His word to us exhibits control, meaning, and presence. It also applies ectypally when human beings communicate to one another. Each of us exerts control by communicating; we have something that we say (truth, or sometimes error); we say it to someone, drawing ourselves into a personal relationship with someone (presence). Receiving a communication involves responding to this control, hearing what the person says (meaning), and listening to the person as he is present with us in the communication.

How does this triad apply to the Bible? The Bible is the word of God to human beings, and hence it ectypally manifests the same triad. In the Bible we undergo transformation by God's control. We hear truth (the word). We meet God (personal presence). We may thus say that the purposes of the Bible are three: for God to transform people, for him to teach the truth, and for God himself to be present.

But, as we might expect, these three purposes are also one. The triad consisting of control, truth (meaning), and personal presence derives from Trinitarian interrelationships. It is an ectype of the Trinity, which is the archetype. The persons of the Trinity are coinherent, so the three aspects are ectypally coinherent. That is, they mutually involve one another. Meeting God always involves knowing something about him, and thus knowing truth. Knowing truth involves knowing God, who is the truth. Meeting God involves being transformed by his presence. We are overwhelmed and cannot remain the same. Even if we rebel against God, we do not remain the same, but become more guilty than we were before (cf., e.g., Ex. 7:5,17; 14:4). If we are transformed, it is only through the power of God working in us (Phil. 2:13; cf. Lam. 3:37–38; Eph. 1:11; Ps. 103:19).[3]

What are the implications for the practical study of the Bible? On the one hand, God has a plurality and richness of purposes for the Bible. We ought not to reduce it all to one monolithic purpose. For example, we ought not to reduce the Bible simply to personal encounter. We are not to be mystics, who try to achieve personal encounter with God without the presence of conceptual truth. Such was the tendency of Pietist in the Bible discussion group. In addition, we do not reduce the Bible to intellectual meaning. We are not to be intellectualists, who try to store up truth without paying attention to meeting God or practical living (doing what it says). Such was the tendency of Doctrinalist. We are not to be pragmatists, who care only for "the bottom line" of visible effects, without attending either to truth or to the God who speaks. Such was the tendency of Cultural-Transformationist.

But in emphasizing the diversity of purposes, we still affirm a unity. Each purpose points to and even encompasses the others. For instance, rightly knowing truth irreducibly involves knowing God, who is the truth (John 14:6). Hence, meaning, properly understood, includes personal presence. Knowing the truth also includes practical effects (2 Cor. 3:18; John 17:3). Hence, meaning includes control. Conversely, response in action, the practical side of obedience, includes cognitive action, that is, knowing truth. Similarly, response is proper only if it is response to the God who comes, response that reaches out in the personal encounter of worship. Thus, the aspect of control encompasses the aspect of personal presence. In a similar way, we can see that each aspect encompasses the other two aspects.[4] The aspects are coinherent.

Now this coinherence has a specific implication. Truth and application are distinguishable, but not isolatable from one another. They are two aspects of a coinherent triad. Truth is the content of Scripture (the meaning aspect), while application is the control of Scripture over our selves, our thoughts, and our behavior (the control aspect). The two coinhere.

God means and intends to communicate certain truths. He also means and intends that the truths be applied. The application is thus an integral aspect of the meaning. Meaning includes application. But, conversely, application includes meaning. Any particular application is an application of something, an application of a truth or truths. It is an application of the meanings of specific words or texts that are being applied. The application illustrates the meaning on which it is based. Moreover, the totality of application includes application in the mental sphere. Applying a verse includes applying it to our beliefs. It includes altering our beliefs so that they agree with what the verse says. That is, it includes attention to the meaning of the verse.

Consider a simple example: "Then in accordance with what is written, they celebrated the Feast of Tabernacles with the required number of burnt offerings prescribed for each day" (Ezra 3:4). "What is written" alludes to Numbers 29:12–38, Leviticus 23:33–43, and other passages in the Law of Moses. An aspect of the meaning of Numbers 29:12–38 is that people should celebrate with certain sacrifices. One implication of that meaning is that the people of Zerubbabel's time were required to do so. The action in Zerubbabel's time was an application of the text from Moses' time. That application was an implication of the meaning of the earlier text, and as such was an aspect of that meaning. But now there is another way of looking at the matter. One application of Numbers 29 is mental application. People should mentally grasp what God is prescribing. When Zerubbabel and others correctly grasp God's law, they grasp its meaning. Meaning is thus application in the mental sphere. Meaning is an aspect of application.

The same intertwining of meaning and application occurs in the foundational text in John 17. The Father has given his word to Christ, and Christ has given the word to the disciples (v. 14). He gives them the word with the intent that the Father will sanctify them by the truth (v. 17). This sanctifying is an aspect of the intention and the effect of giving the word; it is an aspect of the meaning of the communicative act. Conversely, one aspect of sanctifying is mental sanctifying, which is achieved through understanding the meaning. Thus, meaning is an aspect of the application, that is, the sanctifying. Meaning and application are even more impressively intertwined when we consider them on the level of divine action. The control exercised through the sanctifying work of the Father and the truth expressed through the word of the Son coinhere through the indwelling of the Father and the Son in one comprehensive work.

As we might expect, coinherent unity and diversity exist wherever we look in Scripture, whether our focus is on personal fellowship with God, on truth, or on application. Consider first the matter of personal fellowship with God. There is one God, and hence all Christian fellowship is fellowship with one God. Fellowship rests on the unity of the unchanging character of God. Such is the unity of fellowship. There is also diversity: many people enjoy God's fellowship, at many times, in many stages of growth, as 1 Corinthians 12 reminds us.

Or consider the matter of application. We obviously may find diverse applications to the diverse circumstances in which we live. Yet all the applications have a unified goal: they aim at holiness (Heb. 12:14; 1 Peter 1:15–16). They all aim at glorifying God (1 Cor. 10:31). Or, to express it differently, they aim at being like Christ, at conforming to the image of Christ (Rom. 13:14; 2 Cor. 3:18; 1 Cor. 15:49).

Finally, consider the issue of truth. The Bible contains many distinct truths in the distinct assertions of its distinct verses. But all these cohere in the One who is the Truth (John 14:6).

Christ as the Center of Scripture

It is worthwhile to develop in more detail the Christocentric character of biblical truth. A number of passages of Scripture indicate in more than one way that Christ is at the center of the Bible and the truth. John 14:6, "I am . . . the truth," is only one.

Colossians 2:3 says that "all the treasures of wisdom and knowledge" are hidden in Christ. "All the treasures" obviously includes all the truths of all the verses of Scripture. All of them are hidden in Christ.

John 1:1 and Revelation 19:13 indicate that Jesus Christ is the Word of God. As we have seen above, all particular divine words, from the words of creation onward, are manifestations of this one eternal Word.

Second Corinthians 1:20 says, "No matter how many promises God has made, they are 'Yes' in Christ." The promises of God all find fulfillment in him. Of course, only some parts of the Bible have the explicit form of a promise. But perspectivally speaking, all of the Bible contains a promissory aspect, since God commits himself to his people when he speaks to them.

First Timothy 2:5 and other passages indicate that Christ is the unique, indispensable mediator between God and men, by which we are saved and are able to listen to God without dying. Christ is indispensable for our right reception of Scripture. And since Scripture has the function of bringing salvation, it is fundamentally about Christ. "Preaching must be theological. Salvation is of the Lord, and the message of the gospel is the theocentric message of the unfolding of the plan of God for our salvation in Jesus Christ. He who would preach the Word must preach Christ."[5]

The claims in Luke 24:25–27 and 24:44–49 are particularly important. The disciples on the road to Emmaus felt defeated after Jesus' crucifixion. But Jesus rebuked them (vv. 25–27).

> How foolish you are, and how slow of heart to believe all that the prophets have spoken! Did not the Christ have to suffer these things and then enter his glory? And beginning with Moses and all the Prophets, he explained to them what was said in all the Scriptures concerning himself.

Thus, in this discussion on the road to Emmaus, Christ himself indicates that the Old Testament from beginning to end is about himself.

Sometimes people have thought that Christ is claiming only that a verse here and a verse there speak of the coming Messiah. And it is of course true that some verses speak more directly in this way. But the whole of the Old Testament is about God working out salvation. And salvation is to be found only in Christ. So the whole Old Testament, not just a few isolated verses, speaks of Christ. Luke 24:44–47 makes this claim more explicitly.

> He said to them, "This is what I told you while I was still with you: Everything must be fulfilled that is written about me in the Law of Moses, the Prophets and the Psalms."
>
> Then he opened their minds so they could understand the Scriptures. He told them, "This is what is written: The Christ will suffer and rise from the dead on the third day, and repentance and forgiveness of sins will be preached in his name to all nations, beginning at Jerusalem."

"The Law of Moses, the Prophets and the Psalms" cover most, if not all, of the Old Testament. The Jews conventionally divided the Old Testament into three parts, the Law of Moses, the Prophets, and the Writings. The Law of Moses consisted of Genesis through Deuteronomy. The Prophets included "the Former Prophets," or the historical writings of Joshua, Judges,

1-2 Samuel, and 1-2 Kings, as well as "the Latter Prophets," Isaiah through Malachi (but Daniel was customarily reckoned with the Writings). The Writings included all the other books, the most prominent of which was the book of Psalms. Since the Writings were a more miscellaneous collection, they did not until later have a standardized name.[6] It appears that at an early period "Psalms" was used as a convenient designation for this third group.[7] Thus, Jesus probably referred to the whole group of Writings, speaking of the Psalms as its most prominent member. But even if he did not—that is, even if he was referring only to the book of Psalms and not to the other books included among the Writings—he still encompassed the great bulk of the Old Testament within the sweep of his claims.

Note also that verse 45 says, "He opened their minds so they could understand the Scriptures." Here the entire Scriptures are in view, not just some of them, and certainly not just a few scattered messianic texts. Verses 46–47 indicate in what this understanding consists. "What is written"—the substance of the message of the Scriptures—he explained to be that "the Christ will suffer and rise from the dead on the third day." The whole Old Testament, we conclude, has as its central message the suffering and resurrection of Christ. This conclusion confirms what was said in Luke 24:25–27. The whole Old Testament is about the work of Christ, in that it points forward to this work as what "must be fulfilled" (v. 44).

Few would challenge the idea that Christ is the core of the message of the New Testament writings. But Luke 24 is striking in making an analogous claim about the Old Testament. Christ's work is the core of the purpose and import of the Old Testament as well as the New. But how can that be so, and how do we arrive at such an understanding? We do not want simply to force a Christological message onto a text in an artificial way. That would not be "understanding" the scriptural text in question, but simply imposing a meaning from some other (New Testament) text. But neither do we want to avoid taking up the challenge that Luke 24 offers. The alternative to a Christocentric understanding of the Old Testament is not understanding it rightly—not understanding it as Christ desired.

Understanding the Christocentric character of the Old Testament is not easy. The Scriptures are profound, and we cannot exhaust their implications. A good beginning can be made by studying the quotations and more direct allusions to the Old Testament that are found throughout the New Testament. In those passages Christ himself and his apostles instruct us in the proper understanding of the Old Testament. The book of Hebrews is particularly important because, of all the books in the New Testament, it contains the most lengthy discussion of the fulfillment of the Old Testament.

This matter is so important that is deserves a book-length treatment. Indeed, books have been written on the subject of Christ's fulfillment of the Old Testament.[8] Because of the availability of some of these works, we will go on to consider other topics, rather than expounding the Christological implications of the Old Testament in detail.

ENDNOTES

1. These three are a slight variation on John's Frame's triad of authority, control, and presence (with the order of authority and control reversed). See Frame, *The Doctrine of the Knowledge of God* (Phillipsburg, N.J.: Presbyterian and Reformed, 1987), 15–18, 42–48.

2. For further use of the triad of authority, control, and presence, see ibid.

3. One may find many other instances of perspectival relations in Frame, *Doctrine of the Knowledge of God*; Frame, *Perspectives on the Word of God: An Introduction to Christian Ethics* (Phillipsburg, N.J.: Presbyterian and Reformed, 1990); and Vern S. Poythress, *Symphonic Theology: The Validity of Multiple Perspectives in Theology* (Grand Rapids: Zondervan, 1987).

4. See Frame, *Doctrine of the Knowledge of God*, 17–18, for the coinherence of the three aspects in a general context.

5. Edmund P. Clowney, *Preaching and Biblical Theology* (Grand Rapids: Eerdmans, 1961), 74.

6. See Sirach 1:1; Roger T. Beckwith, *The Old Testament Canon of the New Testament Church and Its Background in Early Judaism* (Grand Rapids: Eerdmans, 1985), especially 110–80.

7. Ibid., 111–17.

8. See Clowney, *Preaching and Biblical Theology*; Edmund P. Clowney, *The Unfolding Mystery: Discovering Christ in the Old Testament* (reprint, Phillipsburg, N.J.: Presbyterian and Reformed, 1991); Vern S. Poythress, *The Shadow of Christ in the Law of Moses* (reprint, Phillipsburg, N.J.: Presbyterian and Reformed, 1995); Mark R. Strom, *Days Are Coming: Exploring Biblical Patterns* (Sydney: Hodder and Stoughton, 1989). Older works on typology are of considerable value: see Patrick Fairbairn, *The Typology of Scripture* (reprint, Grand Rapids: Baker, 1975).

CHAPTER 5

THE TRIUNE CHARACTER OF TRUTH

Herman Hermeneut: O.K. So we have achieved some insight into God and into the fact that he speaks. But shouldn't we also consider issues of language? After all, the Bible is written in human language. How does this fact limit what God says? What are the implications? What about considering what the character of truth is?

Missy Missiologist: Language is embedded in human culture. What we understand will depend heavily on the cultural context in which we read the Bible. We need to rise above the limitations of our own cultural context. Otherwise, we are in danger of hearing only what fits our culture.

Oliver Objectivist: But wherever we start, and whatever the biases of our own culture may be, the truth itself remains the same. The fixed, well-defined, objective meaning of the Bible is eternal truth.

Amy Affirmationist: No, I think the Holy Spirit may bring different truths to different people. Each person must find the truth that God gives him.

Dottie Doctrinalist: Human language has its foundation in the doctrine of creation. Let's go to Genesis.

We will now look more closely at truth and language. As we interpret the Bible, we are constantly faced with its language and its truth. But what is language? And what is truth?

Language as Imaging God

The Bible indicates that human beings were created in such a way that they could speak and understand language. Moreover, before human beings were created, God spoke. "God said, 'Let there be light,' and there was light" (Gen. 1:3). Divine language and divine speaking precede human language and human speaking.

Here we have another instance of imaging. Human beings use language because they imitate God, who uses language. God's speaking is the archetype for human speaking; human speaking is the "image" or mirroring of divine speaking.

Truth

Truth in human language also derives from a divine archetype. Jesus says that he is the truth (John 14:6; cf. 18:37). In his divine nature, he is therefore the archetype for all human manifestations of the truth. John's language about truth is closely related to the fact that Jesus definitively revealed God in his incarnation: "For the law was given through Moses; grace and truth came through Jesus Christ. No one has ever seen God, but God the One and Only, who is at the Father's side, has made him known" (John 1:17–18).

Thus, truth is Trinitarian in character. Jesus is the truth. At the same time, he is the truth about God the Father. He is the truth manifested through the power of the Holy Spirit (Isa. 61:1). Of course, we are speaking here primarily of central religious truth about God. But such truth cannot be isolated from all truth. God teaches human beings whatever truth they know, and he is the source of it all (Ps. 94:10; Rom. 11:33–36). Colossians speaks of "Christ, in whom are hidden all the treasures of wisdom and knowledge" (Col. 2:2–3).

We may summarize some aspects of truth using the triad of imaging that we introduced earlier. First, truth in the Father is original reality. Second, truth in the Son is the dynamic manifestation or image of the original reality. Third, truth in the Spirit is the harmony between the Father and the Son through their mutual indwelling. We may say that this truth is the concurrence of the Father with the Son, the presence of each with and in the other. Thus, we have three categories: original reality, dynamic manifestation of the original, and concurrence of the dynamic expression with the original. These categories describe the relations of the persons of the Trinity. But these divine relations are imaged and mirrored in the experience that human beings have of truth. We experience both reality and a particular manifestation or way of grasping that reality through a particular revelation.

We can illustrate this unity in diversity with the four Gospels. The four

Gospels describe one Christ and one series of events in his earthly life. There is a unity to the truth of the four Gospels,[1] but also a diversity in their emphases and in the ways in which they present Christ. In Matthew, Christ is preeminently the Davidic king, so Matthew appropriately begins with the genealogy running through the kings of the Davidic line. In John, Christ is the Son of the Father, revealing the Father. In Luke, Christ is the one bringing salvation to the poor and prophetically proclaiming Jubilee release (Luke 4:18–19). In Mark, the Son of Man comes to destroy the kingdom of Satan. The diversity of the four Gospels is of course the product of the distinct personalities, interests, and situations of the four human authors. But God wills this diversity as well. The diversity is divine as well as human.

The Gospels in their plurality, as well as in their unity, represent God's interpretation of the life of Christ. We do not need to go behind the diversity to find the "real" Christ. A person who reads only one of the Gospels can already know the real Christ, precisely in knowing him in the concrete manifestation in that one gospel with its distinctive point of view. At the same time, that point of view is not the only possible one that is true.

As a result of coinherence, there may be both multiple expressions of truth and, at the same time, unified truth that these multiple expressions express. The diverse manifestations coinhere.

Now compare this approach with popular alternatives. Rationalism expresses a fragment of truth by stressing the unity, stability, and self-consistency of the truth. God is one and is faithful to himself. (This view is an exaggerated form of Objectivist's approach.) But rationalism counterfeits this reality if it then pictures truth in a way that eliminates the personality of God, the diversity of persons in the Godhead, and the dynamic aspect in the Son's relationship to the Father. It then suppresses the diversity and creativity in the manifestations of the truth. The result is that we begin to think that we can find real truth only beyond the diversity of its concrete manifestations. Truth is then an abstraction from the world. It becomes remote.

At the other extreme, relativism expresses a fragment of the truth by emphasizing the diversity of the manifestations and the perspectives of the different persons. (It is an exaggeration of Amy Affirmationist's approach.) But it introduces a counterfeit when it then claims that there is no absolute truth. It falsifies the divine nature by undermining the unity of God and the unity of truth. Truth splits apart into the often contradictory views of different individuals and communities.

In the Trinity, we do not sacrifice unity to diversity or diversity to unity. The Trinity provides an answer to relativism through coinherence. The diversity of manifestations or viewpoints does not imply the destruction or the inaccessibility of truth. Rather, God speaks through the Holy Spirit. Hence, rather than being inaccessible, truth is inescapable!

Let us illustrate again from the Gospels. In reading any one account, we may grasp Christ truly, though not exhaustively. Christ, as the truth, meets us and comes all the way to us in any one gospel, through the Holy Spirit. Moreover, the truth in any one gospel coheres with the truth in the other gospels.

God is one, and does not contradict himself. We may not always be able to give a definitive harmonization of all truths, for we are creatures and our knowledge is limited. Moreover, in sin we may twist and distort the truth. But in the midst of our limitations we may still know Christ, whether through one gospel alone or through all of them together.

We should appreciate the distinctive emphases of any one gospel, but not at the expense of denying the unity of all four. Thus, grasping truth and knowing truth do not depend on our rising above all perspectives and human limitations, but rather on appropriating and enjoying what God supplies to us where we are.

Here we find also the beginnings of an answer to the vexing problems of multiple cultures and contextualization with which Missy Missiologist is concerned. Through the Spirit, who is the Creator, God is present in all the nooks and crannies of each culture. To be sure, human cultures are contaminated by sin. God may confront human beings to judge and punish sin as well as to reveal himself in blessing. But in spite of sin, people do not escape from God. They suppress the truth about him even while they know it (Rom. 1:18–21). They try to run away from him, but they cannot escape from him (Ps. 139). Hence, we do not need to rise above the particularities of Chinese culture, or ancient Hebraic culture, in order to know God truly. We need to be freed from sin, in its cultural as well as its individual manifestations. But God and his truth can come to us right where we are, even in the midst of sin. We do not first disengage the divine truth in the Bible from its cultural setting in the ancient Near East—that would be impossible anyway, since we ourselves are part of a particular culture. Anthropologists may try to rise above all cultures, but their methodologies and tools for doing so belong inextricably to the Western academic subculture of theoretical anthropology! We do not, then, disengage the Bible's truth from the particularities of cultures, but rather grasp the truth as it inheres in its particular cultural setting. Each *manifestational* instance of the truth is a manifestation of *originary* truth. The instances are *concurrent* with the truth that they manifest.

Secular Theories of Truth

From this standpoint, we can also see how secularist theories of truth fare. There are three main kinds of approach: coherence theories, correspondence theories, and subjectivist theories.[2] According to coherence theory, a system of thought is true if it is consistent with itself. God is consistent with himself. His consistency is guaranteed by the unity of God and the indwelling of the persons of the Godhead through the Spirit. If our thought is consistent or coherent with the thought of the indwelling Spirit, it is true.

According to correspondence theory, thought is true if it corresponds to what is the case. The Son, as the image of God, corresponds to or matches the Father. Truth is the correspondence of the Son to the Father. Or, for human beings made in the image of God, our thought is true if it corresponds to, that is, images, the thought of the Son.

According to subjectivist theory, truth has to do with what a personal subject acknowledges. Truth is what God the Father knows. My truth is what I acknowledge, to the degree that it is not I alone but the indwelling Spirit who leads me into truth (John 16:13).

Thus, all three theories in their secularist form have a grain of truth, but they also distort the truth. They become counterfeits of Trinitarian truth.

Truth as Analogical

From the character of God, it follows that truth is inherently analogical. We never completely dispense with analogy and metaphor. Whether a particular piece of our language is mostly literal or mostly metaphorical, it images the divine language of God and the truth of God. The imaging relation is itself analogically related to the original imaging between the Father and the Son. Because God is unique, human beings image God in a way that is analogous to, but not identical with, the way in which the Second Person of the Trinity images the Father. As the Son is not identical with the Father, so the created images are not identical with the uncreated. As the Father and the Son coinhere, so the divine truth coheres with its images in human knowledge. We may never bring God down to the same level as creatures. But the Bible indicates that we may see analogies between what is true of God and what is true of us. For example, John 17:21 compares the oneness of believers with the oneness of the Father and the Son, even though the two kinds of oneness are not on the same level.

Every attempt to dissolve all analogy and metaphor into a single level of purely literal language fails to do justice to this mystery of coinherence.

ENDNOTES

1. Because God is consistent with himself, and because truth is one, the Gospels do not contradict one another. Sometimes we may find *apparent* contradictions, but closer study often reveals a probable harmonization. And even if we cannot find a harmonization through our limited human efforts, there is always a harmonization known to God.

2. See further John M. Frame, *The Doctrine of the Knowledge of God* (Phillipsburg, N.J.: Presbyterian and Reformed, 1987),133–34, 141–42, 149–64.

CHAPTER 6

·

MEANING

Herman Hermeneut: *Now what about meaning? What do we mean by "meaning"?*

Missy Missiologist: *Meaning depends on the culture of the hearer.*

Oliver Objectivist: *I grant that different cultures may have their biases. But meaning is the same throughout all cultures. It is the fixed content of what is said.*

Amy Affirmationist: *But couldn't the same verse mean different things to different people? Couldn't every one of the meanings be the work of the Spirit?*

Curt Cultural-Transformationist: *Meaning has to be worked out in action, or it means nothing—it's mere hypocrisy.*

Laura Liturgist: *Real meaning can be discovered only through participation in worship.*

Doctrinalist: *It's all about what God has in mind.*

Objectivist: *It's all about what the human author has in mind.*

The differences that we have already seen in the Bible discussion group tend to reappear when the issue of meaning is discussed. So we need to consider the question of meaning. If all particular truths cohere with one another and are perspectives on one another, do texts have one meaning or many?

And what do we mean by "meaning," anyway?

Consider a particular example: John 17: 4 says, "I have brought you glory on earth by completing the work you gave me to do." What is the meaning of this verse? How does its meaning relate to other verses of the Bible? What is its meaning for us?

Unity and Diversity in Content

John 17:4 says something definite. Other verses do not simply repeat this one, but say other things. At the same time, all the verses of John and all the verses of the Bible fit together to teach coherent truth. Two verses never contradict one another, but say things in harmony with one another. As there is both unity and diversity in the truth, so there is both unity and diversity in the meanings of different verses. As usual, God's Trinitarian character provides the archetype for our understanding of the unity and diversity in truth and meaning. The truths and meanings of different verses are different, yet together they form a larger whole.

We could understand this unity and diversity by developing an analogy from the earlier idea of one originary truth and multiple manifestational expressions of it. But instead, let us develop a new triad of categories.

The Word, in his incarnate life, manifests who God always is. He is God. Hence, everything he does manifests who God is. At the same time, he is a particular person in the Godhead. So he manifests God in a particular way. He is the Word become flesh. The Son, and not the Father, became incarnate. In the Incarnation, the Son shows that he is a particular person, distinct from the other persons of the Godhead. There is both unity—one God—and diversity—the particularity of who the Son is in his incarnation. We may associate with this unity in diversity a triad of categories.

First, we may express the unity in God by speaking of a *classificational* aspect of the revelation of God in the Word. God is one and the same God throughout history. Every particular act of God is a manifestation of the class "God." It is the same God who is always revealed. The *classificational* as-

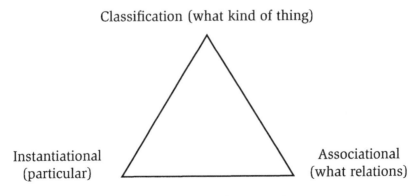

Figure 6.1. Triad of partitioning

pect pertains to the unity in all the instances that reveal who God is. Of course, all three persons of the Godhead remain the same throughout history. But it is preeminently the Father who remains the same, through the diversities of the coming of the Word in flesh and the pouring out of the Spirit at Pentecost. We associate the classificational aspect with God the Father.

Second, we may express the diversity in God's acts by speaking of the *instantiational* aspect of the revelation of God. By this we mean that every act of God has its own individuality. One act is distinguishable from other acts at other times. Each one is an instance of God's action. The Word who became flesh (John 1:14) is an instantiation of God. We associate the instantiational aspect with the Second Person of the Trinity.

Third, we may express the unity in diversity and the diversity in unity by speaking of an *associational* aspect. By this we mean that different instances of God's action are all in harmony with who he is: they cohere with his unchangeable character and they cohere with other instances of his action. In the associational aspect, we focus on the relationship between instances and the general class. The associational aspect is expressed in the statement "The Word was with God" (John 1:1). The Word has an association with God. As we have seen, this association consists of mutual indwelling (John 17:21). It is mediated through the Spirit. So we link the associational aspect with the Holy Spirit.[1]

We thus have three categories: classificational, instantiational, and associational. Together these form a triad of coinherent perspectives.[2]

Now, each particular event in the earthly life of Christ was an instantiation or manifestation of the one God, who is classificationally the same. The presence of the Holy Spirit guarantees that the particular instantiations are all associated with the one God. They manifest who this God really is.

The particular truths about the particular events are like instantiations. One God knows all these truths, which therefore classificationally belong to the single category "truth." Moreover, all the truths coinhere or are concurrent.

Suppose that we consider two truths: God is righteous, and God is all-knowing. These statements are distinguishable and are particular. At the same time, they describe one God. Each casts light on the other. God's righteousness is all-knowing righteousness. And God's knowledge is righteous knowledge. We do not properly understand God's knowledge if we think it is knowledge in unrighteousness; nor do we understand God's righteousness if we do not think it is informed by complete knowledge. Hence, the two statements inform one another and are deeply involved in one another.

Each in a sense presupposes the other. In this way the two statements coinhere. They are aspects of a unified truth, namely, that God is God.

The two statements in their relation to one another therefore show classificational, instantiational, and associational aspects. Classificationally, they point to one unified truth, the godhood of God. Instantiationally, each says a particular thing, distinct from what the other statement says. Associationally, they interpret and expound each other through coinherence.

In like manner, the record of individual events in the life of Christ in the Gospels contains many instantiations. Each individual statement or incident is particular, exhibiting the instantiational aspect. Each also fits into a narrative whole, expounding the character of the one Christ, who is the same in all these events, thus exhibiting the classificational aspect. Finally, the different statements and incidents interpret one another and mutually expound one another, thus exhibiting the associational aspect.

In agreement with the nature of the Trinity, the classificational, instantiational, and associational aspects coinhere in the Trinity. By analogy, they coinhere in the particular manifestation of Trinitarian truth in the Bible. Hence, we know that classificational, instantiational, and associational aspects coinhere in each and every truth found in the Bible, and in each and every meaning expressed in the Bible.

A Triad for Meaning

Now let us apply this triad, consisting of classificational, instantiational, and associational aspects, to a chosen passage of the Bible. Its message has classificational, instantiational, and associational aspects. Because this topic is so important for us, we will employ more terms. We will speak of the sense, the application, and the import of the passage.

Let us call the classificational aspect of a passage the *sense* of the passage. We can reexpress the sense through paraphrase, but we still intuitively know that it is the same sense. Any particular expression of the sense involves a particular series of words or sentences uttered at a particular time and place. We may rephrase the same truth in different words. But the sense that we express remains fundamentally the same. God is the same, and he remains faithful to himself at all times. The truths of God remain the same. Hence, God guarantees the stability of the sense, throughout all the ways that we may choose to express it.

For example, consider John 17:4, "I have brought you glory on earth by completing the work you gave me to do." This verse says what it says. The

Son, not someone else, has brought glory to the Father. He has done so specifically "on earth," not in some other location. He has accomplished a particular work rather than being idle or independent. The particular truth here is the sense of the verse.

Second, let us call the instantiational aspect of the passage its *application*. *Application* is a most apt term to use in the case of imperative passages. "Pray continually" (1 Thess. 5:17) is instantiated or applied when a particular person prays continually. His or her praying is an application of the command in this verse.

We want to stretch the word *application*, however, to cover other kinds of use as well. A teacher may teach "pray continually" either by saying those words, by a paraphrase, or by an illustration. Each such act of teaching is an "application" of the content that is taught. Each inference from a truth of the Bible is an application of the truth. *Application*, in this use, includes not only obedience to commands, but appropriate cognitive, verbal, behavioral, and attitudinal responses to assertions, questions, commands, meditations, and any other kind of communication in the Bible. An application is any instantiation of a passage in word or deed; it is an illustration, realization, or unfolding of the consequences of a passage within a particular context in the world. Now the applications are first of all what God in his wisdom plans and foresees. God knows all possible applications before any human being even hears the text. Applications are ultimately what God has in view, not what human beings succeed in doing.

Finally, let us call the associational aspect *import*. The import of a passage then resides in the multitude of its connections with other passages and other truths, so that each throws light on the other. John 17:4 is a good

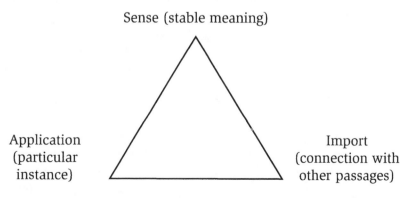

Figure 6.2. Triad of meaning

illustration of this process. In the phrase "completing the work," Jesus alludes to the entire course of his earthly ministry. The meaning of the phrase is filled out by perusing the rest of the gospel of John and seeing what particular works Jesus had in mind. The expression "you gave me to do" is supplemented by all the other passages in John that talk in one way or another about the Father sending and commissioning the Son. By putting 17:4 together with the rest of the gospel of John, we understand more than we could from reading the verse merely in isolation.

Thus, we have a triad of meanings: sense, application, and import. As usual, the three coinhere and offer perspectives on one another. Nevertheless, for many people, "meaning" naively has associations very much like our idea of "sense." "Meaning" is any paraphrased restatement of the main point of a text, taken more or less in isolation. If we chose, we could of course define "meaning" as identical with "sense." The important point is not how we label any of the three elements of our triad, but rather that we see that the three coinhere.

Application presupposes sense. Application is an application of something, namely, the sense. Concrete particulars make sense only in the context of the general meanings or senses that they illustrate. Conversely, sense presupposes application. No sense can be grasped without application—without grasping ways in which it would make cognitive, ideational, and behavioral differences in particular instances. If a child could parrot the words "You shall not steal," but could not paraphrase or explain it and could not exhibit behavior illustrating it, we would rightly say that the child did not yet really understand it.

Sense also presupposes import. Sense exists and is intelligible within a surrounding context, both historical and textual. The context in its relation to the sense constitutes import. Conversely, import presupposes sense, in that import arises from relations among senses. Sense arises out of the particularity of application, and import arises out of the particular senses that relate to one another. Application becomes possible only within a context of import and a context of other meanings that guide the interpretation of the relation of a sense to a particular situation in which it is applied.

It follows that understanding a passage always involves an interplay of sense, particular application, and the associational richness of contexts (import). People instinctively follow this interplay all the time when they read and understand. But some theories would prefer a world in which sense could be rigidly isolated and considered independently of an indefinitely large context of applications and associations.

Depth in Import

The associations of one text with its larger context extend out indefinitely. Hence, sense, though definite, coheres with import that is indefinitely deep. Let us illustrate by considering John 17:4 again. John 17, as we saw, is not merely the word that God speaks to us, but the word that God speaks to God. That is, the Son speaks to the Father.

To be sure, John 17 is written by John to us. It is a record of the speech that the Son gave earlier. But in the record, John points us to the speech itself. Through the perspective or window of John's written record, we hear the speech, not merely a record without value. Since John is inspired, his perspective faithfully reveals the original.

Now, in the divine speech of the Son to the Father, expressions like "I brought you glory," "completing the work," and "you gave me" have infinite meaning. We know that they do because in fellowship the Father and the Son share infinitely rich knowledge, and that knowledge is summed up in the expressions in question. The expressions do not lose anything in their definite sense; rather, they gain in rich allusions.

As human beings, we do not suddenly obtain an infinite depth of knowledge in our reading of John 17:4. But we know that we can grow in understanding indefinitely. As the Lord gives us knowledge of himself through other passages, in the course of our whole life, we come to know God more and more, with more and more depth (John 17:7, 21, 25–26). As we come to know God more, we see more and more of the implications contained in the divine communication between the Son and the Father in John 17:4. Thus, in this passage an indefinitely deep richness extends also to us.

In John 17:4, it is quite evident that sense, application, and import cohere. They are not neatly separable. The applications include all the particular "works" that the Son accomplished on earth. These do not exist in pure isolation, but enjoy what meaning they have in the context of a unified work, "*the* work you gave me to do." The sense of the verse involves this work. All the applications are implications of the one sense, that is, the general claim that the Son makes. By "completing the work," the Son has completed by implication all the particular works. He turned the water into wine, he conversed with Nicodemus, he conversed with the Samaritan woman, he fed the five thousand, and so on. These implications, according to most views, are part of the "meaning," and thus are included in the sense.

But the sense, understood accurately, is not simply any sense that could be attributed to the words in John 17:4. Rather, it is the sense that they actually had when spoken by the Son at a particular time and place. That sense can be interpreted only through context. We are tacitly invoking import when we reckon with the other passages of John that speak of the particularities in the "work" of the Son. Conversely, the import made up of all the passages taken together can be appreciated only by appreciating the sense of each particular passage. Sense, application, and import interpenetrate.

Meaning and Application

How does this view of meaning and application compare with other views? It is important to underline three features of this approach. First, God gives stability to meaning and to sense. Because God exists, and because he is the ultimate source of meaning, meaning is not just mush. It is not just a human invention that we manipulate as we wish.

Second, God is not only the author of the words of Scripture, but also their interpreter. This fact is most obvious when God explicitly speaks to God, as in John 17. But by virtue of the Holy Spirit's role as "hearer" (see John 16:13), we can infer the same conclusion with respect to other passages.

Third, contrary to some popular versions of meaning-application theories, meaning and application coinhere. Each is a perspective on the other, and neither can in the end be understood or even discussed or identified without tacit understanding of the other.[3] God plans and intends that his words should have the effects on readers that they have. This intention includes all the details of all the applications throughout history. The applications are part of God's intention. Hence, in the usual approach that identifies meaning with authorial intention,[4] all the applications are part of the meaning. Conversely, each application, if it is an application at all, is an application of something: it is an expression or instantiation of the intention of God, an intention that covers more than one application. Hence, the very idea of application presupposes a unity of meaning through the unity of God's plan.

In short, we can associate meaning with the classificational aspect, and application with the instantiational aspect. We also have a relation of meaning to application, using the context of other truths and other meanings: we have the context of import.

Evangelicals have rightly maintained that secularist reader-response theories threaten to undermine all stability in meaning, leading to a situation where every man does "that which is right in his own eyes." By contrast, God provides stability to meaning. Since God does not change (Mal. 3:6), neither does the meaning of his word change. God knows the end from the beginning (Isa. 46:10; cf. Ps. 139:16). He possesses all import in the infinitude of his wisdom.

Now one aspect of God's wisdom is his plan for history. Events develop in time. To human beings on earth, import becomes accessible only gradually. We compare later events with earlier ones. By using the import perspective, we can understand the grain of truth in reader-response approaches. The Holy Spirit continues to speak and teach Christians today (2 Cor. 3:16–18; 1 John 2:20–27; cf. John 16:7–16, which applies primarily to the apostles but secondarily to all believers). The canon of the Bible is complete, but redemptive history continues to unfold through the reign of Christ. Consequently, our understanding of the Bible continues to change and grow. This growth takes place through God's continuing to speak through Scripture. What he says does not change, but he continues to instruct us by saying it. In this sense, the communication is not over. From the standpoint of historical development, from the standpoint of the experience of individuals and the experience of the church, the import for human beings is incomplete and changing dynamically. Closure comes with the Second Coming (1 Cor. 13:12).

The Divine and the Human in the Bible

We have derived richness in meaning from reflecting on the fact that it is God who speaks. What now is the role of the human speaker or author?

God made man in his own image (Gen. 1:26–27). Human language mirrors divine language. We may expect that it has a derivative richness mirroring the richness of divine language. Human speaking involves sense, application, and import. Human assertions and commands have a stable sense expressed in a particular manifestation or application, in the context of a larger network of meanings that make up import.

Now what is the relationship between the divine and the human? What is the relationship between the divine and the human in the Bible? Each book of the Bible has a human author as well as the one divine author. Do the two authors, divine and human, mean the same thing or different things?

We may use as our model the way that Christ speaks in John 17. The divine Christ speaks, and simultaneously the human Christ speaks. By virtue of the unity of the one person of Christ, we may rightly say that one person speaks. The particular speech in John 17 is thus a single speech from a single person, simultaneously divine and human. As divine utterance, verses like 17:5 have infinite meaning, as we have seen. As human utterance, they express finite knowledge on the part of the speaker. As God, the Son knows all things (Matt. 11:27); as man, his knowledge is limited (Luke 2:52). How can we possibly comprehend this mystery? We cannot. It is the mystery of the Incarnation.

Through this mystery we may nevertheless come to understand what God has revealed in Christ. We see a harmony between the divine and the human. Christ the man does not know all the details of God's plan, but he does know the basic facts of his own role, including the presence of his divine nature (John 17:5). In his human nature, he knows that there is more knowledge in his divine nature than what he knows. He alludes to that infinite knowledge in John 17:5. In his human nature, he uses language that includes the divine infinite.

Conversely, Christ the eternal Son knows all the details of God's plan. Included in that knowledge is the knowledge of his human nature, and of the concrete role that he plays with respect to his human nature in the events of redemption, "completing the work you gave me to do" (John 17:4), "while I was with them" in the incarnate state on earth (John 17:12). God the Son affirms the particular significance of the actions of his human nature. By implication, he affirms the significance of the limitations in knowledge that accompany the speech of his human nature on earth. Within the infinitude of the divine plan, this and not that bit of knowledge is singled out to be communicated to Christ's human nature—and to his disciples.

What we have here is unique, because it belongs to the uniqueness of Christ's incarnate state. But, at the same time, Christ's unique incarnation reveals who God always is. We have here an instance of the operation of the triad of imaging, consisting in originary, manifestational, and concurrent perspectives. The originary perspective in this instance arises from Christ's divine nature, the manifestational perspective arises from his human nature, and the concurrent perspective arises from the unity of the two natures in one person. Starting with any one of these, we end by affirming all. All are inextricably involved in one another.

To put it another way, the finite meanings of Christ's human nature point to, and are in union with, the infinite meanings of his divine nature. Each is a perspective on the other.

We may now extend the lesson from John 17 to all of the Bible. Christ is the final Prophet (Acts 3:20–26). As such, he is absolutely unique. But he is thereby also the model for how all prophets functioned throughout the Bible. Only through the mediation of Christ may we sinners receive the word of God and yet live. The ministry of other prophets thus presupposes the ministry of Christ and is theologically founded on him.

The prophets, then, tacitly affirm the presence of God in their speaking. When they say "Thus says the Lord," it is not merely they as human beings speaking, but God speaking through their speaking. Conversely, the Lord affirms the significance of the prophets in directing our attention to them and not merely to his voice in bare isolation: "If anyone does not listen to my words that the prophet speaks in my name, I myself will call him to account" (Deut. 18:19).[5]

Second Peter 1:20–21 explicitly combines divine and human action: "Above all, you must understand that no prophecy of Scripture came about by the prophet's own interpretation. For prophecy never had its origin in the will of man, but men spoke from God as they were carried along by the Holy Spirit."

In prophetic inspiration, the divine and human aspects enjoy inner harmony. But the divine and the human are not strictly identical or indistinguishable. Christ as man points beyond the limits of his human knowledge in John 17:5, without having to exceed the finite limits of his human nature. Christ as God knows the limits of his human nature, without being confined to those limits when as God he addresses the Father in this passage.

We cannot, then, strictly limit ourselves to the "human" Christ when we read John 17. Verse 5 explicitly forbids it. What can we infer about Scripture? Christ has a divine and a human nature. Scripture has divine and human speaking. The analogy is not exact. But it is still suggestive. We cannot strictly limit ourselves to the human speaking when we interpret Scripture. The phrase "Thus says the Lord" on the prophet's own lips explicitly forbids it.

Now let us return again to the question of infinite meaning. As we have seen in John 17:5, when God addresses God, we are dealing with an infinitude of meaning.

But an objector says, "Wait! John 17 is the word of John the Evangelist to us. We can limit ourselves to the finite meaning of John the Evangelist." No, we cannot. The Evangelist intends that we should hear the Son speaking. The Son indicates his deity in John 17:5. The Evangelist is then in effect confessing that, although he does not comprehend the depths of infinite meaning in that verse, he invites us to join with him in contemplating that infinitude. His intention is to reveal to some extent an infinitude that he does not himself fully comprehend. To be loyal to the Evangelist's intention we need, as it were, to go beyond his intention, or, more precisely, to go beyond his comprehension. The human mediation of John the Evangelist, like the human mediation of Christ on which it is built, does not block off infinitude, but gives access to it.

We have arrived, then, at a partial answer to Oliver Objectivist. Objectivist located meaning exclusively with the human author, and insisted on the precise stability of one meaning. He is right in seeing the importance of the human in God's message to us. And he is right to insist on stable meaning, that is, stable sense. But sense coinheres with application and import, so that it is illusory to try to deal with sense in pure isolation. Moreover, the human meaning of the prophetic authors coinheres with the divine meaning, so that it is illusory to try to restrict oneself to a purely human level.

Diversity in the Mode of Divine Authorship

John 17 furnishes a model not only for understanding the divine and the human, but for understanding the diversity in divine modes of address. Divine speaking includes the Father speaking, the Son speaking, and the Spirit speaking. They speak to one another and to human beings. John 14–17 reveals a striking diversity in mode of address, because of the plurality of persons in the Trinity.

An analogous diversity appears when God addresses human beings. God can address people in an audible voice, as at Mount Sinai (Ex. 20:18–19). He can write with his own finger on tablets of stone (Ex. 24:12; 31:18; 32:16). He can also raise up a prophetic mediator, like Moses (Deut. 5:22–33; 18:15–18). The prophet can say "Thus says the Lord," and then speak for the Lord in the first person (e.g., Ex. 32:27; Isa. 43:14). He can also quote what the Lord has said to him: "The LORD said to me, 'I have heard what this people said to you'" (Deut. 5:28). And he can also speak back to the Lord in his own voice, "But now, please forgive their sin—but if not, then blot me out of the book you have written" (Ex. 32:32).

Naively, we might suppose that only the speech of God addressed to the prophet is really the divine voice, and that the prophet then speaks in his own voice to the people. But that is not correct. The prophetic speaking to the people is still divine speaking, not merely a quote from the past divine speaking to the prophet. The prophetic word to the people not only quotes God, but carries forward to the people the word of God to the prophet. The prophet passes along what he has heard. This passing along is analogous to what happens in John 17: the Son's word to the disciples passes along the Father's word to the Son. His word is also the Father's word. The prophet's word to the people is also God's word to the people.

Consider another mode represented in John 17. When the Son speaks to the disciples, his speaking includes the Father's speaking by dwelling in the Son (John 14:10). Likewise, the prophet's speaking to the people in the name of God includes God's speaking to the people through the prophet. The Son speaks back to the Father concerning the disciples and the Father's plan for them. Likewise, under inspiration the prophet speaks back to God concerning the people (Ex. 32:32).

We need, then, to head off the idea that only one kind of speech, such as "Thus says the Lord," constitutes the real divine speaking. Within Scripture the genres of speaking are quite diverse. For example, in the Psalms, human psalmists pour out to God their remarkably human struggles, doubts, and expressions of trust. These psalms represent human beings speaking to God. Some interpreters have then taken the next step and concluded that the humanity excludes deity: these psalms, they say, are not instances where God speaks to human beings. But such a conclusion is false. John 17 is the speech of a human being to God, but it is also the speech of God to God. Likewise, the Psalms are speeches of human beings, but these human beings were "carried along by the Holy Spirit" (2 Peter 1:21), so that the words are also divine. The Psalms are perfect examples for the people of God to imitate, examples pointing forward also to the perfect speech of man to God in the person of the God-man, Jesus Christ. The Holy Spirit groaned within the psalmists, after the manner of Romans 8:26–27, so that God and man speak in the same act of communication. However, they do not speak in the same way. The "I" of the Psalms is directly the human suppliant; the Holy Spirit speaks not by being literally the "I," but by instructing the psalmist and us concerning the manner in which we are to pray. The joint speaking is possible because of indwelling, that is, an Old Testament precursor of the New Testament indwelling that we see after Pentecost.

In sum, we need to do full justice to the fact that not all Scripture presents itself to us in the same way. The texture differs according to whether God addresses human beings, or human beings address God, or human beings quote the address of God. We do not flatten all these textures into a boring monotone. The diverse textures, far from eliminating the divine presence, confirm the rich Trinitarian character of that presence.

This richness is wonderful. But it does confront Oliver Objectivist with certain difficulties. On whose meaning do we focus? Not only do we confront the dwelling of the divine in the human, but the dwelling of the divine in the divine. We deal with the distinct voices of the Father, the Son, and the Spirit. We must obviously try to appreciate and understand all three, in unity and in diversity. Such is not the original program that Objectivist had in mind when he used a picture of a single meaning that would be simply one without Trinitarian diversity.

The Concerns of Scholars

The concerns of Objectivist are of broader interest. Objectivist thinks in the same way as many scholars do. Ideally, in their view, interpretation pursues an objective meaning that is "there." By accumulating sufficient information about language and historical background, and by sifting this information with sufficient intellectual acuity, using the proper techniques, scholars may hope to discover the objective meaning. Safety resides in cutting the objective meaning loose from the subjective response of the interpreter. Are the concerns of these scholars valid?

Such desire for objectivity raises many questions. Which is primary, sense or import? Meaning or application? Stability or living interaction in interpretation? Objectivity or subjectivity?[6] Being intellectual or being emotional in our response to the text?

All of these questions seem to produce a dilemma. But they are all false alternatives. In fact, responsible biblical interpretation includes the two seemingly incompatible poles harmoniously. As God purifies us, we as subjects begin to listen humbly to the objective aspects of the textual message. The objective message, in turn, has the power to transform us subjectively. Diligent application leads to sanctification. When we become godly, we obtain a firmer grasp of the sense. Deeper absorption of the sense leads to more diligent application and greater godliness.

Thus, we reject both kinds of one-sidedness. We need sense, application, and import, all three.

First, we need to understand the sense. We need to pursue God by listening to what he says. We need to grasp the sense of each passage more and more accurately and more and more deeply. The Holy Spirit is never in tension with what God has said once and for all. The Holy Spirit speaks "only what he hears" (John 16:13). Moreover, the Holy Spirit, as Creator, has supplied all the good resources that we find in language and culture. The Holy Spirit produces all godly scholarship. Thus, the best tools of godly scholarship play a valuable role in grasping this sense.

Second, the Holy Spirit leads us into application. We do not rightly interpret the Bible if we ignore its demand to be applied. "Do not merely listen to the word, and so deceive yourselves. Do what it says" (James 1:22). Application brings us into conformity to Christ, so that we know his mind. Then we interpret Scripture more accurately.

Third, the Holy Spirit uses import in instructing us. We need to understand the overall message of the Bible, not merely a jumble of details. Lest the Corinthians miss the main point, Paul summarizes the whole of his message in 1 Corinthians 15:1–4.

The Holy Spirit is our teacher in all these aspects (1 John 2:20–27). But we are still on the way. We are not always good at bringing the different poles together. If you will permit me to exaggerate, I will draw the following caricature. The Christian church splits into scholarly and nonscholarly parties. The scholarly party cares only for objectivity, rigor, and the recovery of the Bible's grammatical-historical sense. The nonscholarly party tries to apply devotionally whatever ideas come into the mind when the Bible is read, and does not ask itself whether God could be saying one definite thing. But both of these responses are recipes for stultification.

Fortunately, people do learn from God and from other members of the body of Christ (1 Cor. 12). The potential split that I described is continually being healed. But there are still tendencies in these two directions.[7]

The scholarly party is small in number, but it is educated and privileged. We tend to draw a flattering picture of ourselves. Naturally, as the educated, we "know" what the problem with the masses is and what they need. They need to follow us. We are the leaders, the vanguard. We see and understand the teaching of the Bible more deeply.

I sympathize with one aspect of this picture, namely, the desire that others should profit from scholars' insights. But there are at least two things wrong with this picture. First, we who are scholars are not as well off as we think. We still have spiritual deficiencies. We who are scholars need to know God, and to apply this knowledge to every aspect of our scholarship as well as our everyday lives. The application to our lives, in turn, influences the skills and fruits of scholarship.

The second problem with the scholar's self-portrait is that it subtly depreciates the work of the Holy Spirit among nonscholars. The Holy Spirit dwells in ordinary believers, as well as scholars, and guides them into the truth.

In particular, we need to look carefully at the ways in which nonscholarly people use God-given insight into biblical texts. Scholars tend to see in nonscholarly imagination only ignorance and uncontrolled subjectivity. And of course sometimes they are right. But often something very profound is going on. What looks suspicious to many scholars may actually be a work of God.

Illustrations Using Analogy

When nonscholars engage in the most subjective flights of imagination, they use analogies. A passage in the Bible calls to mind a situation that they once were in, or a saying that they have heard, or a theory that they once had. They can do such things only because they, like the most careful and exacting scholar, are roaming about in the richness of the connections among the truths of God (the associational aspect). They are exploring remote regions of the import of a passage.

Now we must be careful. Human beings on earth are sinful. God does not endorse whatever comes into our minds. But we are dependent on God for our minds. And we are dependent on God for the associations that we can make between truths or between opinions that we take to be true. Even in the midst of our error, we do not escape relying on connections that God himself has established and ordained.

Hence, the connections that people find, however strange, were created not by them, but by God. God thought these connections before any human being ever did. God made sure that these connections were of such a kind, and in such contexts, that people could discover them.

Hence, people can discover truths of God in strange ways. They may wildly misunderstand the sense of a text, and yet arrive at a conclusion endorsed by other parts of the Bible. If we have been in Christian circles for a while, we have seen this sort of thing happen. For example, a newly converted young man reads Acts 18:2, "Claudius had ordered all the Jews to leave Rome." He decides that God is commanding him to move out of his girlfriend's apartment and stop sleeping with her. The conclusion is biblical, but it is supported by other passages, not by Acts 18:2.

Let us consider a more complex example. We start with Isaiah 54:4–5, which says,

> Do not be afraid; you will not suffer shame.
> Do not fear disgrace; you will not be humiliated.
> You will forget the shame of your youth
> and remember no more the reproach of your widowhood.
> For your Maker is your husband—
> the LORD Almighty is his name—
> the Holy One of Israel is your Redeemer;
> he is called the God of all the earth.

I once heard a widow testify how much this passage had comforted her. She said that when she lost her husband, the Lord had given her this passage, promising that he would be her husband.

Scholars who examine the original historical context know that Isaiah is speaking to Jerusalem, pictured as a widow and personified (see Isa.

52:9–10). Jerusalem, in turn, stands more broadly as an exemplar of God's dealings with his people as a whole. The sense of the passage is concerned with the spiritual and physical restoration of Jerusalem and the people of God, not the comforting of a widow in the literal sense.

Thus, the woman's interpretation looks to the scholar like a totally arbitrary leap. But of course there are loose, analogical associations between the various ideas. If there were no such associations, the woman herself would probably not have seen any connection between the passage and her own situation. She would not have been comforted by going back to it.

The analogical associations are associations between various elements in the truths of God. Many of these truths are taught somewhere in the Bible. Other truths we infer from a large number of passages, taken together. For instance, according to 2 Corinthians 1, God undertakes to comfort his people in many different circumstances. Widowhood is one such circumstance. Hence, the Lord did promise to meet the woman's need in her widowhood.

The woman was not wrong in her conclusion. Neither was she wrong to think that there was at least a loose association between the comfort-in-widowhood complex in Isaiah 54:4–5 and the comfort-in-widowhood complex in her own life. She would have been wrong, of course, if she had insisted that the sense of the passage was her comfort. But it is very unlikely that she was actually claiming anything that precise. Rather, she was saying, "This is how the Lord applied the passage to me." Nonscholars do not usually invoke the technical idea of sense. They do not make precise distinctions between sense, import, application, and loose association. The widow does not carefully distinguish these aspects, but unconsciously weaves them all together.

Was the Holy Spirit involved in what happened to the woman? She learned a biblical truth, even though the truth does not attach primarily to the sense of Isaiah 54:4–5. How do we describe this situation? Is it the work of God? Did the Holy Spirit use the loose association to bring home to the woman the biblical truth that God would comfort her in her widowhood?

I say yes. But how do we know? We know because God is sovereign over the operations of the human mind, including this widow's mind. And from 2 Corinthians 1 we know that the final effect is biblical. Her conclusion does not contradict the teaching of Scripture as a whole, but rather conforms to it.

In fact, in this particular case, the loose association with Isaiah 54:4–5 is not so loose as we might suppose at first. Galatians 4:27 indicates that the promise to Jerusalem in Isaiah 54 is fulfilled in the heavenly Jerusalem, the church. Our widow is a believer. She belongs to the heavenly Jerusalem.

The benefits that Christ purchased for the church flow to her also, since she is united to Christ. Christ is the church's husband, as Ephesians 5:22–33 points out. If she is a member of the church, he is a husband to her in particular. The imagery of widowhood in Isaiah 54:4–5 is in fact especially appropriate to her, because she is in need of comfort in a way pointedly analogous to the comfort of which the passage speaks. When we take into account enough biblical context, the passage (with its context) does apply to her, and applies in the way that she understood.

People without professional training are often unable to fill in all of these steps. The widow may not have been able to cite Galatians 4:27 and Ephesians 5:22–33 and set forth a theology of New Testament fulfillment in order to defend her interpretation. But the Holy Spirit knows all these connections and all the possible supporting arguments. Most important, he knows what he is doing with the woman.

In short, this woman's conclusion from Isaiah 54:4–5 is fundamentally sound. But can we endorse everything that people come up with? Clearly not. Sinful human beings can come up with heresies and distortions when they read the Bible. How do we tell the difference between the woman's conclusion and a heretical conclusion? We must go back and examine the Bible, just as we did when we appealed to Galatians 4:27 and Ephesians 5:22–33. The Bible must remain our ultimate standard. Any conclusions in tension with it must be rejected.

Thus, it is not true that anything goes. We do not just accept anything, in the way that Amy Affirmationist is tempted to do. But we can acknowledge that the Holy Spirit sometimes teaches people in mysterious ways, through associations as well as through self-conscious logic.

We can extrapolate from cases like the widow's to even stranger analogies. We may include even the young man's "misuse" of Acts 18:2 to conclude that he stop living with his girlfriend. The Holy Spirit uses texts as a springboard to enlist and stimulate believers' spirits. As Creator and the sovereign ruler over language, he establishes and superintends all associations and analogies. He includes in his domain not only the "tight" analogies used when scholars reexpress the sense of a passage, but the loose metaphoric analogies that we associate with the function of spiritual intuition. Import extends out and ultimately embraces all the truth in the entire plan of God.

If people's spirits are attuned to loving God, and if the Holy Spirit guides them, people arrive again and again at biblical conclusions. Scholars may say that these conclusions are unsound. But the Holy Spirit is Lord, ruling over scholars as well as everyone else. In agreement with scholars, we must acknowledge that there is a distinction between paraphrase and other dimensions of language. We acknowledge the stability of the sense of a passage. In agreement with intuitive nonscholars, we acknowledge that there are a host of other pathways of analogy, all of which may be pathways for discovering the truth of God.

Augustine makes a similar observation:

> Since, therefore, each person endeavours to understand in the Holy Scriptures that which the writer understood, what hurt is it if a man understand what Thou, the light of all true-speaking minds, dost show him to be true although he whom he reads understood not this, seeing that he also understood a Truth, not, however, this Truth?[8]

In the first half of the sentence, Augustine focuses on the concern of scholars for understanding the sense: "that which the [human] writer understood." But in the second half, Augustine acknowledges that God may choose to teach another truth by means of the passage. The legitimacy of the effect is based on the unity of truth in one God. Augustine also says,

> He who knows the Truth knows that Light; and he that knows it knoweth eternity. Love knoweth it. O Eternal Truth, and true Love, and loved Eternity! Thou art my God; to Thee do I sigh both night and day.

> If we both see that that which thou sayest is true, and if we both see that what I say is true, where, I ask, do we see it? Certainly not I in thee, nor thou in me, but both in the unchangeable truth itself, which is above our minds.[9]

We must add one further point that Augustine presupposes: there is a difference between truth and error. We must sift conclusions that we reach, whether we have used logic or whether we have used intuitive connections. Not all the thoughts of all human beings are equally acceptable. Human beings are sinful. God uses preestablished analogies to trap the fool in his folly as well as to encourage the faithful.

Moreover, although there is an antithesis in principle between those who serve God and those who do not, in this world we are all inconsistent. We should not abandon ourselves to all kinds of folly just because we are believers. We must not fondly hope that our imaginations are now so impeccably good that God endorses whatever pops into our heads! We ought not to be naive about our remaining sinful inclinations, the temptations of Satan, and the sin of testing God (for example, when Satan calls on Jesus to throw himself down from the pinnacle of the temple). We ought not to endorse every strong impression, and equate the moving of the Holy Spirit with our feeling that the Holy Spirit is moving us. Church history is strewn with the wreckage of spiritual movements that yielded themselves uncritically to a supposedly direct "inspiration of the Spirit."[10]

How then do we tell the difference between ideas and associations that God endorses and approves, and those that he does not? Once again, God's word itself, the Bible, is our standard. And the more directly available sense of a passage is the proper starting point for further reflection. The Bible is clear: "The statutes of the LORD are trustworthy, making wise the simple" (Ps. 19:7). God disapproves of whatever stands in tension with the Bible's teaching.

We must also bear in mind that God judges attitudes of the heart, not merely outward actions or theological conclusions. Suppose a person uses an outlandish association between texts of ideas, and nevertheless happens to conclude with something that is biblical in content. God endorses the conclusion. But he does not endorse the process of traveling toward the conclusion, as if it were an ideal example of biblical reasoning. Nor does he necessarily endorse the person. People with good, active intuitions may easily use their gifts as an excuse to become lazy. Their attitude is then sinful, even though their conclusions may be orthodox in particular instances.[11]

I conclude, then, that God intends to use, and often does use, loose associations within his system of truth to accomplish his purposes, even the most strange. If these are an aspect of his intention, they are also a part of import. The import and application of Scripture are exceedingly broad. In their outermost reaches, they encompass the entire truth that God teaches in the Bible. The truth of the whole in this sense coheres with any one passage. At the same time, and in harmony with this expansive import, the sense is stable. All of God's purposes are stable, having the very stability of God.

We can reinforce the same conclusion by pointing to our earlier reflections on concurrence. All of God's truths dwell in him, since he indwells himself exhaustively. They are then concurrent with one another. The thought of any such truth leads naturally, through its revelation of the divine being and glory, to the thought of all other truths, insofar as these are accessible to human beings, that is, insofar as the Holy Spirit may reveal them to us. All "leaps" from one biblical truth to another, however strange they may appear to scholars, have their ontological basis in the unity of God's plan and the unity of his wisdom. Every truth is concurrent with every other one, on the basis of the omnipresence of God and his self-presence to himself through the Spirit (1 Cor. 2:10).

Creativity

We should also remember that God is the Creator. He can surprise us with what is new. He is not the prisoner of mechanism. What he says at a particular time is not merely a mechanical effect of what he has already said. God addresses new circumstances. His love and faithfulness guarantee that what he says to us will be accessible to us. But what he says becomes accessible through his presence as a person, as well as through the stability of the content of his words. Content and personal presence are complementary perspectives on communication, and neither can simply be eliminated in favor of the other.

Hence, in God's communication, the import of a whole passage is indicated by its parts and its context, and simultaneously exceeds purely mechanical calculation. We gain access to this import through the operation of rational faculties and simultaneously through the creativity of the human spirit and the superintendence and control of the Holy Spirit.

People have from time to time touched on these realities when they say that interpretation is an art, not a science. That is, it is not mere mechanical technique. It is not a procedure that can be carried through with confidence and accuracy regardless of our spiritual state. For that matter, science and scientific study are themselves not mere technique. But we would deflect from our main point if we pursued this claim.[12]

Hence, we may view present-day interpretive "leaps" from the standpoint of creativity. When such leaps land on results and applications that are biblical in character, we may see them as the creative work of the Holy Spirit, who superintends the creativity of the human spirit. But, as we have observed, leaps do not always land in safe places! Only some, not all, conform to Scripture.

Diversity in the Body of Christ

Finally, we must reckon with the diversity of the body of Christ. Although the sense of a passage is unified, its applications are diverse. There are diverse people to whom the passage applies, and there are diverse circumstances to which each person applies the passage. Missy Missiologist is right in stressing that applications may differ from culture to culture.

Applications can arise from one passage or from many taken together. When a passage is tied to a particular application by close and obvious analogical connections, we are comfortable in saying that the application is an application of this one particular passage. For example, if I refuse to cheat on my income tax, that is an application of "You shall not steal."

In other cases, we come to a conclusion by listening to many passages. For example, I have to decide how many cars to have in my family, when to buy a new or used car, and what kind to look for. God guides me in the Bible through instructions about materialism, use of money, use of gifts, care for one's family, care for the poor, reliance on God, the importance of motives, the value of other people's counsel, prayer, and so on. All these instructions I bring to bear on circumstances that in their details are not quite the same as anyone else's. "You shall not steal" has broad implications for the care of property, both mine and other people's; hence, many godly decisions about property are in a sense applications of that commandment. But the application requires creativity, imagination, and vision in understanding God and how he sees my needs in my circumstances.

A closer examination even of an easy case, like income tax, shows that it is not a trivial application. Contextual elements from other places in the Bible come to bear. I need Romans 13:1-7, Matthew 22:15-22, 1 Peter 2:13-17, and similar passages to teach me that the government has a legitimate right to taxes, instead of taxation itself being a form of theft that I ought to resist. Such passages become even more important if the government is using my money for unrighteous purposes, such as to support atheism or abortion. I may also be helped by reflecting on the truthfulness of God, and seeing that I ought to tell the truth on my income tax report.

Thus, it is hard to find a case that is merely an application of a single passage, giving no attention to a larger sweep of context. In fact, in the strict sense it is impossible, since it is impossible even to take the first step in deciding the most basic sense of a passage without some interaction with the truth of God, and hence some interaction with all kinds of contextual dimensions. Even the simplest-looking applications of one passage invoke more than this one passage; they rely most basically on knowledge of God. Application depends on contextual relations, that is, on import, the larger family of truths.

Conversely, it is hard to find a case of application, even the most complex, that does not amount to an application of one of the Ten Commandments. All discussions of theological doctrine are applications of the commandment "You shall not give false testimony against your neighbor." As John Frame argues, each of the Ten Commandments can be seen as a perspective on who God is and what his will is for all of life.[13] Hence, all of life is an application of each one of the commandments.

Inevitably, interpretation differs from person to person and from culture to culture. Through Scripture, God speaks to each person in order to apply his word to that person in many particular situations. The applications differ from person to person, and even from one time to another in a given person's life. The implications of God's word are not exhausted by any one person or any one time of life. They include God's entire plan for the entire course of history. At the same time, God discriminates between good and evil. His word distinguishes righteousness from unrighteousness. Not all supposed applications are legitimate. All legitimate applications harmonize with the sense of Scripture.

Remember that God is intimate with us. A human speaker may be skillful enough to speak to a diverse audience so that everyone in the audience remains interested and receives something, but not all receive the same thing. Jesus' parables illustrate an analogous effect in the case of God's communication. But now we can see that at the level of detailed application, God's communication always works in this way. It differentiates its effect into the many diverse applications made by different people.

The oneness of God's being is the irrefragable foundation for the oneness of his truthfulness, the oneness of his purpose, and the stable oneness of the sense of his words when he speaks to us. But we may also affirm the reality of plurality. The mysterious Trinitarian plurality in God's being is the foundation for the plurality of the world, the plurality of history, and the plurality of particular purposes that God accomplishes in history. The diversity of types of people in the body of Christ images the richness of God's Trinitarian love. The diversity of applications in different people's lives does not contradict God's unity, but rather is in harmony with it.

Of course, some people may use these facts as an excuse for reasserting human autonomy. They may say, "I may do whatever I want, since my behavior does not have to match anyone else's." We need to remind such people of the distinction between God's approval and his disapproval. I have been speaking about "applications," but I have in mind legitimate applications, approved applications. Genuine applications take place in obedience to God. Not all supposed "application" is genuine obedience. We must be alert to the devil's deceit and the possibilities for our own self-deceit. Excuse-making may conceal sin from human beings, but not from God.

When God traps the sinful and the foolish in their self-deceit, he is also using his word to do so. Hence, even sinful misinterpretations of the Bible are "applications" in this broad sense. However, they are not applications with which sinners should be comfortable! In such cases of application, the word brings sinners into judgment and curses them. The word applies to them as the two-edged sword of the warrior, which brings destruction as well as grace. We find salvation from our folly only as God pursues us so that we may begin to pursue him.

The Positive Role of Scholarship

Although I have said a good deal about the possibilities for the Spirit's work among ordinary people, it should be clear that I affirm the value of sense. And with that affirmation I also affirm the value of scholarly study of the Bible, when such study is conducted in a godly fashion, subject to the word of the Lord. Scholarly study helps refine the whole church in its grasp of the sense of Scripture. That was true particularly during the Reformation; it can be true now.

We must avoid driving a wedge between creation and redemption, favoring one and despising the other. The Holy Spirit plays a key role in both creation and redemption. He was instrumental in creation (Gen. 1:2; 2:7). The Spirit is the source of all intellectual gifts and faculties in creation. He is also the source of true redemptive understanding (1 Cor. 2:8–16). Appreciating the Spirit implies appreciating both his creational and his redemptive gifts—including intellectual ability, as well as humility, spiritual discernment, and ability to fight the devil's deceits.

The unbelieving scholar makes a mistake when he prizes intellectual gifts, but neglects repentance, humility, spiritual discernment, and renewal of the mind (Rom. 12:2). But, conversely, the believing simpleton makes a mistake when he prizes repentance and spiritual discernment, but neglects intellectual gifts as if they were innately "worldly." In fact, gifts relating to teaching and communicating the gospel have a particularly prominent and leading role in the total process of the growth of the body of Christ, as Paul indicates by singling out such gifts in Ephesians 4:11–16. But the relative prominence of such gifts does not undermine the importance of the fact that "each part does its work" (Eph. 4:16). The two sides belong together, in exactly the manner in which they appear together within a single body, as described in Ephesians 4:11–16.

ENDNOTES

1. For further discussion, see Vern S. Poythress, "Reforming Ontology and Logic in the Light of the Trinity: An Application of Van Til's Idea of Analogy," *Westminster Theological Journal* 57 (1995): 187–219.

2. These three categories are closely related to my earlier terms *contrast, variation,* and *distribution,* respectively, which are used in Vern S. Poythress, *Philosophy, Science and the Sovereignty of God* (Nutley, N.J.: Presbyterian and Reformed, 1976), 123; and Vern S. Poythress, "A Framework for Discourse Analysis: The Components of a Discourse, from a Tagmemic Viewpoint," *Semiotica* 38, no. 3/4 (1982): 289–90. The earlier categories derive from Kenneth L. Pike's terms *feature mode, manifestation mode,* and *distribution mode,* in Pike, *Language in Relation to a Unified Theory of the Structure of Human Behavior,* 2d rev. ed. (The Hague: Mouton, 1967), 84–93; see also Kenneth L. Pike, *Linguistic Concepts: An Introduction to Tagmemics* (Lincoln: University of Nebraska Press, 1982), 41–65. I employ a new terminology here in order to make my meaning more transparent, to emphasize the basis for the categories in the Trinitarian revelation of John 1:1, and to expand the potential range of the application of the categories. My newer terms express aspects of God, and they pertain analogically to anything in creation. They have the generality of Pike's earlier terminology. However, the terms *contrast, variation,* and *distribution* are customarily narrower: they denote three aspects of the description of linguistic units. They are thus the expression of classificational, instantiational, and associational aspects in a particular area, namely, in the description of a single linguistic unit.

3. See John M. Frame, *The Doctrine of the Knowledge of God* (Phillipsburg, N.J.: Presbyterian and Reformed, 1987), 83, on the intertwining of meaning and application. Frame uses the two terms interchangeably, while I distinguish them. Although our use of terms differs, our views are very similar, since I hold that meaning and application coinhere and thus are inseparable.

4. E.g., E. D. Hirsch, *Validity in Interpretation* (New Haven: Yale University Press, 1967). One may find similar positions widely held among evangelical interpreters and analytic philosophers. For a brief argument in favor of the coinherence of meaning and application, see Frame, *Doctrine of the Knowledge of God,* 83–84, 97–98. Frame says, more provocatively, that meaning *is* application (p. 97), and he proposes to use the two words interchangeably (p. 83), while I distinguish them in their nuances and make them perspectivally related. I do not think that there is a substantive difference here.

5. See further Vern S. Poythress, "Divine Meaning of Scripture," *Westminster Theological Journal* 48 (1986): 241–79.

6. Frame, *Doctrine of the Knowledge of God,* has much valuable material on the tendency to introduce false polarities between objectivity and subjectivity.

7. Note the discussion between Oliver Objectivist and Peter Pietist. Pietist represents the pole emphasizing application. Objectivist is only one example of an emphasis on grammatical-historical objectivity. Dottie Doctrinalist and Fatima Factualist might be other examples.

8. Augustine, *Confessions,* in *A Select Library of the Nicene and Post-Nicene Fathers of the Christian Church,* ed. Philip Schaff (reprint, Grand Rapids: Eerdmans, 1979), 12.18.

9. Ibid., 7.10; 12.25.

10. See Richard F. Lovelace, *Dynamics of Spiritual Life: An Evangelical Theology of Renewal* (Downers Grove, Ill.: Inter-Varsity, 1979), 262–69.

11. Augustine returns to this point again and again: "But because they [disputants] contend that Moses meant not what I say, but what they themselves say, this I neither like nor love; because, though it were so [!], yet that rashness is not of knowledge, but of audacity; and not vision, but vanity brought it forth. And therefore, O Lord, are Thy judgments to be dreaded, since Thy truth is neither mine, nor his, nor another's, but of all of us, whom Thou publicly callest to have it in common, warning us terribly not to hold it as specially for ourselves, lest we be deprived of it" (Augustine, *Confessions,* 12.25).

12. See, for example, Michael Polanyi, *Personal Knowledge* (Chicago: University of Chicago Press, 1958); Stanley L. Jaki, *The Road of Science and the Ways to God* (Chicago: University of Chicago Press, 1980); Cornelius Van Til, *Christian-Theistic Evidences* (Nutley, N.J.: Presbyterian and Reformed, 1976); Vern S. Poythress, "Science as Allegory," *Journal of the American Scientific Affiliation* 35 (1983): 65–71; Harry Van Der Laan, *A Christian Appreciation of Physical Science* (Hamilton, Ont.: Association for Reformed Scientific Studies, 1966); Thomas S. Kuhn, *The Structure of Scientific Revolutions,* 2d ed. (Chicago: University of Chicago Press, 1970).

13. John M. Frame, "The Doctrine of the Christian Life," unpublished classroom syllabus, Westminster Theological Seminary in California, Escondido, California, n.d.; Vern S. Poythress, *Symphonic Theology: The Validity of Multiple Perspectives in Theology* (Grand Rapids: Zondervan, 1987), 32–34.

CHAPTER 7

■

TERMS

Herman Hermeneut: In our discussion, we have to be self-conscious about the terms we use. Do we know what we are doing when we use words? This becomes especially crucial when we use key words in theology. For example, what do we mean by the word God?

Fatima Factualist: We mean what the dictionary says it means.

Dottie Doctrinalist: No, we have to let God define himself. A dictionary can't capture the full range of what God teaches about himself.

Laura Liturgist: We must encounter God in worship.

The insights that we have gained concerning meaning can also be applied to meaning at a low level: the meaning of terms.

Infinite meaning belongs to the total discourse in John 17. Does such infinitude belong also to the term "glory" in John 17:5? "The glory I had with you before the world began" is infinitely rich. "Glory," in the context of the utterance, appears also to be infinitely rich, in that it encompasses and evokes the infinitely rich knowledge of Christ's preexistent glory. Thus, individual terms confront us with mysteries analogous to what we already saw in John 17 as a whole.

Terms and Naming

What are the terms and names that we use, and where do they originate? God's name identifies himself. By analogy, God gives names to creatures and to aspects of creation. We understand the names and terms for creatures by analogy with the name of God himself. Since the name of God

95

is Trinitarian (Matt. 28:19), we expect other names to be dependent on the triune God.

To put it another way, human words are ontologically dependent on the eternal Word, revealed in John 1:1. Human words exist according to the pattern of the eternal Word. Hence, human words show classificational, instantiational, and associational aspects.

For example, consider the word *camel*.

First, *camel* has an instantiational aspect. It occurs in various instances. It may be pronounced rapidly or slowly. It may be used to refer to any of a number of different creatures in the camel class, both one-humped dromedaries and two-humped Bactrian camels.

We learn the word *camel* through instances of its occurrence in certain contexts and associations. Perhaps we see some pictures of camels. Or we just hear a verbal description. Either way, the particular pictures or the particular verbal descriptions are instances or "instantiations" that are necessary for learning what a camel is.

Frequently, if not always, the particularities color our subsequent knowledge. Immediately after we have learned the meaning of the word *camel*, it means for us "an animal like the ones I saw in the pictures," or "an animal matching the description that I heard and the impression that I formed in my mind." We may of course modify our knowledge by further experiences in which we see camels, smell them, or have them mentioned to us. But these later experiences involve more instantiations. The further instantiations modify the impact of the initial instantiation. We never simply dispense with instantiations.

Second, *camel* has a classificational aspect. Every instance or occurrence of the word *camel* belongs to the class "camel." We classify a particular occurrence as an instance of the word *camel*. There is a unity belonging to all such instances, namely, the unity of the one word *camel*. That word is recognizable in and through all the individuality of its particular occurrences.

As an expression of this classificational unity, we recognize this word as distinct from other words in English. It is distinct in pronunciation. It is identifiable as a certain sequence of sounds or letters ($c + a + m + e + l$) in contrast to other possible sequences. It is distinct in meaning. It singles out large mammals of the genus *Camelus*, with their characteristic features, in contrast to other kinds of animals. It contrasts with other words, such as *dog*, *horse*, and *pig*. Contrast is an integral feature of the classificational aspect of words.

Third, *camel* has an associational aspect. The word occurs in many different verbal contexts. It is used in various situations that may help to make plain which camel is being referred to—contexts of human communication in which we speak, listen, and think. It occurs in the context of the English language and speakers of English. We learn the word *camel* as children by observing contexts in which it is used.

Our word *camel* presupposes God's word governing the creation of camels. The word is one in all its occurrences because God is stable and self-consistent; his word concerning camels has unity. The human word *camel* has a diversity of particular occurrences because God in his creativity and fecundity ordains a diversity of occurrences. There is an associational context of human words because any particular word of God has an associated context in a whole plan, according to the unity of God's wisdom.

The three aspects, namely, the classificational, the instantiational, and the associational, coinhere. Any particular instance of the word *camel* must be identified as an occurrence of this word, rather than some other word. Hence, the instantiational aspect presupposes the classificational aspect. We can talk about the class "camel" only if we are able to produce particular occurrences or instances of the word. Hence, the classificational aspect requires the instantiational—and so on.

In principle, we could conduct a similar analysis of any word in any human language. All words have classificational, instantiational, and associational aspects.[1] This situation derives from the fact that human language and human words are dependent on God's language. God's speech is necessarily Trinitarian, trimodal, and coinherent. Human speech is dependent. Since it provides access to real knowledge of God, it is necessarily trimodal and coinherent by analogy.

We can see similar effects when we look, not at words and language, but at earthly creatures. Camels themselves, as creatures, were created through a Trinitarian operation. The Father is the Creator (1 Cor. 8:6), the Son is the Creator (1 Cor. 8:6; John 1:3; Col. 1:16), and the Spirit is also the Creator (Gen. 1:2; note Ps. 104:30, where there is a providential action analogically related to the original creating activity of God). What are some of the implications of this?

First, in accordance with the classificational aspect, all camels are camels. According to Genesis 1:24, they reproduce "according to their kinds." In accordance with the faithfulness of God, they hold to a common pattern fixed by the word of God, the pattern of being a camel. Camels thus display the faithfulness, the self-consistency, and the unchangeability of God, as Romans 1:20 indicates. The Word is who he is from all eternity (John 1:1). So, derivatively, analogically, camels are what they are in constant conformity to the pattern that God specified in the constant word.

Second, in accordance with the instantiational aspect, each camel is particular. Each one is itself and no other. Each camel is an instantiation. It is a particular being, not simply "camelness," nor simply a camel, but *this* camel.

The Word is himself particular, in relation to the category of God. Derivatively, analogically, the Word calls forth particular creatures (Pss. 104:30; 147:15). These creatures exist and are sustained in conformity with the word that creates them (John 1:3; Heb. 1:3). Each camel displays the control of God over details, and each camel displays the creativity of God through its uniqueness in being what it is.

Third, in accordance with the associational aspect, all camels exist in contextual associations. Camels live in certain ways, eat certain foods, and are used by people for certain purposes. The eternal personal association of the Word is the original to which all creatural associations analogically relate. The existence of a camel in association with other things displays the universal presence of God, by which he holds all things together (Col. 1:17).

Word and Thought

So far we have focused almost wholly on words and expressed language, rather than on thought. Do the same considerations apply to thought as well as to language?

In God there is a close relationship between thought and word. His speech is in accordance with his thought. Isaiah 46:10 illustrates this: "I make known the end from the beginning, from ancient times, what is still to come. I say: My purpose will stand, and I will do all that I please." In the clause "I make known . . . ," God speaks of what he is making known to human beings, and hence he includes his words to them. In the later clauses, "My purpose will stand" and "I will do all that I please," he speaks of his will—his inward thought, if you will. Clearly his word conforms to his thought.

We might infer the same conclusion from John 1:1. The Word of God is an expression of his thought, in analogy with the fact that the words of human beings express their thoughts. In this close relationship between thought and word, the thought belongs preeminently to the Father, while the Son is his Word. On a human level, we may say that the relationship between human thought and human word is analogical to the relationship between the Father and the Word. Consequently, the same fundamental mysteries confront us with respect to both thought and word. If we wished, we could analyze thoughts as well as words in terms of the classificational, instantiational, and associational aspects.

In both thoughts and words, we deal with profound mysteries. In both cases we deal with matters that reflect the Trinitarian character of God. In neither case can we be complacent about our own supposed mastery.

ENDNOTE

1. One may see further development of these concepts in a linguistic context in the tagmemic theory of Kenneth L. Pike. Note the use of the terms *feature mode, manifestation mode,* and *distribution mode* in Kenneth L. Pike, *Language in Relation to a Unified Theory of the Structure of Human Behavior,* 2d rev. ed. (The Hague: Mouton, 1967). The terms *contrast, variation,* and *distribution* appear in Kenneth L. Pike, *Linguistic Concepts: An Introduction to Tagmemics* (Lincoln: University of Nebraska Press, 1982), 39–63.

■

CHAPTER 8

COMMUNICATION

Herman Hermeneut: *Do we need to consider the audience to which God addressed the books of the Bible?*

Peter Pietist: *I don't see why. God speaks to us today through the Bible. That's all we need.*

Dottie Doctrinalist: *We need to concentrate on what God says, not on the ancient audience or on ourselves as a modern audience. The audience is sinful and prone to error. Only God is trustworthy.*

Curt Transformationist: *But we need to reckon with how God wants the audiences to respond, to change themselves, and above all to change the world.*

Missy Missiologist: *In order to apply the Bible properly, we must take into account the cultural setting. God gave particular commands to the first-century church, within the Roman Empire. But in another culture, obedience may take another form.*

Now we need to enlarge the picture to look at communication among people.

When people communicate through language, they usually speak *to* someone. Hence, we can distinguish the speaker, the speech, and the audience. Or, for written communication, we can distinguish the author, the text, and the readers.[1] Which of these is the key to the communication as a whole? Secular circles studying literature hotly dispute the answer. Different schools advocate different approaches, with radically differing results. Some people say that readers must create meaning afresh each time they read. Others make the author's intention the standard. Others look only at the text, in isolation from the author.[2]

God Speaking

Human speech images divine speech. So there is a divine archetype for the human triad of speaker, speech, and audience. In John 1:1, God the Father is the original speaker. God the Word, the Second Person of the Trinity, is the speech. By analogy with Psalm 33:6, the Holy Spirit is like the breath carrying the speech to its destination. But what is the destination? When God speaks to human beings, they are clearly the destination, the audience. In the New Testament, God promises to send the Holy Spirit to dwell in believers, in order that they may properly receive his speech (1 Cor. 2:9–16).[3] In some important respects, the Spirit stands with believers in the process of hearing God's word.

Most often, the Bible speaks of the Spirit as the speaker or an instrument or one who empowers the speaker of God's word (e.g., Acts 1:16; Isa. 61:1). But can we also conceive of the Spirit as the hearer or audience for God's word? First Corinthians 2:10 says that "the Spirit searches all things, even the deep things of God." Thus the Spirit is a recipient of knowledge. John 16:13 is even more explicit, indicating that the Spirit "will speak only what he hears." The Spirit hears in order to speak. What does he hear? He hears the truth from God, the truth that is described as "what is mine [Christ's]" (v. 14). These biblical texts speak about the imparting of redemptive truth. They describe God as acting in history for our benefit. But, as always, God's action in history is in accord with who he is. Thus, by analogy, we infer that there is an eternal hearing by which the Spirit hears the Word spoken from all eternity by the Father. In this intratrinitarian communication, the Father is the speaker, the Son is the speech, and the Spirit

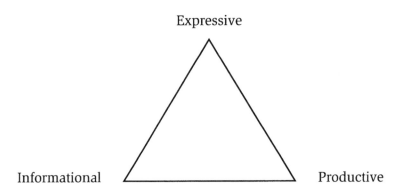

Figure 8.1. Triad of communication

is the hearer or audience. This Trinitarian speech is the archetype to which human communication is analogically related and which it images.

We may reexpress the truth in another way by speaking of three aspects of communication, namely, the expressive, the informational, and the productive aspects. The *informational* aspect has to do with the fact that communication makes or implies assertions. It has informational content. The *expressive* aspect has to do with the fact that speakers express something of themselves, their views, and their feelings. The *productive* aspect has to do with the fact that communication is designed to produce an effect on hearers. It may persuade, amuse, shock, or move people to action. The expressive aspect ties in closely with the speaker; the informational aspect with the speech, and the productive aspect with the hearers, in whom an effect should be produced. God's speech includes all three aspects. Divine speech is expressive, revealing the Father. It is informational, containing the wisdom hidden in Christ (Col. 2:3). And it is productive: through the power of the Spirit, who is the "breath" carrying it along, it arrives at its chosen destination and produces effects.

The persons of the Trinity coinhere. Analogously, the aspects of communication coinhere. The informational aspect expresses what the speaker believes, and hence it is tacitly expressive of who the speaker is. The expressive aspect reveals who the speaker is and so implies information about the speaker. The productive aspect indicates what the speaker wants to effect and hence is tacitly expressive of the speaker. The productive aspect provides information about what is desired as an effect and so is tacitly informational in character—and so on.

Because of coinherence, the speaker, the speech, and the hearer can each provide a perspective on the whole of communication. The speaker is a speaker only because he is speaking something—the speech. And he is a speaker only because he is speaking to someone, even if it be the special case of speaking to himself in soliloquy. Thus, the very idea of a speaker makes no sense apart from a tacit acknowledgment of the presence of both speech and hearer. Similarly, each point of view presupposes the presence of the others.[4]

Hence, speaker, speech, and hearer are not even intelligible in isolation. Understanding one inevitably involves the tacit presence of all three in relation to one another. Moreover, this coinherent triad is itself intelligible only through the presence (inherence) of God, whose archetypal speech grounds our own.

Most modern theories of interpretation are predominantly speaker oriented, discourse oriented (speech oriented), or audience oriented. Likewise, when communication takes written form, we find author-centered approaches, text-centered approaches, and reader-centered approaches. Most of the fights among these approaches are vain. All three types of approach are important. In a sense all are right, and in a sense all are wrong.

On the one hand, each approach has an element of truth. Speaker, speech, and audience are each involved in the process of communication. Moreover, each can be the starting point for a perspective on the whole. It can in a sense account for everything. Coinherence guarantees that in a sense nothing of significance escapes if we pursue our starting point far enough and expand its vistas wide enough.

On the other hand, each approach distorts the truth. When our relationship with God is distorted, we introduce counterfeiting in our theories of interpretation. The human author becomes the godlike master of meaning and communication, or else the text is made into a god, or the readers are treated as gods, each substituting for the true God.

Author, Discourse, and Reader

But let us consider in more detail how an author-centered, discourse-centered, or reader-centered approach could really be valid.

First, consider an author-centered approach. God is the primary author of the Bible. He not only knows what he intends, but is the very standard for our interpretation. Human authors may manage the media of communication imperfectly, but God controls the media perfectly. He is able to express and accomplish what he wishes (cf. Isa. 46:10). An author-centered approach means simply a God-centered approach, and such an approach is surely valid.

But we still encounter dangers of misunderstanding. In our sin, we may presume to know God so well that we are overly confident of our own insight. We may cease to pay attention to the details of the texts, the readers, or the human authors. Some of the wilder instances of allegorical interpretation, such as Mary Baker Eddy's "Key to the Scriptures," involve such presumption.[5]

Second, what about a discourse-centered approach? The text of the Bible, what is written, is divinely authoritative (2 Tim. 3:16, "all Scripture," *graphe*). Inspiration extends to the text, not merely to the thoughts behind the text in the author's mind. Hence, focusing on the text in principle leads to receiving what God says. But again, there are dangers of abuse. We may treat the text in isolation, as if the author or the circumstances did not matter. Then, in the absence of a definite context, almost any set of words is capable of sponsoring an indefinite number of meanings.

Third, consider a reader-centered approach. Can we say that the effects on readers are a sufficient focus for interpretation? Such an approach may seem problematic. After all, readers may misinterpret, as many examples in the Bible show (e.g., Matt. 22:29; 15:1–9; 2 Peter 3:16; 1 Tim. 1:3–7; 2 Tim. 2:23–26; 4:3–5). If readers are our final reference point, everyone does what is right in his own eyes. How then can a reader-centered approach ever harmonize with the Bible's claim to authority?

Misinterpretations as an Aspect of Divine War

We may see the harmony in more than one way. First, the Spirit is involved in the productive aspect of communication, that is, in the production of effects. The Spirit interprets God's word infallibly. Hence, the Spirit, as the divine reader, provides the standard of authority. Because the Spirit interprets infallibly, whatever effects the Spirit produces in readers are in accord with the divine purpose. Not all readers interpret accurately. But the Spirit, as a reader, interprets accurately. His interpretation is the norm according to which all other readers' interpretations are judged.

We may also approach the issue from the standpoint of Christ as the divine warrior, the one who wars against sin and evil. When evil enters the world, God is zealous to fight against it. The Lord is a warrior on behalf of righteousness, that is, on behalf of himself (Ex. 15:3). The climactic picture of divine war occurs in Revelation. Christ appears as the divine warrior in Revelation 19:11: "With justice he judges and makes war." Motifs of war pervade the rest of the book as well. Christ executes judgment by his word, which is symbolized by the "sharp sword" coming out of his mouth (Rev. 19:15; 1:16; cf. Isa. 11:4; Eph. 6:17).

Hence, the word of God may have judgmental as well as saving effects (2 Cor. 2:15–16). God pronounces judgment and punishment as well as blessing through the words of the prophets. The judgment may take the form of blindness and lack of understanding.

> Go and tell this people:
> "Be ever hearing, but never understanding;
>   be ever seeing, but never perceiving."
> Make the heart of this people calloused;
>   make their ears dull
>   and close their eyes. (Isa. 6:9–10)

Jesus' teaching in parables has a similar effect. Outsiders do not understand (Mark 4:1–20). By God's design, some are hardened and do not understand; others understand and profit.

In all these situations, God accomplishes his purposes: "So is my word that goes out from my mouth: It will not return to me empty, but will accomplish what I desire and achieve the purpose for which I sent it" (Isa. 55:11). God's plan is comprehensive (Lam. 3:37–38; Ps. 103:19; Eph. 1:11). His accomplishment of his plan is also comprehensive (Dan. 4:34–35; Isa. 46:9–10). The effects of God's word are in exact accord with his plan.

Hence, the supposed problems with readers are in fact a display of the character of God's communication. The diversity and even the contradiction between different readers fulfill and illustrate the character of the communication. This very diversity, in all its dimensions, shows who God is, what he is saying, and what power there is in his speech. He has power to save and to destroy, power to enlighten and to blind (Ex. 4:11; Isa. 6:10; Rom. 11:7–10; John 9:39–41).

The divine war again sin is ultimately Trinitarian. We have already illustrated this fact. The effects on readers are Spirit-worked effects. The divine warrior is Christ. The warrior executes the comprehensive plan of God the Father.

ENDNOTES

1. There are subtle differences between communication using an oral medium and communication using a written medium. But for the moment we shall focus on some common features.

2. For a critical survey of the implications for biblical interpretation, see Anthony C. Thiselton, *New Horizons in Hermeneutics: The Theory and Practice of Transforming Biblical Reading* (Grand Rapids: Zondervan, 1992).

3. Much of the language in 1 Corinthians 2:9–16 may apply preeminently to Paul and to other inspired bearers of revelation. But the continuation in 3:1–3 shows that Paul expects the Corinthians to draw some inferences about their own ability or lack of ability to understand. Their understanding depends on whether they are "spiritual," that is, whether they enjoy in themselves a teaching operation of the Spirit similar to that described in 2:9–16.

4. We understand a speech only if we infer a speaker. (If there is no personal origin, we have just a random series of sounds or marks.) And a speech is nothing but sound waves or marks without someone to hear and understand it. Even if there is no human hearer, God hears it. Finally, the hearer is a hearer only in the act of hearing something. That something may be a mere noise, such as the rustling of leaves. But the hearer is a hearer of human communication only if he hears something that is intelligible, coming from a personal source.

5. Mary Baker Eddy, *Science and Health with Key to the Scriptures* (Boston: Trustees under the Will of Mary Baker G. Eddy, 1934), 501–99.

CHAPTER 9

·

STEPS IN INTERPRETATION

Herman Hermeneut: Could we come up with a "how-to" list for interpreting the Bible?

Dottie Doctrinalist: That would definitely be useful, provided it were based solidly on the Bible.

Oliver Objectivist: We certainly need such a list, in order to be rigorously objective in our interpretation and to eliminate subjective biases.

Peter Pietist: I'm not so sure. Wouldn't a method interfere with my personal communion with the Lord?

Laura Liturgist: I'm just as uneasy as Peter. Does "method" mean something purely academic? Or would it include participation in worship?

Missy Missiologist: I can see both advantages and disadvantages. We certainly need to take steps in order to make sure we are not blinded by the blind spots of the culture in which we were raised. But we need to be careful. Our focus on method can introduce a Western bias. The idea of having a technique or assembly-line process for producing the right meaning seems natural within an industrialized society, where we pursue technique.

The pattern of speaker, discourse, and hearer provides us with a framework for developing some specific principles in biblical interpretation.

First, on a broad scale, God speaks the entire canon of Scripture to the entire people of God throughout the entirety of history.[1]

The study of the Bible involves all three aspects: God the speaker, the Bible as his speech, and the people to whom he speaks. In view of coinherence, we may focus on any of the times involved: the original time, when God first gives the word to people; the intermediate time, during which it is passed on; and the present time, when we now hear it.

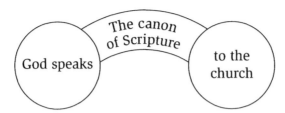

Figure 9.1. God's global communication

As usual, these foci are perspectivally related. Even at the earliest time, when God first spoke a particular message belonging to the canon, he designed that message in such a way that it could serve people of future generations as well as the immediate audience. When we focus on the earliest time, we find that God's word includes an intention extending to later times. The intention thus tacitly includes the later times. Conversely, suppose that we begin with God's address to us now, in the present time. God intends now that we recognize that part of his plan involves a historical development. Hence, we find ourselves forced to reckon with how the message came about through an earlier process. Finally, when we focus on the intermediate times, and the process of transmission, we cannot ignore the purpose of what is being transmitted, a purpose that includes both an origin and a goal, that is, the earlier and the later times. All three foci, properly understood, include tacit acknowledgment of the other foci.

We can see the importance of these perspectives by showing how they derive naturally from the very character of God.

God's Presence Today

Consider first the perspective that focuses on the modern time and the modern hearer. God is present and active today, as he has promised (Matt. 28:18–20). His presence today is the basis for focusing on his communication to present-day hearers.

God is present as his word comes to us today. He speaks to us when we read the Bible. How is this so? The original manuscripts of the Bible are the word of God. Copies and translations may be imperfect, but they are the word of God insofar as they express the message of the original. The same applies to preaching, teaching, and other means of communicating the word of God. As ordinary Christians come to know the Bible, they communicate its contents to one another. Colossians 3:16 says, "Let the word of Christ dwell in you richly as you teach and admonish one another with all wisdom, and as you sing psalms, hymns and spiritual songs with gratitude in your hearts to God." Paul is here addressing the whole group of Christians at Colossae. "The word of Christ" is to "dwell in you richly," and you are to "teach and admonish one another" through the presence of this word. Modern preachers and modern Christians are not infallible. When they attempt to convey the word of God, they can mix it with merely human notions, or even with heresy. But fragments of it may remain even in the midst of serious deviations. And when the church is spiritually healthy, the word of God dwells in Christians with greater consistency. The word of Christ is present among Christians as they teach and admonish one another. As God says, "I will put my laws in their hearts, and I will write them on their minds" (Heb. 10:16).

Our fallibility and failures contaminate the word. But the word does not cease to be present in the midst of this contamination. The word of God cannot be muzzled or shut up (2 Tim. 2:9), particularly now that the Holy Spirit has been poured out on his church. In the modern transformations of the word of God, including translations, commentaries, and counseling, we may genuinely hear and encounter God.[2] The Westminster Confession of Faith affirms this truth.

> But, because these original tongues [Hebrew and Greek] are not known to all the people of God, who have right unto, and interest in the Scriptures, and are commanded, in the fear of God, to read and search them, therefore they are to be translated into the vulgar language of every nation unto which they come, that, the Word of God dwelling plentifully in all, they may worship Him in an acceptable manner; and, through patience and comfort of the Scriptures, may have hope. (1.8)

Classic Roman Catholicism fears this catholicity of the word, because it seems disorderly, unstructured, and productive of heresies. And indeed God in his love does startling things. The Word of God incarnate suffered abuse and torture during the years of Jesus' earthly life. In similar manner, false teachers try to subject the written word of God to abuse and torture to the end of the age.

But one of the purposes of Pentecost was that God would write his word on our hearts and we should all be prophets (Acts 2:17–18). Acts 2 opens the door to "prophetic" ministry on several levels. First, the apostles speak the word of God definitively and infallibly. Second, God commissions other ministers of the word, like Timothy, who are not infallible. Third, at another level, people without ordination may spread the word (Acts 11:20?). As we have seen from Colossians 3:16 and Hebrews 10, all Christians should have the word dwelling richly in them. We are to honor and respect those whom God has appointed leaders and overseers (Heb. 13:7; 1 Thess. 5:12–13). But the people as a whole, not just the leaders, receive the Holy Spirit, and the people as a whole have the law written on their hearts (Heb. 10:16). We must respect the freedom that Christ has given to his people and not erect a paternalistic hierarchy that attempts to restrict other people's access to the word of God.

The lesson here is relevant also for many anticharismatic Protestants. The charismatic movement, like all other sectors of the church, has its share of problems, aberrations, and doctrinal confusion. Critics may legitimately warn us about these problems. But they should not ignore the strengths resulting from the charismatics' appreciation of the presence of the Holy Spirit and the priesthood of all believers.

God's Truthfulness

Consider next the perspective that focuses on the time when biblical words originated. In this case, we consider God's truthfulness and holiness. His word, not ours, is authoritative. This reality impresses on us the importance of attending to what he said and the circumstances in which he said it. Not every word claiming his sanction actually has it (see Jer. 28). God calls upon us to trust in him and not in man (Ps. 146:3). His word vindicates his holiness by testifying against the people (Deut. 31:26). In the Old Testament, the worship of Molech, Baal, and Ashtoreth demonstrates the possibility of radically false religion. The corruption of the priesthood and the appearance of false prophets demonstrate the possibility of enormous confusion. In the New Testament, the scribes, the Pharisees, and Christian heretics illustrate the same danger. Even genuine Christians can succumb for a time to the temptations of false doctrine (1 Cor. 15; Gal. 1:6; 3:1; 5:10).

Hence, the holiness of God calls us to sift and reject human tradition by listening again to God. God is the standard, and his word is the standard by which we test the prophets (Deut. 13; 18; 1 John 4:1–3). But how do we identify God's word? The word, we have said, dwells among Christians, but how do we gain deeper discernment of what is and what is not this word? We need access to the word of God uncorrupted by sinful distortion. That is, we need that word deposited to testify against the people as well as (sometimes) on their behalf. In other words, we need the canon of Scripture. God so loved his people throughout the ages that he gave them clear instruction. He declared not only that Moses was his spokesman (Deut. 5:22–33), but that later spokesmen could be identified through the canon of Moses' words (Deut. 18:17–22). This word cannot be broken and remains with perfect reliability to the end of time (John 10:35).

The canon of Scripture is now complete. It is the standard by which all modern communication is judged. But it is not only a standard. It expresses the inexhaustible fullness of what God communicates to us in redemption, for in it the Holy Spirit unfolds that full revelation of Jesus Christ, the one in whom "all the fullness of the Deity lives in bodily form" (Col. 2:9). As Hebrews says, "In the past God spoke to our forefathers through the prophets at many times and in various ways, but in these last days he has spoken to us by his Son, whom he appointed heir of all things, and through whom he made the universe" (Heb. 1:1–2).

Of course, we still have much to learn from the Bible. And we can learn much from the world that God governs. God can teach us in ordinary or in extraordinary ways. But the heart of wisdom is in knowing Christ. Those who lust after "further revelations" make a great mistake, because they are deficient in love for the person revealed in this one great completed redemption. And being deficient in love, and blinded by sin, they are in no condition to sift properly the modern voices that they examine.[3]

Modernism resists this apostolic exclusiveness and Christocentric definiteness of the word. Modernism trims down the word, adjusting it to what modern culture says is within the bounds of acceptability. Contemporary Roman Catholicism, Eastern Orthodoxy, and Pentecostalism in their varying spheres exhibit a spectrum of attitudes. Some people within these circles would agree with me, but others would not. In some quarters we find theoretical or practical denial of the exclusiveness of biblical authority. Papal teaching or church tradition or the contemporary voice of the Spirit may function to supplement Scripture, even though in theory it remains subordinate to Scripture. The uncertain trumpet hinders us from preparing for battle.

How do we find our way? In principle, we may learn from many sources. We may learn from modern scientific investigations or from philosophical reflections. We may learn from ecclesiastical tradition. We may learn from the saints of past ages, because they too received the Spirit. We may learn from our fellow Christians today, because they are being taught by the Spirit. All of these sources have some value. But they are all fallible. So we must sift the modern ideas, the tradition, and the spiritual voices by the divine standard.

God's Control

Consider finally the perspective that focuses on the process of transmission from ancient to modern times. Here we need to reflect on God's control. God's control over history is the basis on which we can understand the way in which the ancient word relates to the modern age. We must reckon with God's plan for the whole of history and the working out of this plan, if we are rightly to assess how the coming of Christ has brought the Old Testament to fulfillment and also has made obsolete some of the particular applications of Old Testament law. We must reckon with God's plan and control as we wrestle also with the phenomena of textual criticism: how do the later copies point to an earlier autograph, within a universe governed by God?

Smaller Acts of Communication

We have considered the whole Bible as a single, great act of communication. But this one great act includes many smaller acts of communication. Each book of the Bible, and indeed each paragraph of each book, constitutes something distinct. As might be expected, the many acts of speaking cohere with the one overall act.

Each smaller act of communication has the same threefold structure that we have already seen. It has its origination in a speaker, transmission in a specific medium, and reception by a hearer. Let us take a specific example: the book of Micah.

First, Micah the prophet wrote the book of Micah to his contemporaries, most probably in the days of Hezekiah or shortly afterward (Mic. 1:1).[4] The speaker (or writer) is Micah, the message is the book of Micah, and the hearers are Micah's contemporaries in Judah. However, we must also remember that God is the primary author, in addition to Micah's secondary authorship.

Second, people in modern times copy, translate, preach, and study Micah. Many writers and speakers endeavor to bring the message of Micah to bear on themselves and others. Through the Holy Spirit, God gives teaching gifts, so that he speaks the message of the book of Micah today through noninspired spokesmen.

Third, between the original time of writing and today, God has provided the means and the media for transmitting his message: both the primary means of copying the text and various secondary means. God sustains his people so that they discern the importance of the message and endeavor to digest it, apply it, and preserve it. God providentially preserves other information about the ancient world, so that we may have more confident and accurate understanding of Micah.

Let us picture communication as an arch. We can then represent the full process of biblical communication as a single big arch, together with smaller arches at both ends and smaller arches all along the span. The single big arch is from God and his spokesman, Micah, to the people of God of all ages. The author and originator stands in Micah's time, the arch travels over all times, and the hearers and readers stand in our own time.

What do the smaller arches represent? A smaller arch at the beginning of the big arch represents Micah's communication to his contemporaries. A smaller arch in our modern time represents the many-sided communication of modern interpreters of Micah. And in between are many arches representing many people down through the centuries who have interacted with the book of Micah.

The Bible itself describes in a general way such a process of transmission.

> He decreed statutes for Jacob and established the law in Israel, which
> he commanded our forefathers to teach their children, so the next

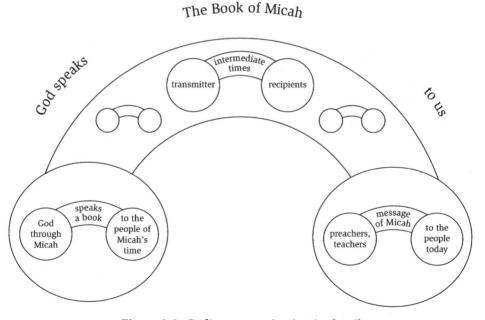

Figure 9.2. God's communication in detail

generation would know them, even the children yet to be born, and they in turn would tell their children. Then they would put their trust in God and would not forget his deeds but would keep his commands. (Ps. 78:5–7)

And the things you have heard me say in the presence of many witnesses entrust to reliable men who will also be qualified to teach others. (2 Tim. 2:2)

Passages like these tacitly assume that corruption can enter in during the course of transmission. Scripture explicitly warns us about corruption in Deuteronomy 31:27–29 and in Jesus' criticism of the human traditions of the Pharisees (Matt. 15:1–20; 23). Thus, it is important to listen continually to the speaker and to the original communication. But the application to one's own circumstances is also important. In Psalm 78, the goal of the process of transmission is that people "would keep his commands" (Ps. 78:7).

Explicit Hermeneutical Procedure

The hermeneutical arch, along with its subarches, suggests the beginnings of formalized hermeneutical procedure. There are three steps in understanding a biblical text. They deal successively with the three time periods of the arch, namely, the origination of the message, the transmission of the message, and the reception of the message by us. We may lay out the steps (again, for the book of Micah) as follows:

Step 1. Understand what God said to Micah's original audience, the people of Micah's time. Find out about Micah the prophet, his words, and his audience.

Step 2. Understand how God has preserved the book of Micah through a period of historical development up to the present. Include in this understanding not only textual transmission, but additional words of God through later Scriptures and the historical and redemptive developments issuing in the work of Christ and the formation of the New Testament church.

Step 3. Understand what God says to us now. Find out about yourself, the church of Christ, the gifts of the Spirit, and the role of teachers and preachers in order to assess the ways in which the church as a whole is digesting the message from Micah. Assess your culture in the light of the Bible. Respond to what God is saying; apply the message to yourself, your circumstances, and your neighbors.

As we have already observed, if step 3 is not controlled by step 1, the church loses its moorings. She begins to distort the message of Micah or even replace it with another message of her own devising. On the other hand, if step 3 is omitted, we are not obeying God, and our profession of being the church is hypocritical (Rev. 3:1; James 1:22; Matt. 7:24–27). Moreover, if we do not love God, as exhibited in step 3, our perceptions become clouded with sin and we cease to make good progress with step 1.

We must also remember that the steps we have distinguished are not, in practice, isolated from one another. We continually return to the source (step 1) in order to critique our present applications (step 3), and we continually return to application (step 3) in order to purify our hearts and minds to understand the source (step 1). Each of these cycles of coming and going is directed by our understanding of God's plan for the entire course of history, and this plan is revealed in the canon as a whole (step 2). In all this work, we are not on our own. God gives us direction by sending the Spirit to guide us.

In fact, the expressive, informational, and productive aspects are coinherent. That is, author focus, discourse focus, and reader focus coinhere. Hence, we cannot take any one of the three steps without tacitly involving the others. For example, when we explore the meaning of the past (step 1), *we* are the ones doing the exploration. We must reckon with ourselves as persons who live in the present (step 3). Moreover, our study of the past is already an attempt to reform our cognitive processes, and thus it is a form of application in the present. Godly interpretation always takes place in the presence of God, and hence involves present fellowship with him, even when we are consciously focusing on the past.

Conversely, any application of the message of the Bible to the present involves receiving the message as a message coming from God, who has plans for all of history. Thus, we cannot dispense with an overall understanding of history. Action in the present presupposes knowledge of the past. In the next chapter we shall consider this coinherence in greater depth.

Further Subdivisions

Scholarly, technical study of the Bible often focuses on only a small part of the whole. This small part may belong to any one of the three steps above. For this purpose, we might proceed to subdivide the three steps almost indefinitely.

For example, under step 1 we can introduce several substeps. First, with an expressive focus, we analyze the author. Who was Micah, what was his background, and what were his characteristics? Next, with an informational focus, we analyze the text. What are the words? In what order do they occur? What do they say? Next, with a productive focus, we analyze the hearers and their situation. What was going on in Micah's time, where was Micah located, and what people surrounded him? What does the text set out to achieve? Finally, we analyze the total communication. What does God do with these words that were given through Micah to the people of Micah's day?

We may analyze the modern interpretation of the Bible in a similar way. Who is the human speaker? What are the words and what do they say? What is the situation (the facts)?[5] What does God do with these words to the hearers through the speaker? Suppose that you yourself are striving to speak on God's behalf, whether in a sermon, a commentary, or a private exhortation. Before speaking or writing, or while doing so, you endeavor to understand the people to whom you are speaking, the message of Micah, and yourself as a person with capabilities, weaknesses, and sins. You speak to an audience. You try to fashion your words so that they as persons receive a normative guidance in an intelligible form that is relevant to them and their situation.

God's Work in the Whole Process

As we have said, the broad context of God's communication in history exhibits three aspects: the expressive, the informational, and the productive. The canon as a whole is the message, representing the informational aspect. The whole of history worked out under God's control represents the productive aspect. And God's prophets, apostles, and other spokesmen are the mediating persons, representing the expressive aspect.

In a deeper sense, however, Christ himself is the archetype for all three aspects. First, consider the informational aspect. Christ is the focus of the content of the Scriptures. In him "are hidden all the treasures of wisdom and knowledge" (Col. 2:3). The Scriptures, as the utterance of God's wisdom, express only what is already contained in him.

Consider next the productive aspect. The supreme effect or application of the word of God lies in the earthly life of Christ. He is the supreme fact of history. His incarnation, life, death, and resurrection provide the hinge on which all of history turns. They are also the factual center of Scripture, around which, in God's providence, all the other events are organized and find their fulfillment (see Luke 24:44–49).

Finally, consider the expressive aspect. Christ is the personal mediator of all God's words. All the prophets are images of Christ, who is the final and greatest prophet (Acts 3:22–24). All the apostles act on Christ's authority and with the impetus of his Spirit. As the Second Person of the Trinity, Christ is the author of all the Scriptures. As Savior, he has acted in redemption in order that we could hear the word of God and not die (Deut. 5:22–33). Christ is thus the archetypal prophet.

Thus, interpretation of the Bible is Christocentric in several ways. We must interpret Micah in conformity with God's purposes for the book. And his purposes center on the accomplishments of Jesus Christ.

Step 2 of our hermeneutical procedure can be subdivided in a way that acknowledges these various contexts. We try to understand the context of the persons doing the transmission, namely, the people of God in various ages (the expressive aspect). We try to understand the transmission of the message of Micah (the informational aspect). We try to understand the situations through which the transmission has gone (the productive aspect).

These aspects are structured by God so that they are not mere featureless deserts across which the transmission glides, but God-ordained historical developments focused on Christ. Let us consider the expressive, informational, and productive aspects.

First, consider the expressive aspect. Focus on what happened to the people who transmitted the Scriptures. Through Christ, God maintained communion with his people down through the ages. At Pentecost, God transformed them into the Spirit-filled body of Christ, in which the message of the Old Testament lives. We need to understand what happened to God's people at the coming of Christ, and how all scriptural interpretation is now mediated by the presence of his Spirit, who is transforming us into the image of Christ (2 Cor. 3:12–18).

Second, consider the informational aspect. Focus on the message that people transmitted. In Old Testament times, God commissioned spokesmen in Christ's image to give further words interpreting the earlier words and further unfolding God's mind. Christ himself climaxed the message. He was himself the eternal Word (John 1:1) and spoke the words of life (John 6:63, 68). After his resurrection, the apostles proclaimed the gospel, whose content centers on Christ.

Third, consider the productive aspect, connected with the facts of history. Focus on God's acts in history. He accomplished redemption and fulfilled his promises through the death and resurrection of Christ. All of the events of the Old Testament anticipated Christ's work, and all of the New Testament reflects on it and shows its implications for present and future facts. God's purpose has been "to bring all things in heaven and on earth together under one head, even Christ" (Eph. 1:10).

Hence, interpreting Micah involves seeing how God used its words in further interpretation, reflection, and expansion in later canonical books (the informational perspective). It involves seeing how the words of Micah were fulfilled in later history (the productive perspective). It involves seeing how people have been affected by its message (personal involvement).[6] Above all, it involves seeing how Micah is fulfilled in Christ. Christ is the final word, the fulfillment of the truths and norms expounded by the book of Micah. Christ is the final fact to which Micah's factual promises and predictions looked forward. Christ is the final mediatorial person, the prophet to whom Micah the prophet was analogous.

The sort of focus that we have on step 1, step 2, or step 3 influences to a great extent what kind of questions we ask and what kind of answers we seek.

In step 1, we focus on the origination of the message. We want primarily to understand what a particular book or a particular passage in that book says. But we may still ask the question in a manner that prepares us to move forward toward application. How does God's word to people in Micah's day fit into the larger picture? Answering this question leads primarily to exegesis, commentaries, and expository sermons.

In step 2, we focus on the transmission of the message. We want primarily to understand, not what a particular book or a particular passage says, but how God builds up the total message of the gospel and the total message of Christ to us over the course of time. Even if we consider a smaller passage, we ask, How does this passage from Micah fit into a growing corpus of canonical communication destined to be completed with the coming of Christ and the writing of the New Testament? Answering this question leads primarily to biblical theology and reflection on the historical unfolding of redemption.

In step 3, we focus on the reception of the message. We want primarily to understand God's total communication to us. Even if we consider a smaller passage, we ask, How does this passage fit into the total teaching of the Bible on topics or issues with which I am struggling? What does the Bible teach about sin? about Christ? about marriage? about use of the tongue? about Christian growth? about the Second Coming? Answering these questions leads to systematic theology and books on Christian devotion and practice.

The interpretation of a particular passage of the Bible is never finished. Responsible obedience to God involves loving him with all our heart, soul, strength, and mind. Such love desires to understand and obey all of God's instruction. If we are to understand with thoroughness and depth, we must relate all the passages of the Bible to all the steps set forth above. We can never in one lifetime complete everything ourselves, but many others aid us. The church labors corporately to grow "until we all reach unity in the faith and in the knowledge of the Son of God and become mature, attaining to the whole measure of the fullness of Christ" (Eph. 4:13).

We can at this point summarize our results by listing the various steps and aspects that we have enumerated.

Steps in Interpretation

Step 1. Original time and context
   a. Understand the person who is God's spokesman (the personal perspective).
   b. Understand the text itself (the normative perspective).
   c. Understand the circumstances of the audience (the situational perspective).
   d. Understand the total import of God's message.

Step 2. Transmission and its context
   a. Understand the people who transmit the word: official tradition bearers and, more broadly, God's people.
   b. Understand the transmission of the text and its message (the normative perspective). Both textual criticism and the history of interpretation are involved.
   c. Understand the situation of transmission. Understand narrowly the concerns of scribes and broadly God's plan for history.
   d. Understand the total import of God's speaking to the whole church through the Scripture.
   (1) Understand with different foci.
      (a) Understand later use of the passage (the exegetical focus).
      (b) Understand how the passage fits into the body of growing revelation (biblical theology).
      (c) Understand how the passage fits into an entire body of teaching on various topics and issues (systematic theology and Christian living).
   (2) Understand Christocentrically.
      (a) How does Christ fulfill the passage by climaxing its truths and embodying its wisdom, righteousness, and holiness?

    (b) How does Christ fulfill the facts of the passage by fulfilling its promises and predictions and bringing to a climax the historical struggle to which the passage relates?

    (c) How does Christ fulfill the personal aspect of communication (the prophet as mediator)?

Step 3. Modern context

    a. Understand what God is saying now through the text and the larger context of biblical and systematic theology.

    b. Understand your situation, as controlled by God.

    c. Understand your gifts and capabilities and those of other speakers or hearers with whom you are communicating.

    d. Understand the total import of God's call to you as speaker and/or hearer.

Within each of the three major steps, subdivision d contains the more synthetic overview of the entire process. Particularly there we are analyzing God's action and his speech. Hence, knowing God, the author, is in each step an implied part of the task.

These steps in interpretation are similar to what can be found in many textbooks on hermeneutics and in many summaries of interpretive procedure. But there is a significant difference in our analysis. The three steps and their subdivisions originate in the triad of author, discourse, and reader, or the closely related triad of the expressive, informational, and productive perspectives. These perspectives, in turn, are based on the Trinitarian character of God. The three perspectives are coinherent; they are mutually involved with one another and presuppose one another. As a result, the steps are inevitably coinherent and mutually involved with one another. The steps not only influence one another, but also interpenetrate one another. They are not neatly separable in time, in subject matter, or in conception. Each step, rightly understood, encompasses the others.

Nevertheless, we can distinguish the steps. We have three distinct steps, and they belong in a certain distinct order. The order derives from an analysis that spreads out God's speech in time. For example, God speaks through Micah in the time of Hezekiah (correlating with step 1), the message is transmitted down through the centuries (step 2), and the message is received in our own time (step 3).

Let us call these three steps, taken together, the *transmission perspective* on interpretation. Is this the only way of analyzing interpretation?

ENDNOTES

1. Who are the recipients of God's communication in the Bible? The Bible is a covenantal document, representing God's communication to his servants (see Meredith G. Kline, *The Structure of Biblical Authority* [Grand Rapids: Eerdmans, 1972]). In a broad sense, the Bible is relevant to all human beings, but there is a definite focus on God's redeemed people. God's relationship to Adam and Eve at the beginning and the covenant with Noah in Genesis 8:21–9:17 affect all people. Other biblical covenants are addressed primarily to God's people, that is, the people whom God takes to himself in a special relation of intimacy and love. These focused covenants also have broader relevance, since they mention the destiny of other nations (Gen. 12:3; Deut. 4:6–8; Mic. 4:1–3). It is expected that other people, who are initially outside the circle of intimacy, may and will hear and read the covenant. This broader reading is appropriate not only because all people are responsible to God, the Creator and Consummator, but also because God's covenants of redemption promise that his purpose is to reach out and save people "from every tribe and language and people and nation" (Rev. 5:9).

2. The Second Helvetic Confession says, "Hence when today this word of God [referring to Scripture] is proclaimed in the church by preachers lawfully called, we believe that the word of God itself is proclaimed and received by believers" (Proinde cum hodie hoc Dei verbum per prædicatores legitime vocatos annunciatur in Ecclesia, credimus ipsum Dei verbum annunciari et a fidelibus recipi). But I would go further than this confession, which restricts its discussion to "preachers lawfully called."

3. I do not want to conceal complex questions that arise concerning the nature of the canon and its recognition. However, discussing the role of the canon and its completeness could easily require a whole book. See Herman N. Ridderbos, *Redemptive History and the New Testament Scriptures*, rev. ed. (Phillipsburg, N.J.: Presbyterian and Reformed, 1988). Neither can we discuss in detail at this point the issues of textual criticism.

4. Micah 1:1 indicates that Micah prophesied during the reigns of Jotham, Ahaz, and Hezekiah. The book probably includes prophecies from this entire span of time. If so, the final written form must be later than all of the oral prophecies. Many critics attribute parts of the book to later authors and editors, but their evidence is flimsy. We cannot enter into these debates at this point. We are assuming here that the book is a unified work written by Micah.

5. These three aspects correspond roughly (but only roughly) to Frame's existential, normative, and situational perspectives. See John M. Frame, *The Doctrine of the Knowledge of God* (Phillipsburg, N.J.: Presbyterian and Reformed, 1987).

6. On the perspectival relationships, see ibid., 62–75.

.

CHAPTER 10

ALTERNATIVE HERMENEUTICAL PERSPECTIVES

Herman Hermeneut: So now we have it. Three Steps. Is everyone satisfied?

Missy Missiologist: Do people from every culture go about interpretation in the same way? Might we have overlooked important cultural differences?

Amy Affirmationist: Even within our culture, I don't think that every Christian goes about it that way. Could the Holy Spirit give people more than one method?

We can represent God's speech as spread out in time. But since God is present with his people in all times, this particular manner of representing the communication is not exhaustive. Let us continue to consider the book of Micah. If we wish, we can represent the entire hermeneutical process as taking place within the sphere of the presence of God in Micah's time, speaking to all subsequent generations in a single act. Or, equally, we can represent the entire hermeneutical process as taking place within the sphere of the presence of God with us now. Let us see how these two approaches work.

An Alternative Perspective: God Speaking to His People Once for All

God, through Micah, wrote to the people of Micah's time. But God is the Lord of time. Unlike human beings, he does not limit his vision to the events or customs or thoughts of one time or culture. But even human beings can write books or leave records for posterity. People have at least a limited ability to think about other times and to communicate forward to later times. This ability is, of course, an image of God's eternity, his mastery of all times, and his presence at all times. God certainly has the ability to write to subsequent generations as well as to the people of one time. Has he ever done it? According to the Scriptures, he has.

> These things happened to them as examples and were written down as warnings for us, on whom the fulfillment of the ages has come. (1 Cor. 10:11)

> For everything that was written in the past was written to teach us, so that through endurance and the encouragement of the Scriptures we might have hope. (Rom. 15:4)

> After Moses finished writing in a book the words of this law from beginning to end, he gave this command to the Levites who carried the ark of the covenant of the LORD: "Take this Book of the Law and place it beside the ark of the covenant of the LORD your God. There it will remain as a witness against you. For I know how rebellious and stiff-necked you are. If you have been rebellious against the LORD while I am still alive and with you, how much more will you rebel after I die! (Deut. 31:24–27)

God purposed to include later readers. We can apply this truth to Micah. God included all the readers of all future generations in the audience that he addressed when he wrote the book of Micah.

From this viewpoint, the task of interpretation is simply to realize that we are part of the original audience and to identify with the audience of Micah's time. The whole process of interpretation seems to collapse into step 1. But the collapse is only apparent. Once we focus on the composition of the audience, all the differentiations in steps 2 and 3 reemerge.

Let us think first about human authors and their intended readers. Good authors know that there are differences of knowledge and viewpoint among their intended readers. Authors may deliberately include a spectrum of materials in order to appeal to a broad spectrum of readers. They know that not everything will appeal equally to all their readers at once. In addition, some authors may deliberately include allusions or secrets or more precise formulations that can be detected and fully understood by only some readers. I know one Christian speaker who tries to give as many as three messages at once, one to non-Christians, one to comparatively ignorant Christians, and one to theologically informed Christians—in order that all three groups in his audience may stay interested and be further challenged and informed.

Similarly, it is in principle possible for God to provide a different fullness of truth and communion to different portions of his audience. In fact, we know that he sometimes does. In the parable of the sower, Jesus reveals to his disciples "the secret of the kingdom of God," while veiling that secret from others (Mark 4:11–12).

Thus, we must be prepared to differentiate among various parts of the total audience. The differentiation can take place along many lines, including intellectual gifts, loyalty versus antagonism to God, spiritual maturity, social status, gender, and historical circumstances. Fullest absorption and appreciation of God and his word occur when the different parts of the audience share their insights, impressions, and emotional responses with one another. Such, indeed, is what the church does, according to Ephesians 4:11–16 and 1 Corinthians 12.

Of course, direct communication backward in time is not possible. But it is still useful and important to project ourselves back in time, as it were, in order to imagine what people then would have understood. People from earlier times cannot give fresh responses, beyond what has been preserved in literary form and in other material evidence. But the process of imaginative projection still has important similarities to the attempt to understand the people whom we meet and talk to today. In both cases we try to some extent to see things from the other person's point of view. And that attempt frequently allows us to learn what we might not learn if we were rigidly confined to our own individual experience.[1]

To put matters theologically, communion with the saints includes not only communion with the saints who are now alive and are part of our local church, but also communion with others through other means of communication. We are in communion with the saints of past ages.

The apostles of Christ may serve as our primary example of this communion. Christ gave the apostles to the church partly for the purpose of being definitive, authoritative witnesses to his life and his resurrection (Acts 1:21–22). Today we may have church planters and highly respected leaders, but in the nature of the case we have no more apostles. Have we then lost forever one of the necessary aspects of church life described in Ephesians 4:11? No, for although the apostles have died, their voice lives on through their writings. We still receive their foundational instruction again and again. In a subordinate way, the gifts of understanding, teaching, and ministry that God gave to saints in past ages are not useless to us, either. Their gifts helped to build the church and helped it to persevere until our time, and the gifts of understanding and teaching often survive through their writings.

Bible study today should include communion with the apostles, of course. They laid the indispensable, inspired, authoritative foundation for our faith. But Bible study needs also to be a dialogue with the saints of all previous ages. Indeed, we must include the people of Old Testament times as well as those of New Testament times, for there is only one way of salvation. Abraham is an example to encourage our faith (Heb. 11:8–19, 39–40; 12:1).

The hermeneutical arch and the three hermeneutical steps discussed in the previous chapter are spread out in time. So it is interesting to ask how the total audience of the Bible is differentiated in time. There are many ways in which the passage of time and one's situation in time make a difference. We need only dwell on the areas that are more obvious.

First, people are in different situations. Cultural differences exist between the Hebraic cultures of the Old Testament, the Judaic and Hellenistic cultures of the New Testament, and modern cultures. More important, the coming of God's new redemptive acts, especially the coming of Christ in the flesh, makes a decisive difference in the world's situation. Christ's resurrection is the firstfruits of the final resurrection and the renewal of the world. It is truly cosmic in its implications. One of the implications is that, although Mosaic Israel was required to keep the special food laws, we are not. Jesus has made all foods clean (Mark 7:19). In fact, the implications are quite profound, for the whole law is not only fulfilled, but transformed through its supreme expression in the righteousness of Jesus Christ.[2]

Second, people differ in their persons. At Pentecost, Christ pours out the promised Holy Spirit on his church. The reading of the Old Testament is now illumined by the Holy Spirit (2 Cor. 3:15–18) and by the law written on the hearts of believers (Heb. 8:10). Of course, the Holy Spirit was at work in Old Testament times, but not with the fullness with which he comes at Pentecost (compare Deut. 29:4 with 1 John 2:20–27). He now comes bringing the resurrection power of Jesus Christ and uniting us to Christ Jesus in his heavenly glory.

Third, people differ in their access to the word of God. Inspired writings appeared after Micah's time. People who have been alive since then have been able to compare Micah with a fuller set of communications from God. The total import of a passage depends on what kind of literary context and how much literary context an author provides. If the author provides quantitatively more context, the readers may be able to learn more about the author and thereby understand more deeply the import of a particular passage. Similarly, later readers of Scripture may have greater knowledge of God through the contribution of later inspired writings. Moreover, later writings and later redemptive events may throw light on promises and prophecies that originally were less specific in character.

These differentiations in the audience that God addresses mean that steps 2 and 3 in the transmission perspective are tacitly still part of the total process of interpretation. The changes in situation imply that it is legitimate to break off the modern audience for special reflection in step 3. The changes in access to the canon imply that we may ask questions about systematic theology from the whole canon. The changes in situation and in persons with the coming of Christ and Pentecost imply that it is wise to ask many questions about the Christocentric fulfillment of Scripture. Hence, this new perspective on God's speech potentially includes all the aspects given in the former perspective, the transmission perspective. It includes in principle the concerns of the three hermeneutical steps. It differs mainly in the arrangement of them. Instead of viewing God's speech as a process of transmission through a long period of time, consisting of three distinct speech acts, we view God's speech as a single, unified affair. Instead of a transmission perspective we have a *once-for-all perspective.*

This new perspective has several advantages. First, it expresses more forcefully and vividly than the transmission perspective that God's intention in speaking is united and coherent, and that his speaking to his people is a unified act. By contrast, the transmission perspective may give the misimpression that God's speech is divided into three unrelated acts or stages. This impression, of course, is only an artifact of the picture. God, being the Lord of all history, holds all time together in his speech.

Second, the once-for-all perspective emphasizes more vividly the importance of the original context and the authority of God's speech in that context. The understanding by all subsequent audiences is still bound to this one time of utterance.

Third, the once-for-all perspective promotes an appreciation for the role of the Holy Spirit in understanding God's word. The Holy Spirit is the one who unites us with believers of all ages, who distributes his gifts to these believers, and who enables us to enter into fellowship, communication, and spiritual communion with them through the records that they have left behind. Without the Holy Spirit, all we would receive today would be a merely human tradition about what God spoke long ago.

Fourth, the once-for-all perspective indicates more explicitly that interpretation is a spiral process. It involves the growth of the whole people of God together through a complex communion. By contrast, the transmission perspective can easily be misunderstood as involving a merely linear movement from ignorance to knowledge to application.

But the once-for-all perspective also has some disadvantages. Unless we are alert, we may underestimate the changes that take place in the reception of God's word over the ages. For example, we can make the mistake of assuming that everything in the Bible addresses us now in exactly the same way that it addressed all people of previous centuries. We might fail to observe that the Mosaic covenant was a shadow of a new and better one (Heb. 8:7–13; 10:1), and that we are not called to observe it in the same manner as were Israelites in Mosaic times. Or we could easily turn this view into a caricature, in which God drops a book from heaven. We might picture God as if he were not involved in history, as if he totally ignored it. The heavenly book would then present a system of ethical rules or propositional theology, but would not announce what God has done. The rules would speak in a completely uniform manner to people in any and every situation. Of course, there are universal ethical rules and propositions in the Bible. But we must not flatten everything out as if the coming of Christ in history did not make a decisive difference.

Fortunately, whatever view we start with, the Bible itself is capable of correcting our misunderstandings. Hebrews, for example, teaches us about the relation of earlier words to later ones. It shows both that the earlier words have lessons for us now and that the coming of the new covenant in Christ has superseded what was shadowy in the old.

An Alternative Perspective: God Speaking Now

Next, we can use still another model, in which the entire process of interpretation involves God speaking now. We may start with Paul's affirmation:

> But the righteousness that is by faith says: "Do not say in your heart, 'Who will ascend into heaven?'" (that is, to bring Christ down) "or 'Who will descend into the deep?'" (that is, to bring Christ up from the dead). But what does it say? "The word is near you; it is in your mouth and in your heart," that is, the word of faith we are proclaiming: That if you confess with your mouth, "Jesus is Lord," and believe in your heart that God raised him from the dead, you will be saved. (Rom. 10:6–9)

Paul repudiates the idea that the gospel is confined only to the Jews or only to Palestine. Undoubtedly he would also repudiate the idea that one would have to travel backward in time. We do not literally have to stand with Moses at Mount Sinai to hear God speaking. Since God's word has been recorded, we have it available now. Paul focuses in particular on the word of the gospel. It is the word of God, and it is clearly available now.[3] It is actually in those who believe: "The word is near you; it is in your mouth and in your heart" (Rom. 10:8). This near word might superficially appear to wipe out all consciousness of time. But actually it calls upon us to grow in Christ and to grow in knowing God in all the ways that we have observed earlier.

The word to which Paul refers is the word of the gospel, the word that involves proclaiming and confessing that "Jesus is Lord" and that "God raised him from the dead" (Rom. 10:9). The lordship of Jesus Christ, when truly acknowledged, implies that we are servants and that we submit to his lordship. Jesus requires us to "obey everything I have commanded you" (Matt. 28:20). The aspect of authority here, along with our own creatureliness and sinfulness, drives us back to the issue of whether we are really obeying Christ and his word, or whether we just project a word out of our own present consciousness, and then call upon ourselves to obey our own projection. If the latter—that is, if we obey only ourselves (as with Kant's categorical imperative)—we are still our own master, and we are worshiping ourselves, not Jesus, the Lord.

Thus, Christ's authority forces us to acknowledge an external authoritative word, the word of Scripture. Moreover, the word of the gospel says that "God raised him from the dead," and this proclamation alerts us to the indispensability of God's work in history. The Bible proclaims that God worked salvation out for real people in real time and space. God, speaking authoritatively to us in the Bible in the present, tells us that time is significant. Fellowship with Christ involves fellowship with the Jesus of the past who accomplished his work for us once and for all.

Hence, God's speaking in the present calls upon us to make the differentiations in time that have already been made using our previous two models. God himself instructs us about how he speaks. He speaks not only in the present moment, but in the present through a message given, preserved, translated, and applied through time. Because of the fullness of God's presence in his present speech, we know him. And knowing him, we know him as the Lord of time, space, and history. We hear his word as a word that controls and transmits itself through all times. His word has the textures of its transmission embedded in it at the very moment and in the very way in which he speaks to us now.

Let us take a simple example. Right now God says to you in the book of Micah, "The word of the LORD that came to Micah of Moresheth during the reigns of Jotham, Ahaz and Hezekiah, kings of Judah—the vision he saw concerning Samaria and Jerusalem" (Mic. 1:1). Right now God instructs you that this is not an undifferentiated address to your present moment. It is an address to your present moment, to be sure (Rom. 15:4). But it is differentiated as an address that was initiated at an earlier time and place. God in the present tells you a story containing a notice of how he dealt with people in the past.

This final model, which we will call the *present-time model*, has advantages and disadvantages relative to the other two models. First, it has the advantage of vividly emphasizing the presence of God, his intimacy with you here and now, and therefore also the necessity of application.

Second, the present-time model can emphasize the universal and intimate claims of God and of Christ on you. You cannot remain an academic observer, merely analyzing information that does not concern you personally.

Third, the present-time model can emphasize the centrality of the gospel. For this message is the central thrust of Scripture to you here and now.

Fourth, like the once-for-all model, the present-time model makes more explicit the spiral character of hermeneutics. A central commitment to Christ, growing in strength, depth, and purity, controls the entire hermeneutical process, and is in turn nourished by the word that God speaks.

But the present-time model also has some disadvantages. It can be perverted by existential theology (including neoorthodoxy) into subjectivism. In this view, the word of God can supposedly never be "objectivized," but only comes to you in the moment of personal encounter with the Wholly Other. Kant's transcendental ego encounters God in an ineffable noumenal realm. But existential theology radically suppresses the truth about what the word of God is (cf. Rom. 1:18). Jesus is Lord. Neoorthodoxy and liberalism, despite protestations to the contrary, evade the fact that Jesus is Lord over the standards, facts, and personal motives in modern science, modern historical investigation, modern biblical interpretation, and modern efforts at systematic theological reasoning. People may of course rebel against the Lord now. But even when they rebel, they remain subject to his judgment and punishment. Liberalism, by failing to reckon adequately with Christ's lordship, has swallowed modern philosophy as its fundamental guiding framework. It does not submit to the instruction of Jesus in Scripture.[4]

The Nature of Alternative Models of Interpretation

Any of the three models that we have considered can be perverted. But when used carefully, the transmission model, the once-for-all model, and the present-time model are actually complementary approaches to the same realities of the word of God. The once-for-all model starts with God's authority and the giving of the word in its permanence and universally normative character. God's word has fixed propositional content and fixed ethical demands. The present-time model starts with God's presence now. It focuses on the mystery of human consciousness operating only in the present. The transmission-model starts with speech spread out in time through God's control over speech and history. It focuses on the external, historical context of God's speech.

Each model emphasizes one of God's attributes. The once-for-all model emphasizes God's authority and truth. The present-time model emphasizes his presence. The transmission model emphasizes his control. As usual, these emphases lead to complementary approaches. Each approach, rightly understood, affirms and embraces the others. Law (truth), consciousness (presence), and history (transmission) interlace each other. God is one in the manifold richness of his being. Hence interpretation is also one, in the midst of its manifold richness.

In principle, then, the three approaches should lead in the same direction. But human sinfulness corrupts our interpretation, and we do not always live up to the potential of any one of these approaches. Each approach, as we have already observed, is open to certain dangers and misunderstandings. Moreover, our hearts are constantly tempted to produce new idols. We can make idols out of the law, the facts, and/or the persons in interpretation. Law, facts, and persons belong together in harmony, and each functions together with the others to display God's truth, control, and presence. But in the hands of idol makers, they are distorted. Secularistic rationalism idolizes law or the rules of interpretation. Secularistic empiricism idolizes facts and interprets everything in terms of visible effects. Secularistic subjectivism idolizes persons and tries to subject everything to the mastery and decision-making of supposedly autonomous human subjects.[5]

Errors in secularist approaches to interpretation are so blatant that they are fairly easy to detect. But subtler forms of the same errors and the same idolatries beckon to Christian interpreters. Let us see how each of these three hermeneutical models can be misused in an idolatrous direction.

The once-for-all approach focuses on God's authority and the origination of his speech. It can therefore be distorted into an idolizing of rules.

Secularistic rationalism tends to idolize rules of interpretation and tries to make interpretation into an objective science. In a more subtle form of rationalism, people ignore the historical context of the Bible and view it merely as an infallible source of doctrine, a collection of propositions about God, man, and salvation. They do not relate it to what God is actually accomplishing in history.

Similar inclinations may also influence our personal response to the Bible. Look at Dottie Doctrinalist. We may become doctrinalists, who think that orthodox doctrine is the heart of Christianity. And of course there is no denying that truth is absolutely essential to Christian growth (Eph. 4:15). But so is love. Doctrinalists run the danger of distorting and flattening the Bible by ignoring some of the multidimensionality of divine communication. They also run the danger of using pride in their orthodoxy as an excuse. They conceal from themselves their fear and reluctance to change subtle attitudinal sins of the heart. They develop a false dogmatism, overconfidence in themselves, and harshness toward those who do not agree with them. They excuse these attitudes by calling them zeal for the truth. With this excuse they make their attitudes into yet another source of pride.

The present-time approach focuses on God's presence and the reception of his speech now. It can therefore be distorted into an idolizing of the human recipient, the human subject. Secularistic subjectivism blatantly idolizes the hearing, reading, and analyzing subject. But once again there are more subtle forms. Look at Amy Affirmationist, who continually affirms everyone's point of view. Christians may read the Bible only for what it says to them now. Group Bible studies may be conducted in which the only question is, What does it mean to you? All viewpoints, even those contradicting one another, may be endorsed as equally valid "for you." Everyone may feel cozily "accepted," but no one is challenged by the piercing authority of God's discipline and the ways in which he contradicts our sinful ideas.

Similarly, some charismatic groups subtly idolize the emotions of the moment of worship. Subjective feelings in the moment of worship are all that matter to them. Their vision never extends to the times and moments and wisdom of the Bible's past or (for that matter) to other individuals and groups, like scholars, in the present. Despite the presence of real gifts of the Spirit within the group, it seldom moves beyond articulating to itself what it already knows, and further extending the implications along lines to which it is accustomed and with which it is comfortable.

These inclinations may also influence people's personal response to the Bible. They become pietists, who think that personal devotional life and prayer are the heart of Christianity.[6] Remember Peter Pietist? Of course, personal devotion, commitment, and fellowship with Christ are essential to Christian growth (Col. 2:6–7). But so is criticism and rebuke from the truth. Pietists run the danger not only of reading the Bible one-dimensionally for its devotional nourishment, but also of avoiding the doctrinal and practical wrestling necessary for fully acknowledging Christ's lordship over our minds (Matt. 22:37).

Lastly, the transmission approach focuses on God's control over the entire historical process of transmission. But it can be distorted into empiricism or historicism, in which the facts (or really, the interpreter's expectations concerning factuality) are idolized. Secularistic empiricism is more blatantly idolatrous. But Christians may also fall into more subtle forms of the same approach. They may use the fact of historical and cultural distance between biblical situations and modern situations in order to make the Bible only distantly relevant to our lives and responsibilities. Only the broad principles of the Bible (or only the person of Christ vaguely defined) are allowed to give binding direction for our situation. In actual fact, the modern situation, or rather our conception of the situation, obtains primacy of place in application. Pragmatism and worldliness creep in.

We see, then, how people can twist the hermeneutical models in doctrinal, emotive, or pragmatic directions. Combinations of these failings and sins are of course also possible.

Scholarship and intellectual gifts do not protect us from these sins, especially the more subtle and sophisticated forms of them. In fact, intellectuals can easily use their cleverness to develop sophisticated forms of sin that are less easy to detect. We invent sophisticated excuses for our practices and find holes in the arguments of our critics. The pride that we have in our intellectual ability prevents us from listening carefully to critics. Pride says that we are intellectually superior to the critic, and so the critic's arguments are worthless. Pride says that we are free from sin anyway, so that the critic could not possibly be right. Pride builds defenses, carefully concealing weak points from the critics' view. First Corinthians 1:27–31 and 3:18–21 should long ago have taught us the danger of intellectual idolatry.

In particular, teachers of the Bible and theology face intellectual temptations. Teachers of systematic theology, on the average, are more likely to be doctrinalists, because they focus on the derivation of doctrine from the Bible. Teachers of practical theology, because they focus on present application, are more likely to be pragmatists and pietists. Teachers of biblical studies (Old and New Testament), because they focus on the historical distance between situations, are more likely to be historicists.

But there are many variations. Whatever their research specialty, people with a more rationalistic, syllogistic intellectual bent are more likely to be comfortable with once-for-all hermeneutics. They exhibit a doctrinalist bias. Next, the informed scholars, those in touch with great masses of fact and multifaceted argumentation from modern scholarship, are likely to see the many problems and complexities associated with the many aspects of transmission hermeneutics. This complexity may encourage them to overall tentativeness, tolerance, sensitivity, and civility, but paralyzes them when it comes to condemning false doctrine or advocating definite, vigorous practical action. They are still caught in a subtle form of historicism. Finally, consider the people absorbed in the society of the present, particularly the bureaucratic, institutional church facing secular society. They are more comfortable with the pragmatics of church growth, the principles of business management, or secular psychological theories of personal counseling. They fall victim to a subtle form of pragmatism.

Explicitness in Hermeneutics

Are we helped by the once-for-all model, the transmission model, or the present-time model? Clearly, any one of these or all three of them together may be useful in encouraging us to study some aspect of God's communication that we have previously neglected. Through any one of them we may detect areas in our thinking or in our application that have previously been sinful and untransformed by the power of God's word. Within the diversity of gifts and members of the body of Christ, as set forth in 1 Corinthians 12, we welcome people whose gifts lead them to focus special attention on particular areas.

But no method is a panacea. No method in and of itself guarantees sanctification. Christ washes us through the word and the Spirit (Eph. 5:26; 2 Thess. 2:13; 1 Peter 1:2), not through method as such. In fact, method can be a subtle snare. We can pervert orthodox doctrine, good and sound as it is, into an idol. Doctrinalists begin to shift trust from Christ and his promises to the doctrinal system over which they are masters. Likewise, we can pervert good hermeneutical method into an idol. Self-conscious interpreters begin to shift trust from Christ and his promises to trust in the hermeneutical method, which supposedly assures them that they will arrive at correct interpretations. Self-conscious interpreters may trust in themselves, their training, their learning, their brilliance, their methodicalness, or their self-consciousness, and thus be ensnared in pride and idolatry. In addition, pride may keep them from admitting that at all costs they need intellectual and hermeneutical repentance in their innermost depths.

Rationalism and the ideal of scientifically dominating the world grew out of the Enlightenment. They tempt us to desire to dominate interpretation and to make it transparent by exhaustive intellectual insight. Rationalism rejects out of hand the intuitions of the charismatic and the possibility of depth significance in texts. But such rationalism is tainted with Enlightenment idolatry, namely, the worship of the transcendent self. We end up in overconfidence and arrogance. And the divine warrior will war against that pride (Prov. 16:18; 11:2).

There is also a converse truth, namely, that the entire hermeneutical method becomes a tacit, subconscious tool for the godly person. To know God is already to know the entire process of interpretation tacitly. For interpretation, as we have seen, grows out of who God is as the speaker of his word. To know God is to know many things about his ways with the world, without necessarily being able consciously to articulate all that knowledge. To know the Lord of history means understanding the intricacy and fidelity and presence of his speech. Or, to put it another way, knowing God promotes wisdom, that is, the practical skill of serving him faithfully in every area of life. One develops hermeneutical skill without necessarily being self-conscious about a series of hermeneutical steps. One finds oneself taking all the steps of the transmission model without self-consciously distinguishing them or even knowing that one is taking them.

To know Christ is to know the one "in whom are hidden all the treasures of wisdom and knowledge" (Col. 2:3). To know Christ is to be bonded to those who are in Christ, and so to stand with them as the audience for God's word. Hence, one experiences tacitly the benefits of the once-for-all approach. To know Christ is to have the key to the purpose of history (Eph. 1:10). Hence, one experiences tacitly the benefits of the transmission approach. To know Christ is to hear him speak (John 10:3–5, 27). Hence, one experiences the benefits of the present-time approach. To know Christ is to be filled with the Spirit who writes the law on our hearts (2 Cor. 3:3). The Spirit is in fact the ultimate Method, and his ways are past finding out. When we fellowship with Christ, we have the mind of Christ, and hence we exercise true rationality. We have the wisdom of Christ, and so exercise true skill with respect to our situation. We have the love of Christ, and so exercise true subjectivity in the Spirit. We know the author, we know his Word, and we know the power of the Resurrection that is transforming us through the Spirit of Christ.

But we need to grow in that knowledge (Phil. 3:10–14).

ENDNOTES

1. The potential fruitfulness of a second person's perspective is a major concern in Vern S. Poythress, *Symphonic Theology: The Validity of Multiple Perspectives in Theology* (Grand Rapids: Zondervan, 1987).

2. See Vern S. Poythress, *The Shadow of Christ in the Law of Moses* (reprint, Phillipsburg, N.J.: Presbyterian and Reformed, 1995), 251–86.

3. One thinks also of the great affirmation of "now" in 2 Corinthians 6:2.

4. On the philosophical roots of neoorthodoxy and other versions of theological modernism, see Royce G. Gruenler, *Meaning and Understanding: The Philosophical Framework for Biblical Interpretation* (Grand Rapids: Zondervan, 1991).

5. See Vern S. Poythress, "God's Lordship in Interpretation," *Westminster Theological Journal* 50 (1988): 37–39.

6. Historically, the earlier pietists were very involved in love, good works, and missions, but the modern ones that I am describing often have narrower horizons.

CHAPTER 11

·

EXEMPLARS AND ANALOGY

Fatima Factualist: I am uneasy about our discussion because we have focused so much on the principles of interpretation. We have become too abstract. It's all floating in the air. Let's talk about particular examples.

Peter Pietist: I too am uneasy, because when we generalize we can leave out the individual and the uniqueness of his personal communion with the Lord.

Missy Missiologist: Maybe we should consider an example, a case study coming from a particular culture.

The resurrection of Christ is the central event in God's dealings with us. As such, it provides a pattern for understanding his plans throughout history. That is, the resurrection is an *exemplar,* a crucial example through which we understand the whole. This use of an exemplar is so crucial that it deserves separate discussion.

The Role of Exemplars

The Bible characteristically teaches by using exemplars, that is, crucial examples. The Exodus from Egypt is God's exemplar to teach Israel what it means for him to save. Later acts of redemption are analogous to the Exodus. The creation of Adam and Eve is God's exemplar to show that he is the Creator of each one of us. The later providential acts by which he brings each of us into being are analogous to the earlier creation. Christ himself is the exemplar for righteous living and the destiny of the righteous person.

Christ's resurrection is the exemplar for the future resurrection of the saints. The crucifixion of Christ is the exemplar of God's righteous judgment against sin, in that Christ bore our sin (1 Peter 2:24).[1]

I use the word *exemplar* rather than *example* because we are dealing here with more than mere examples. These are the crucial examples. They involve real historical events that, in their detailed texture, are unique and unrepeatable. These unrepeatable events, then, are the foundation for all the rest. They furnish general, repeatable patterns for whole series of events. For example, one event becomes the foundation for all later events in which God creates human beings. Another event becomes the foundation for all events of redemption or resurrection. Since the one crucial event is unrepeatable, other events are not identical to it, but only analogous to it. But since the other events do genuinely relate to the exemplar, the analogy is genuine and important.

In this way, the Bible teaches us by a combination of generality and particularity. The Bible includes general statements about how God redeems, and also includes an account of the Exodus, with its particularity. Each helps to interpret the other. Similarly, the Bible includes general statements about how God gives life, and also includes an account of Christ's resurrection. The general truth gets fleshed out through the particular instance. The particular instance receives additional significance through general statements that indicate its relation to a general pattern. Moreover, the Bible is not merely a book of philosophy or dogma. It announces the historical events of Christ's life, the particulars of which are the very basis for our salvation. Since Jesus is the Lord of all, the particulars of his life have significance for all people and all history. Since Jesus is the one who is the Lord of all, the generalities about the world and its history rest inextricably on the Jesus of first-century Palestine.

Moreover, the earthly life of Jesus is the exemplar for who God is. The life of Jesus is the most crucial of all exemplars. As such, it is an exemplar for how other exemplars work in the Bible. Because Christ is truly central to the Bible (Luke 24:44–49), we should be able to extend the list of exemplars almost indefinitely. Within the framework of the Old Testament, the tabernacle is the exemplar for God's dwelling with Israel. Moses is the exemplar for the prophets (Deut. 18:18–22). David is the exemplar for kings (cf. 1 Kings 11:4). Solomon is the exemplar of a wise man (1 Kings 4:29–34). Abraham is the exemplar of faith (Gen. 15:6).

Each of these exemplars is rich in particularity. Each is unique. Each is in some crucial ways unlike the other instances of the pattern of which it is the exemplar. We see this uniqueness especially in the case of Christ. Christ is both God and man. Being God, he is unlike any other human being. And yet, he is not only one man among many, but *the* man, the representative and pattern for a new humanity (1 Cor. 15:45–49).

Using Analogy

We are thus confronted with an analogy, but not pure identity, between Christ and other human beings. Christ's resurrection is analogous to, but not identical with, our being raised to new life in the Spirit (Col. 3:1). Christ's resurrection is analogous to, but not identical with, the coming resurrection of the bodies of the saints (1 Thess. 4:13–18).

In any analogy, there are points of similarity and points of difference. When we are dealing with exemplars, the analogies are richly structured and multifaceted. There are thus many small points of analogy integrated into a larger pattern. But the larger pattern still leaves room for points of striking difference.

How then do we judge the character and the extent of an analogy? How do we judge what the points of similarity and the points of difference are? Can we do it only if someone explicitly enumerates all the points of similarity? An explicit, exhaustive enumeration occurs neither in the Bible nor in most ordinary analogies that people use. Rather, we grasp the main character of the analogy and naturally include in it some degree of detail. But other details remain vague. We are often content to let the boundaries of an analogy remain somewhat unclear.

We are able to make judgments about analogies because we have a context. For example, the Bible provides much teaching about God. This larger context of teaching provides a context that enables us to understand any one particular analogy for God, such as that God is the great king. As other parts of the Bible confirm, God issues orders, has the authority appropriate to his position, and has power to rule. In these respects, he is like an earthly king. But unlike an earthly king, his power is unlimited, his domain is the whole universe, and his rule is always just. He is not subject to the typical limitations of a human king. We are confident of all these conclusions because we already know something about God and something about earthly kings.

In general, analogies work because we have some context for grasping the implications of an analogy. The same holds true when we read an analogy in the Bible. We grasp its implications through knowledge of the context and through knowledge of the author of the analogy, namely, God himself. Hence, our general knowledge of God influences in subtle ways what we make of an analogy. In many cases, it may not noticeably influence the more obvious, large-scale features and implications. But it will influence the subtleties. It affects just what further, more distant implications we draw, and it affects our judgment concerning more subtle similarities and differences.

Thus, using analogy makes sense only against a background of tacit knowledge. We must know God and know something of his creation. Even though analogies are open-ended and nonexhaustive, we can be confident that we understand them because God knows all things exhaustively, because he has made us in his image, and because he has made a world in which there are many fruitful analogies.

A Triad of Attributes

To understand the structure of exemplars and analogies, we may fruitfully employ the triad of classificational, instantiational, and associational aspects, developed previously. These categories are themselves analogical in character. They apply first of all to an exemplar, namely, God in his Trinitarian character. They apply subordinately to the creation and to aspects of it.

We understand God by analogy. For example, how do we understand the associational aspect of God's being, that is, the mutual fellowship and indwelling within the Trinity? It is a great mystery. But we have an analogy within our experience. God consents to have fellowship with us through the work of Christ and the Holy Spirit. Preeminently, God the Father sends the Holy Spirit to dwell in us (Rom. 8:9–11). Through the Spirit, Christ dwells in us (Rom. 8:10)—and the Father as well (John 14:23). God dwells in himself in a manner that is analogous to his dwelling in us. God's dwelling in himself is the archetypal indwelling. His dwelling in us is an ectype. The two are analogous, but not identical (John 17:23).

We also understand instantiation analogically. The Word is eternally the instantiation of God. By analogy, the Word became flesh and "instantiated" God in time and space (John 1:14). We understand this eternal instantiation by analogy with the temporal one.

We understand classification analogically. God reveals himself to us as one God. His revelation reveals his oneness. The revealed oneness is analogically related to the oneness that he has in himself.

The use of exemplars in God's teaching also expresses the classificational, instantiational, and associational aspects. First, an exemplar, like the Exodus, is a particular event or thing. It is an instantiation. Second, an exemplar is an instantiation of a general pattern, a classificational generality. The Exodus instantiates the classificational pattern of redemption. Third, an exemplar enjoys an associational relationship with a larger context, through which we come to understand it. The Exodus is an exemplar for a pattern of redemption that is embodied in another instances. By seeing the relationship with other instances, and with general statements, we grasp how the Exodus functions as an exemplar.

ENDNOTE

1. Thus, I am not agreeing with an exemplary theory of the atonement. Christ is our example, to be sure, but he is much more as well. He is the exclusive penal substitute for sin.

CHAPTER 12

.

HISTORY

Herman Hermeneut: So we can talk about particular examples. But how do the examples fit into the larger whole?

Fatima Factualist: Something like half of the Bible is about history and events. We had better know what history is about.

A sense of history is indispensable in biblical interpretation. God created a world that has history. The great events of God's redemption took place in history. In addition, history is the context for the steps in interpretation laid out in the transmission perspective. The once-for-all perspective on interpretation focuses on the original speech of God, within its original historical context, thus demanding that attention be given to history.

So what is history? How do we reckon with it? The coinherence of the three steps in the transmission perspective raises questions about the character of history. Coinherence suggests that the historical moment of the past, the original point when God spoke, cannot be rigidly isolated from the present. The coinherence of the transmission perspective with the once-for-all perspective and the present-time perspective suggests the same thing. In addition, exemplars show that there are complex connections in history. How do we obtain a sound understanding of history?

Remember where we started when we developed the transmission perspective. We started with God's communication. The Father speaks the Word through the Spirit. He speaks to the Spirit as hearer. We can use this same starting point for understanding history. God's speaking and acting go together. In particular, God's speaking offers a perspective on all events in history. Creation took place through God speaking: "And God said, 'Let there be light,' and there was light" (Gen. 1:3). "By the word of the LORD were the heavens made, their starry host by the breath of his mouth" (Ps. 33:6). All events proceed according to his word: "Who can speak and have it happen if the Lord has not decreed it? Is it not from the mouth of the Most High that both calamities and good things come?" (Lam. 3:37–38; cf. Eph. 1:11).

If history matches God's verbal decrees, we would expect that the events of history show a structure similar to what we have already found with respect to God's speech. Moreover, human beings, made in the image of God, reflect aspects of God's character in a particular way. Hence, we expect that human action will reflect the characteristics of divine action. Divine action always includes divine speaking. Hence, human action on a broad scale should have a quasi-linguistic character.[1]

Unity and Diversity in History

For example, according to our earlier discussion, there is unity and diversity in meaning. By analogy, we would expect that there is unity and diversity to the character of historical events. Many different truths about many different subjects hold together within the unity of God's plan. In this sense we find unity and diversity in the truth. This unity and diversity includes truth about historical events. To historical events we can apply the partitional triad: the classificational, instantiational, and associational aspects.

First, in accordance with the classificational aspect, each historical event is classifiable. It belongs to one or another kind of event. We find events of war, celebration, agriculture, birth, death, marriage, and so on. We understand the past partly by comparison with our own experience. We know about war, celebration, agriculture, and so on, in our own time. Because human beings are made in the image of God, there is a certain constancy to human nature. Even though cultures and times differ, they differ within limits. The element of constancy guarantees that understanding other people in other times is possible.

Next, consider the instantiational aspect. Each historical event is particular. It is this event, at this time and this place, never identical with any other event in all its details—if only because the other events happen at other times or places.

Third, the associational aspect indicates that history hangs together. The events affect one another in causal ways, and their overall meaning depends on their fitting together as complementary events in a total plan of God for history (Eph. 1:11).

As usual, the three aspects hold together. They coinhere. Any one aspect offers a perspective on the others; no one aspect can really be understood except as it presupposes and encompasses the others.

Perspectives on History

The perspectives from transmissional hermeneutics can also become perspectives on understanding history. Thus, we have potentially three alternative perspectives on any historical event. According to the once-for-all perspective, each event takes place in order to provide a development and a significance for the whole rest of history. All the rest of history becomes a kind of "audience" addressed by the one event. The event "speaks to" and affects all subsequent ages.

Second, we may use the transmission perspective. According to the transmission perspective, history is a development in time, in which each event takes place to affect its immediate future, and that later situation affects a still later situation, and so on. The interaction is spread out along a time line.

Third, according to the present perspective, all understanding of history takes place now, in our present meditation on the record of the past. The past is available to us only in the present, through records that still exist in the present, and through memories of the past that exist in the present. Interpreting history is a responsibility that confronts us in the present.

Modern secular approaches to history refuse to acknowledge that God is the Lord of history. So it is difficult for them to acknowledge or appreciate the coinherence of these various perspectives. In a truncated form of the transmission perspective, history remains connected only by immediate antecedents and immediate succession, not by an overall plan. In the Bible, by contrast, the end or consummation recapitulates aspects inherent at the beginning (Rev. 22:1–5). The new creation is a new paradise, a new Garden of Eden. The resurrection of Christ in the past forms the foundation for the spiritual resurrection of Christians to eternal life in the present (Col. 3:1). And it forms the foundation for the bodily resurrection of Christians in the future (1 Cor. 15:22–23, 49). Such a view depends on our knowing that God is one, that he has a plan for the whole, that the plan is unified, and that it will not fail to be accomplished.

In other words, events in history are related to one another, not only to events immediately before and after, but to the whole of history, working out according to the comprehensive plan of God. Each particular event is significant because it has a place in the whole and is connected to the whole. The resurrection of Christ has an effect not merely on the apostles to whom

Christ first appeared, but on us who are united to Christ by faith. We experience resurrection power from that resurrection (Phil. 3:10). The Resurrection does not merely set off a short-term causal sequence, but touches us directly today. Moreover, in one sense the pattern of the Resurrection extends backward as well as forward in time. God reckoned beforehand with the events that were still future (Rom. 3:25). He was gracious and forgiving to people in the Old Testament because of the sacrifice of Christ that was still to come. He put in place animal sacrifices in the Old Testament that prefigured the coming sacrifice.

In a whole host of ways, the associational perspective is significant. Typological or symbolic patterns reappear over long stretches of history. Within the biblical view, then, history contains connections of many richer kinds than what the modern secularist conceives. Modern secular treatments still acknowledge in some fashion that each event is unique (the instantiational perspective). They acknowledge that each event can be classified according to more general patterns (the classificational perspective). But they tend not to appreciate the associational perspective. We shall therefore devote particular attention to it.

We have already briefly considered the death and resurrection of Christ, which are at the very center of history and which cast their light and the power of their effects on all history. But let us consider how the associational aspect belongs even to minor examples.

An Example in 2 Kings 14:5

In 2 Kings 14:5 we read, "After the kingdom was firmly in his grasp, he [Amaziah] executed the officials who had murdered his father the king." This one event is intelligible in relation to other events. For the benefit of our understanding, we should take into account all kinds of relations. This event was related to preceding and succeeding actions. The preceding assassination provided the judicial and emotional basis for Amaziah's decision. Amaziah's knowledge of the Law of Moses may also have been a factor.[2] What about the consequences of Amaziah's action? The narrator does not note any obvious consequences. But we know that the Scripture commends Amaziah's action as righteous. And other biblical texts indicate that God blesses the righteous; hence, any of a number of subsequent events may have been effects of Amaziah's righteous act.

We know from the Bible, as well as from modern experience, that one of the effects of punishing crimes is to induce in others a fear of committing that crime (Deut. 19:20). As people saw Amaziah's righteousness in action, they would have been more ready to submit to his rule and more fearful of attempting further assassinations.

These, then, are the more immediate connections in time. There are also more remote connections. As with language, so with history, the connections extend in many directions and many dimensions.

Amaziah's action is connected with all other attempts throughout history in which monarchs punish assassins and would-be assassins. It is connected with all the power plays and calculations by which people attempt to obtain or increase political power. It is also connected, by way of contrast, with the failures of weak people in power to maintain control. By way of 2 Kings 14:6, it is connected with all the penal sanctions of the Law of Moses. All these instances offer manifestations of the way in which people deal with the issue of justice and fitting punishment for wrongdoing.

This event involving Amaziah is connected with the ups and downs of Israelite history in 1 Kings and 2 Kings. We see a succession of more or less righteous kings, and more or less evil kings, ending with appalling failure in the Exile. Amaziah's one action was righteous, and he is evaluated as basically a good king with a significant failure (2 Kings 14:3–4). But his reign was marked by a disastrous defeat (vv. 11–14), which presaged the Exile to come. Note the close parallel between earlier and later destruction. In 2 Kings 14:13–14, much of the wall of Jerusalem is destroyed, and captives and treasure are taken. In 2 Kings 25:1–21, there is still greater destruction and the captivity and desolation of the Exile. Hence, the issue of true righteousness looms large in the narrative of 1 and 2 Kings. Amaziah's one action was righteous. It may have stemmed the assaults on David's throne for a time. But was it enough to stem the broader tide of national rebellion against God? Ultimately it was not; unrighteousness crept into Amaziah himself when his pride kept him from listening to Jehoash's warning (14:9–11).

First and Second Kings, by ending with the gloom of the Exile, cry out for an answer. David's descendants failed utterly, and were finally saved from total ruin by an outsider's mercy (2 Kings 25:27–30). In the long run, the throne of David needed to be established in a manner that would be free from both assassination attempts and internal corruption of the heart. So Isaiah 9:5–7 answers by promising an everlasting king from the line of David.

Thus, the action in 2 Kings 14:5 is typologically related to the reign of Christ. Amaziah put down his father's assassins, but it was only a temporary measure, a stopgap. In his resurrection, Christ put down his own assassins and established a righteousness that would be permanently free from both external assassination and internal corruption. The kings and rulers plot assassination "against the Lord and against his Anointed One" (Ps. 2:2). They appear to succeed for a time by assassinating the Anointed One (Acts 4:26–28). But God answers:

> The One enthroned in heaven laughs; the Lord scoffs at them. Then he rebukes them in his anger and terrifies them in his wrath, saying, "I have installed my King on Zion, my holy hill." (Ps. 2:4–6)

Christ, established as King, executes perfect justice.

> With righteousness he will judge the needy, with justice he will give decisions for the poor of the earth. He will strike the earth with the rod of his mouth; with the breath of his lips he will slay the wicked. Righteousness will be his belt and faithfulness the sash around his waist. (Isa. 11:4–5)

In Christ's kingdom, the sons of the kingdom are not liable for the assassination carried out by their fathers, that is, the sinful sons of Adam. After mentioning the assassination of the King, for which we are guilty (Acts 3:13–15), Peter says, "Repent, then, and turn to God, so that your sins may be wiped out, that times of refreshing may come from the Lord" (v. 19).

The connection between Amaziah's action and the resurrection of Christ is not merely coincidental or external, but real. Amaziah acted righteously, in accordance with the Law of Moses. But Mosaic law is a reflection of the righteousness of God. And the righteousness of God is supremely revealed in the resurrection of Christ, which is not only *his* legal vindication but ours: "[He] was raised to life for our justification" (Rom. 4:25).

We can arrive at the same conclusion by considering goodness instead of righteousness. It is good for people to be under a righteous ruler. It is a blessing (Prov. 28:12; 29:2; Eccl. 10:17). We have already observed that swift justice to assassins tends to enhance the stability of a kingdom, and may thus be one means of increasing peace and prosperity.

Now the Bible teaches that good things like these always come from God (Acts 14:17; James 1:17). God manifests his goodness in Amaziah's act of justice. Moreover, this goodness comes to people who do not deserve it, for they are sinners. Hence, we must see here not only the goodness of God, but also his mercy. God has been merciful to the people of Israel by causing Amaziah to act in a righteous way. How has God found it possible to be both merciful and just? In mercy he appears to overlook sins (Rom. 3:25), while in justice he must punish them. The solution is found in Christ: "God presented him as a sacrifice of atonement, through faith in his blood" (v. 25). Hence, he is "just and the one who justifies those who have faith in Jesus" (v. 26). The crucifixion and the resurrection of Christ are therefore the ultimate basis for mercy, even in Old Testament times. They are the basis, then, for God's display of goodness and mercy through Amaziah.

Amaziah, then, is a mediator of God's goodness, mercy, and justice. He is also a king in the line of David, the line in which God focuses the promise of the great messianic king. Hence, in the providence of God, the action of Amaziah is linked like a foreshadowing or a type to the greater, climactic action in Christ's resurrection.

Other Kinds of Connections

Events are also connected to one another by the ways in which they display the attributes of God. For example, God is always just. He acts in the events of history. From the expressive perspective and from the perspective of personal presence, we expect that God will display his justice in every event. Hence, all events show common patterns that belong to God's justice.

Similarly, all events show common patterns belonging to God's redemption. He liberates, he conquers evil, and he operates on the basis of substitution and forgiveness founded in Christ. He gives life, accomplishes propitiation and reconciliation, and reveals wisdom.

All these ways of describing redemption are true. But none is merely a pat formula. They describe a work of God that is infinitely wise and deep. We do not comprehend any one description exhaustively, nor do we comprehend fully the relations of the various descriptions to one another. God's wisdom in language is unfathomable, and likewise his wisdom in historical action is unfathomable. The patterning of history is not reducible to a pat formula.

Moreover, God exercises his creativity in history. Hence, every historical event is unique. The patterns are multidimensional and interlocking. We never arrive at a complete list of all possible dimensions of patterning. Rather, we must read the Bible again and again. We must understand in increasing depth what God has done. And, subordinately, we are called upon to understand what he is doing in our lives, in our communities, and in the extrabiblical history of past eras.

Classifying Connections

Although we can never exhaust the possibilities for kinds of connections, we can begin to make some simple classifications. What kinds of connections does this historical event have with other events? For convenience we may organize our discussion using another perspectival triad, namely, the triad of unit, hierarchy, and context.[3]

First, each historical event or incident has a unity and identifiable features. It is a coherent *unit*. It belongs to a distinct class of events. Amaziah's righteous act belongs to the class "punishment of assassins."

Second, each event or incident is embedded in the larger context of a historical and cultural situation. It belongs in a *context*.

Third, each event is a small part of a *hierarchy* of progressively larger events that are spread out in time. For example, Amaziah's pronouncement of judgment is a small event within the larger complex of events that includes the entire process of dealing with the aftermath of the assassination. The aftermath of the assassination is one part of the total time of Amaziah's reign. His reign, in turn, is a small part within the rule of the Davidic line. And this line of rulers is one act within the larger history from Creation to the incarnation of Christ. The progressively larger complexes of events form a hierarchy of events.

Let us take as our exemplar the resurrection of Christ. It is a unique event or unit of history. But in an obvious way it is connected with all other instances of bodily resurrection:[4] the raising of the son of the widow of Zarephath (1 Kings 17:17–24), the raising of the Shunammite's son (2 Kings 4:18–37), the raising of Jairus's daughter (Matt. 9:18–26), and the raising of Lazarus (John 11:17–44). It belongs to the class "bodily resurrection."

A second type of connection is a connection by contiguity or hierarchy. The resurrection of Christ is one incident in a series of incidents in the life of Christ. These incidents are grouped into larger and smaller groups of incidents. The Resurrection is part of a larger series of incidents including the events of burial and the incidents of Christ's post-Resurrection appearances. These incidents, in turn, form the denouement to a larger narrative encompassing the whole earthly life of Christ. And the earthly life of Christ is at the center of a larger history spanning centuries.

The third perspective is the contextual perspective. Within this perspective we focus on metaphoric or analogical connections between the resurrection of Christ and other events. The analogies are of many kinds. For example, Isaac is to be sacrificed, and then is received "back from death" in a figurative sense (Heb. 11:19). When Noah is rescued from the Flood, and when the Israelites are rescued from the Red Sea, they receive life after passing through the waters of death. Jonah comes back from a watery death (Jonah 2:5–7). Jeremiah is raised up from the pit (Jer. 38:6–13).

Now let us generalize. A unit in language or an event in history enjoys connections with other units sharing the same features. It belongs to a class of units of the same kind. The older linguistic terminology of "paradigmatic relations" is an aspect of this kind of connection. Thus, the unital perspective is closely related to the classificational perspective. The archetype for units is the unity of God, which is especially associated with God the Father.

Units in language and events in history may be grouped together on the basis of contiguity in space and time. In the older linguistic terminology, this kind of connectivity was called "syntactic" or "metonymic." The ultimate historical exemplar for connectivity based on time and space is the incarnation of Christ. Connection by contiguity thus rests on the instantiational perspective, deriving from God the Son.

Units in language and events in history may also be grouped together contextually on the basis of metaphoric and analogical relations. The presence of analogy enables us to see one truth or one event through the perspective of another, by virtue of their associations and their theological "concurrence" in the plan of God. The connection through analogy rests on the associational perspective and God the Holy Spirit.

As usual, the three aspects (unit, hierarchy, and context) are perspectivally related. They are correlative to one another and coinherent. The same holds true for the three kinds of connections: connections by common features, connections by contiguity, and connections by analogy or association. Units always occur in a hierarchy of smaller and larger units in which they are embedded. They and their identifying features are intelligible and identifiable only through hierarchy and context. And of course hierarchy and context have no content without units to fill them. In the end, all three mutually involve one another.

Now let us illustrate with some further examples.

The Sin Offering in Leviticus 9:8–11

Consider the sin offering described in Leviticus 9:8–11. First, we find connections of elementary classification closely related to unit. This particular event is an instance of a sin offering. It is connected with all sin offerings made by Aaron, and more broadly with all sin offerings whatsoever.

All sin offerings are also connected with the other types of animal sacrifice described in Leviticus 1–5 and with the sacrifices of the patriarchs before the time of Moses. These different kinds and instances of sin offerings have complex relations of similarity and dissimilarity to one another. All animal sacrifices have some similarities (e.g., the fat and the blood are never eaten). Sin offerings have some distinctive characteristics. For example, some of the blood is put on the horns of the bronze altar or the altar of incense. The flesh is not eaten by the one presenting the offering, but neither is it burned on the altar. The particular sin offering in Leviticus 9:8–11 has features that distinguish it from all other instances of sin offering (in particular, the time and particular circumstances are distinct).

Second, there are part-whole relations, that is, relations governed by hierarchy. The entire act of making the sin offering has connections with the various subordinate steps within the whole. For example, we see Aaron slaughtering the calf, his sons bringing the blood, Aaron dipping his finger in the blood and putting it on the horns of the altar, Aaron pouring out the rest of the blood, Aaron burning the fat, and Aaron taking the carcass outside the camp and burning it. The whole event can be decomposed into smaller parts. Likewise, this particular sin offering is a part belonging to a larger whole. The sin offering goes together with the burnt offering (Lev. 9:12–14), offerings for the people (9:15–21), Aaron's blessing (9:22), and God's response (9:23–24). Together these actions fit into the total rite for consecrating Aaron and his sons (Lev. 8–9). This rite of consecration fits into a larger cycle of events affirming and honoring the holiness of God's presence among the Israelites (Ex. 25–Lev. 27).

Many of the more interesting sorts of connections have to do with contextual connections. For instance, animal sacrifices are related to creation, to redemption, and to consummation.[5]

Let us consider creation first. The institution of animal sacrifice depends on elements in creation in several ways. Animals are what they are according to God's word of creation. On the sixth day, God created the animals and defined the unique existence of each kind. To be an animal is to be subject to God's creative word concerning animals. Moreover, God gave man dominion over the animals. This dominion becomes one of the reasons why it is fitting for people to offer animal sacrifices.

The sin offering presupposes the existence of sin. Since there was no sin in the original created order, the detailed significance of the sin offering has no direct analogue in creation. But there are still some noteworthy elements of analogy. Adam in his disobedience was a representative for all his descendants (Rom. 5:12–21). By analogy, the animal sacrifice represents the worshipers.

Next, consider the consummation. The way in which animal sacrifices are appointed to deal with sin anticipates the final elimination of sin in the consummation. God adopted a symbolic form of judgment and reconciliation with the sin offering. He will achieve consummate judgment and reconciliation at the Last Day.

The sin offering has the closest analogies with redemption, since sin exists in the world only in the period from the Fall to just before the consummation. The animal sacrifices, including the sin offering in particular, were instituted by God to point forward to the sacrifice of Christ (Heb. 13:11–12).

The entire span of time in which redemption takes place extends from the fall of Adam to the second coming of Christ. Within this time span, sin offerings are connected most obviously with the crucifixion of Christ (Heb. 13:11–12). But we may also inquire how they are related to the beginnings of sin and redemption in the Fall, how they are related to the completion of redemption in the Second Coming, and how they are related to any event in between.

Sin offerings are related to the Fall by the fact that it introduced sin. Sin offerings were ordained in response to this problem. Moreover, in the narrative of the Fall, the promise of God (Gen. 3:15) and the gracious action of God (v. 21) hint at the coming of an eventual remedy for sin. The initial symbolic level of remedy involves the use of dead animals (v. 21), which is related at least distantly to the later use of animals in sacrifice.

How are sin offerings related to the Second Coming? At the Second Coming, Christ will remove sin from the world by triumphant war. This removal of sin is analogous to the symbolic removal of sin from the people by means of the sin offering. When Christ returns, the whole world will be made holy; hence, sin must be completely removed (Matt. 13:40–43).

Sin offerings are connected to individuals, the community, and the cosmos. In the first place, the technical details of sin offerings indicate that different types of sin offerings were given for the high priest, for the community as a whole, for a leader, and for an ordinary member of the community (Lev. 4). On the day of his consecration, Aaron offered one sin offering for himself and a second one for the people (Lev. 9:8–11, 15). But even the sin offering for himself was concerned with his capacity to serve as high priest, in which capacity he represented the people before God. Hence, the sin offering for Aaron was indirectly relevant to the people as well. The sacrificed animal represented Aaron as a single person. But through Aaron, who represented the people, it came to represent the people as well.

Now consider the sin offering offered for the people. It was still Aaron who did the officiating. He did so in his official representative capacity. The status of priest and the status of people were bound up together. The animal represented the people first of all. But subordinately it was related to Aaron. And because it was a whole animal with its own singularity, it expressed the unity that belonged to the community.

Each sin offering pointed to the other, and both were part of a larger complex dealing with the intertwining aspects of sin. Sin is both individual and communal in its effects and in the ways that it spreads. Hence, by analogy with this situation, Christ's one final sacrifice cleanses both individual Christians and the church, the community of faith (Eph. 5:25–27).

So far we have discussed how a sin offering can have connections with both an individual and a community. How can it have connections with the cosmos? Christ's sacrifice is the basis for the renewal of the whole universe (Rom. 8:18–22). The subhuman elements of the universe are not themselves sinful, but were "subjected to frustration" (v. 20) because of the Fall. Sin affects them, and renewal affects them as well.

The cosmic implications of sacrifice are tacitly included in some of the associations of the sin offering in Leviticus 9. To see this, recall that the tabernacle was made according to the pattern that Moses received on Mount Sinai (Ex. 25:9). Both the tabernacle and the Solomonic temple were images of God's heavenly dwelling (1 Kings 8:27; Heb. 8:5). The sin offering was slaughtered in the court, and the blood was presented on the horns of one of the altars. This procedure must have had a heavenly analogue. Correspondingly, Christ was put to death on earth but ministers in the heavenly sanctuary (Heb. 8:2; 9:11–14). By the blood of the Old Testament sin offering, the worshipers and the tabernacle were cleansed with respect to symbolic defilement (Lev. 4:20, 26, 35; 16:16, 19–20; Heb. 9:9–10, 13, 21–22). By the blood of Christ, worshipers and the world are cleansed (Heb. 9:23; 10:14).

Central Connections and More Distant Connections

So far, we have focused on the task of simply enumerating various kinds of connections. But we should emphasize the centrality of Christ's work. The Old Testament as a whole testifies beforehand to Christ (Luke 24:44–47).

The animal sacrifices in particular point forward to Christ (Heb. 9:9–14). They do so by showing parallels or analogies to Christ's work (vv. 13–14).

Before his crucifixion, they served as channels whereby the benefits of his crucifixion came to the faithful. At the same time, they were in themselves insufficient and imperfect. They thereby testified that something better and more permanent was to come (Heb. 10:1–22). God ordained the animal sacrifices in order to fulfill these purposes (Heb. 9:8–10). Hence, Christ is the key to understanding the significance that God intended for those sacrifices.

We can also observe that through Christ the particular event in Leviticus 9:8–11 is distantly related to an endless host of other events. Christ's sacrifice, in its very uniqueness, forms the pattern that is manifested in various ways throughout history. God liberated us once and for all in Christ's resurrection. Hence, a pattern of God acting to liberate occurs throughout history. God warred against evil in Christ's crucifixion. Hence, a pattern of holy war occurs throughout history.

Old Testament sin offerings foreshadowed some of Christ's work. This pattern of Christ's work, in turn, is reflected throughout history. Hence, the sin offerings were patterned in a way that we find reflected throughout history.

The sin offering was concerned with the removal of retribution and punishment. Hence, penal substitution, forgiveness, propitiation, and reconciliation seem to be suggested more than some of the other concerns. Penal substitution, forgiveness, propitiation, and reconciliation were accomplished once and for all in Christ's sacrifice. But that once-for-all accomplishment is the very foundation for working out substitution, forgiveness, propitiation, and reconciliation on a human level, among different groups of human beings in their relation to one another as well as in their relation to God. As people are united to Christ, they receive forgiveness and reconciliation with God. They are then to forgive and be reconciled to one another. Hence, human relations throughout history show correlations with the sin offering by imitating it on a lower level.

Analogies Between Historical Events

The sin offering in Leviticus 9:8–11 is only one example. We see through this one example the kinds of connections that a particular historical event enjoys with other events. We could have chosen some other example. To be sure, a sin offering has some advantages. The book of Hebrews makes explicit some of its connections with other events, and with Christ's work in particular. Sin offerings played a prominent role in the whole tabernacle system, which foreshadowed Christ's redemption in an elaborate way. Not everything in the Bible has an identical function or enjoys identical significance. Some elements are more prominent, and some have a more direct function of serving as "shadows."

Because Christ's work is central to history, any event whatsoever has important connections with the work of Christ. The connections may sometimes be less obvious, less striking, or less thorough. We may even see connections between the work of Christ and the false redemptions of false religion. Such connections are to be expected.

First of all, connections must exist because of the character of God. There is one plan of God for all history, and this plan displays the unity of his wisdom. God is present and active in all events. All events therefore display his deity, "his eternal power and divine nature" (Rom. 1:20).

Second, connections exist because of redemption. Sin and its perverse results, wherever they occur, need the same remedy. And there is only one remedy, namely, Christ.

Third, connections exist because of the presence of persons. All human beings are made in God's image. As such, they present us with similar patterns of action. They image God, particularly the divine Son, who is the original image (Col. 1:15).[6]

Because God is infinite and infinitely wise, the connections in his thought are infinitely rich and ramified. The creation is finite, not infinite, but it displays the wisdom of its infinite Creator. Hence, the connections among historical events are incredibly rich, pervasive, and ramified.

But this richness is not chaotic. Some connections are more salient and more prominent. For example, sin offerings are not related equally strongly to every event in the Gospels; they are related preeminently to the Crucifixion (Heb. 13:11–12).

In addition, the kinds of connections can be classified. We can distinguish various kinds of connections from one another, and we can understand what sorts of things we are comparing in any particular case.

For instance, when we compare one sin offering to other sin offerings, we understand that we are comparing events that had the same label or classification in the eyes of the Israelites. They clearly displayed common sequences of events and the common use of various animal parts. On the other hand, when we compare a sin offering to the sacrifice of Christ, we understand that we are comparing an insufficient, preliminary shadow to the all-sufficient, final reality. There is not necessarily an exact one-to-one correspondence between each step in the sequence of a sin offering and each step in the crucifixion of Christ. And even when we find a more detailed correspondence, it passes from one sphere of action to another, from animal to person, from earth to heaven.

An Example of Warfare: 1 Samuel 13:5

Consider now an example from 1 Samuel 13:5:

> The Philistines assembled to fight Israel, with three thousand char-
> iots, six thousand charioteers, and soldiers as numerous as the
> sand on the seashore. They went up and camped at Micmash, east
> of Beth Aven.

This text fits naturally with other cases of war between Israel and Philis-
tia. In the Old Testament, God enters into war, bringing Israel to victory. And
when Israel is disobedient and falls away from God, he brings them to defeat. The theme of divine holy war thus stands behind human warfare.

Moreover, the theme of kingship is important. God appointed Saul to
be Israel's king in response to the people's desire. In this passage, we are
about to see what Saul would do, in response to the people's desire that
their king lead them in war. First Samuel is largely devoted to the question
of the right and wrong kind of king, as represented by David and Saul, respectively. God wins a decisive victory for Israel through David's contest
with Goliath (1 Sam. 17). This victory for David foreshadows God's eschatological war, in which Christ defeats Satan, both on the cross and at the
Last Day.

In 1 Samuel 13:5, the Philistines gather in a threatening way, probably
in response to the earlier challenge to their authority described in verses 3–4.
Their movements challenge Saul and his men to engage in battle. What will
Saul do? In addition, what will God do through Saul, as part of his overall
purpose of waging war against his enemies in behalf of his people? Jonathan's
successes through faith indicate on a small scale what God will do in the future for the whole world. But can we find a man who will have the faithfulness of Jonathan rather than the inconsistency of Saul? David then appears.
The impermanent and partial character of David's successes, not to mention
his eventual moral failures, make us look to the future messianic king (Isa.
11:1–9) and the war that God will wage by himself (Isa. 27:1).

Hence, through the theme of holy war, the passage in 1 Samuel 13:5
enjoys linkages with the entire scope of redemption. These linkages are not
necessarily the only or most prominent ones, but they nevertheless exist.

Consider then a few of the ways in which 1 Samuel 13:5 is connected
to other passages.

First, there are connections through common features. The Philistine
challenge is connected to all other challenges brought about by military

movements. It is connected first of all to other conflicts between Saul and his enemies, then more broadly to conflicts between the people of God and their enemies, then still more broadly to all conflicts whatsoever.

Second, there are part-whole relations (hierarchy). This challenge could in principle be analyzed into smaller parts, involving the assembling, the going up, and the encamping. We could watch the movement of individual warriors. There are also larger wholes of which verse 5 is a part. Verse 5 is part of a movement-and-response package in 1 Samuel 13:5–10. But the response eventually aborts when Saul fails to keep faith (v. 9). This whole series of events in 13:5–10 is, in turn, part of a larger engagement with the Philistines in 1 Samuel 13:2–14:26. This larger engagement is itself part of the larger history of Samuel, Saul, and David in 1–2 Samuel.

Third, there are contextual connections. As with animal sacrifice, so here, we can ask about relations to creation, redemption, and consummation. The Philistine military action presupposes the abilities of organization, planning, weapons manufacture, and dominion given to man in creation. Yet the air of conflict contrasts with the originally peaceful created order.

The connection with the consummation is also mostly one of contrast: in the consummation there is final peace (Isa. 2:4). The redeemed nations assemble to honor God and become his people, rather than to dishonor him and war against him (Rev. 21:26–27).

The connection with redemption can be divided into three principal stages: the Fall, the earthly work of Christ, and the second coming of Christ. The Fall originates the hatred that leads to killing and war (Gen. 4:8, 24; 6:4–5), as well as the focused enmity between the holy offspring and the offspring of the serpent (Gen. 3:15; 4:4–5; 6:9–11). The roots of holy war are found in the promise of enmity in Genesis 3:15. As wickedness grows, the wicked assemble themselves in their thousands, with the weapons produced by their growing power. The climactic assembly of the wicked takes place at the Crucifixion (Acts 4:25–26). In Revelation 20:8, the wicked assemble one final time and experience their final defeat.

The connections are individual, corporate, and cosmic.

First, they are corporate. First Samuel 13:5 focuses on the corporate conflict between two peoples, the Philistines and the Israelites.

Second, the connections are individual. The conflict comes to a focus in the conflict between two representative individuals, David and Goliath (1 Sam. 17). Even before it reaches this point, Saul and Jonathan function as representative individuals, whose faith or lack of faith determines the outcome for their troops.

Third, the connections are cosmic. The cosmic significance of the conflict is not explicit; it is well in the background in 1 Samuel 13. But in the ancient Near East generally, people thought that the gods participated in battle. When Israel was fighting the Philistines, the conflict included a struggle between the God of Israel and the gods of the Philistines. (Note the conflict with Dagon in 1 Sam. 5 and the mention of gods in 1 Sam. 17:43.) Thus, the conflict included the spiritual sphere as well as earthly armies. Saul recognizes the importance of sacrificial offering in 13:9. Jonathan explicitly appeals to the Lord's involvement in 14:6.

An Example of Praise: Ezra 3:11

Another example is provided by Ezra 3:11, which says,

With praise and thanksgiving they sang to the Lord:

"He is good;
 his love to Israel endures forever."

And all the people gave a great shout of praise to the Lord, because the foundation of the house of the Lord was laid.

Ezra 3:11 occurs within the account of the restoration of temple worship, as part of the restoration from captivity. The restoration is a veritable deliverance, inaugurated by an "anointed" leader (Isa. 45:1). It thus parallels the deliverance from Egypt (Isa. 51:9–11). The idols of Babylon correspond to the earlier idols in Egypt. As in Exodus 15:17, the victory of God, the warrior, results in the people possessing his inheritance and building a sanctuary. Praise is one aspect of celebrating the victory. Moreover, the actual words of praise in Ezra 3:11 are connected to the words used repeatedly in celebrating God's past victories (Pss. 118; 136). Thus, this passage evokes an element in a larger pattern, the pattern of divine war, victory, and celebration.

We could therefore follow the linkages with the theme of divine war. But in Ezra 3 there is undoubtedly more emphasis on the theme of worship and the theme of the temple as the place of God's presence. So we will look at the connections of this kind.

Ezra 3 stresses the connections with the Law of Moses (v. 2), thereby making one think of the parallel with the construction of the tabernacle. There are also links with the establishment of worship in the time of David and Solomon (1 Chron. 16:34; 2 Chron. 7:3).

As usual, we can roughly classify the different types of connections.

First, there are connections of classification. The praise in Ezra 3:11 is related to other instances of praise, some using almost the same words, and some using quite different words. The singing links the passage with the entire book of Psalms.

Second, there are connections of part and whole. The action in verse 11 can be further analyzed or subdivided into parts, such as the individual lines sung by the Levites, the shout of the people, and the preceding action of laying the foundation of the temple. Verse 11 mentions actions that fit into larger wholes: the entire incident of laying the foundation in Ezra 3, the ups and downs of the restoration in Ezra 3–6, and the entire story of restoration in the book of Ezra.

Third, there are connections by contextual association. Ezra 3:11 is connected to other celebrations of God's triumph, victory, and presence.

The praise in Ezra 3:11 is related backwards to creation. Of course, in creation God gave human beings the capacity to appreciate him, to praise him, and to build in his honor. But the connections do not end there. In the creation of the world, God built a macrocosmic house to dwell in (Ps. 104:1–3; Amos 9:6; Job 38:4–6). The angels sang praises in response (Job 38:7), and God in a sense "praised" his own work by pronouncing it "very good" (Gen. 1:31).

Ezra 3:11 is related forward in time to the consummation. The consummation builds a new temple, the New Jerusalem, in which perfect praise comes to God (Rev. 19:5–8; 21:1–22:5).

The praise in Ezra is related also to the redemptive work of Christ on earth. Through his resurrection and the pouring out of the Spirit, Christ builds the new temple, the church (Matt. 16:18; 1 Cor. 3:10–17). Christ himself praises the Father, and the church joins in praise (Heb. 2:12; Rom. 15:5–13).

Within the total scope of redemptive history, we can distinguish various stages. For example, we may ask about what happens at the Fall, at the time of the Crucifixion, and at the final conflict at the Second Coming, as well as at any intermediate points.

The Fall was a turning away from true thanksgiving to God. Instead of thanking God for the bounty of the garden, Adam and Eve seized the fruit illicitly. They were cast out of the Garden of Eden, the original sanctuary (cf. Ezek. 28:13–14). In Genesis 4:26, we see praise beginning to be restored, but only in a small way. Similarly, the restoration after the Exile was small and disappointing (Ezra 3:12).

At the Second Coming, a faithful remnant will praise God for his deliverance of them from an unfaithful world (Rev. 7:9–12; 19:1–4). The book of Revelation calls the faithful to persevere in the true worship of God even when they feel small and weak and surrounded by impressive opposition (Rev. 3:8; 13:5–10).

The Clustering of Divine Action

In the examples given above, we have dealt with the time from the Fall to the Second Coming only in a superficial, schematic way. We have singled out three foci, the fall of Adam, the crucifixion and resurrection of Christ, and the Second Coming. To be sure, these three events are absolutely crucial in understanding history as a whole. But the Bible records much that took place between these events. Much happened (and is still happening) that the Bible does not record.

We must not imagine that the landscape in between these three crucial events is simply flat. Neither does it rise slowly and uniformly toward a peak. Rather, God's crucial works cluster in groups. There are crucial periods: the time of Noah's flood; the time of the patriarchs Abraham, Isaac, Jacob, and Joseph; the time of the Exodus and the Conquest; the time of David and Solomon; the time of the destruction of Jerusalem; the time of restoration. The thematic and contextual connections that we have explored may be expected to be stronger when we come to the great acts of redemption, especially the Exodus.

Even within Jesus' earthly life, there are several discernible periods: the time prior to his baptism; his public ministry, including healing, teaching, and exorcism; the journey to Jerusalem; the last days; the Crucifixion, Resurrection, and Ascension. In Acts we find a development from Jerusalem and Judea to Samaria and the ends of the earth (Acts 1:8).

When we are sensitive to historical connections, we do not overlook the different periods in which events occur. We try to understand the uniqueness of each event, and the uniqueness of clusters of events as well. The connections do not undermine uniqueness, but are fully compatible with it.

We have seen how history is interconnected, using fairly small and apparently insignificant events within the Old Testament. It should be apparent that connections are important in the case of the more outstanding and significant biblical events. Creation, the Exodus, restoration from Babylon, redemption in Christ, and the consummation are all woven together in a remarkable way in the prophecies of Isaiah 40–66. The tabernacle, sacrifice, and redemption are woven together in Hebrews. Imagery from the whole Old Testament is woven together in Revelation. Building on such biblical

resources as these, we also have today any number of works in biblical theology that endeavor to sensitize us to the richness of the connections.[7]

Grammatical-Historical Interpretation

We see that rich connections exist among the historical events in the
Bible. Now what do we do with these connections in our interpretation?

Interpretation of the Bible involves both a linguistic side, focusing on
the language of the Bible, and a historical side, focusing on the events and
the contexts in which they occur. As the once-for-all perspective reminds
us, the authority and holiness of God demand that we pay attention to the
original context of God's speech, in both its linguistic and its historical aspects. Thus, we may speak of *grammatical-historical* interpretation. Grammatical-historical interpretation focuses on the original context. But, as we
have shown, its reflections cohere with the later transmission, the modern
reception, and the significance of events in the total plan of God. Thus, grammatical-historical interpretation, rightly understood, is a perspective on a
total engagement with God. It is a total process that interacts with everything that we know about God and includes our transformation into the
image of Christ (2 Cor. 3:18). The grammatical aspect of the original context coheres with the speaking of God throughout history. The historical aspect of the original context coheres with the action of God and the plan of
God throughout history. And our understanding of both aspects undergoes
progressive transformation in our own individual and corporate history in
the church today.

But most scholars do not understand grammatical-historical interpretation in this way. Rather, they suppose that grammatical analysis isolates the
facts of ancient languages and the meanings that a text sets forth by means
of them. Language is reduced to a highly complex but essentially mechanical system. Likewise, they suppose that historical analysis isolates ancient
events within their immediate environment in space and time. They rigidly
exclude any reckoning with divine purpose or with distant events (such as
Christ's crucifixion and resurrection). Pure isolation is in fact impossible,
and the attempt to produce isolation introduces distortions.

The modern scene presents us with still other options. Some represen-
tatives of New Criticism or the reader-response approach reject grammatical-historical interpretation, seeing it as an undesirable goal.[8] Some forms
of liberation theology reject grammatical-historical interpretation as an inauthentic flight from the necessity of taking a stance against oppression in

the contemporary political struggle. Others have radically different conceptions of what grammatical-historical interpretation means. What do we do with our modern situation?

So far, we have concentrated single-mindedly on developing a form of interpretation that is based on the Bible's teaching about itself and about God. And such a focus is crucial. But eventually we must turn our attention to this modern situation. We must understand at least in a summary way what disagreements there are over interpretation, and how we may sift through them. In particular, we may see how radically our Bible-based approach differs from the main modern approaches, even some that are advocated by evangelicals.

The basic differences arise from spiritual warfare, and so we start by reflecting on the character of spiritual warfare, as set out in the book of Revelation.

ENDNOTES

1. In *Language in Relation to a Unified Theory of the Structure of Human Behavior,* 2d rev. ed. (The Hague: Mouton, 1967), Kenneth L. Pike shows how verbal communicative behavior is a subdivision of human behavior in general. Human communication in language and other forms of human behavior share common general features, which he works out in detail in his book. The discipline of semiotics also tries to exploit analogies between natural language and other kinds of human action. The common structure of action derives from the unity of God and the unity of his actions with his speaking.

2. Second Kings 14:6 is an important contribution, but does not contain a full discussion. We need to note the clear-cut prescription of the death penalty for premeditated murder (Num. 35:30–34) and the instructions to kings and judges to abide by the Law of Moses (Deut. 17:18–20) and not to avoid imposing the just penalty out of a false sense of mercy (Deut. 19:11–13).

3. This triad was first developed in the context of language analysis. Unit, hierarchy, and context are explained in Vern S. Poythress, "A Framework for Discourse Analysis: The Components of a Discourse, from a Tagmemic Viewpoint," *Semiotica* 38, no. 3/4 (1982): 277–98, and are closely related to Kenneth L. Pike's feature mode, manifestation mode, and distribution mode, respectively. See also Kenneth L. Pike, *Linguistic Concepts: An Introduction to Tagmemics* (Lincoln: University of Nebraska

Press, 1982); Kenneth L. Pike and Evelyn G. Pike, *Grammatical Analysis* (Dallas: Summer Institute of Linguistics, 1977), 1–4.

4. I am not overlooking the point that Christ's resurrection body is transfigured, according to 1 Corinthians 15:35–57.

5. For a similar analysis of the connections of the tabernacle, see Vern S. Poythress, *The Shadow of Christ in the Law of Moses* (reprint, Phillipsburg, N.J.: Presbyterian and Reformed, 1995), 96–97.

6. Students of triads will note in the above three successive paragraphs the application of the triad of meaning, control, and presence.

7. I would cite as starting points Edmund P. Clowney, *The Unfolding Mystery: Discovering Christ in the Old Testament* (Colorado Springs: Navpress, 1988); Geerhardus Vos, *Biblical Theology: Old and New Testaments* (Grand Rapids: Eerdmans, 1966); O. Palmer Robertson, *The Christ of the Covenants* (Grand Rapids: Baker, 1980); Mark R. Strom, *Days Are Coming: Exploring Biblical Patterns* (Sydney: Hodder and Stoughton, 1989); George E. Ladd, *A Theology of the New Testament* (Grand Rapids: Eerdmans, 1974); Richard B. Gaffin, Jr., *The Centrality of the Resurrection: A Study in Paul's Soteriology* (Grand Rapids: Baker, 1978); Herman Ridderbos, *The Coming of the Kingdom* (Philadelphia: Presbyterian and Reformed, 1969).

8. For an analysis of modern theories, see Anthony C. Thiselton, *New Horizons in Hermeneutics: The Theory and Practice of Transforming Biblical Reading* (Grand Rapids: Zondervan, 1992).

·

CHAPTER 13

IDOLS AS COUNTERFEITS

Dottie Doctrinalist: You know, the Bible talks about getting wisdom and the enlightening of the mind. It warns that sins corrupt understanding and lead to darkening of the mind. I think that our troubles and disagreements are not simply innocent differences in viewpoint. They originate from sinful corruptions that remain within us.

Amy Affirmationist: I don't think we have to be gloomy about it. God promised that the Holy Spirit would guide us.

Peter Pietist: Yes, but accurate guidance comes to the pure in heart. God must purify us, and we must in response purify ourselves. It's worthwhile looking at secret sins, the "hidden faults" of Psalm 19:12.

Missy Missiologist: Some sins characterize whole cultures. A whole culture can have blind spots in looking at God's message. For instance, in the United States we dislike the idea of suffering. We tend to discount the parts of the Bible that say that Christians can expect to suffer.

Curt Cultural-Transformationist: It's also a matter of institutionalized sin. We are in a spiritual war with cosmic dimensions.

The central portion of Revelation, from chapter 6 to chapter 20, deals with holy war.[1] Satan and his agents war against God. "They will make war against the Lamb, but the Lamb will overcome them because he is Lord of lords and King of kings—and with him will be his called, chosen and faithful followers" (Rev. 17:14).

The Combatants

According to Revelation, the earth and the inhabitants of the earth form the setting for a cosmic battle of superhuman dimensions. God wars against

Satan, and Satan against God. Human beings experience effects from the grace and judgment of God, and from the deceit and domination of Satan. God and Satan are morally antithetical. But, ironically, Satan and his agents are also dependent on God. God not only predicts the whole course of the battle, but also makes plain the certainty, the inevitability, and the completeness of Satan's defeat. Moreover, Satan and his agents are counterfeiters. At their most terrifying, all they can do is produce deceiving counterfeits of the true glory of God.

As others have recognized, the satanic forces in Revelation counterfeit the Trinity.[2] Satan is preeminently a counterfeit of God the Father. The Beast, a kind of pseudo-incarnation of Satan, is a counterfeit, unholy warrior opposed to Christ, the holy warrior (compare 13:1–10 with 19:11–21). The False Prophet is a counterfeit of the Holy Spirit. By his deceiving signs, the False Prophet promotes worship of the Beast. His actions are analogous to the manner in which the Holy Spirit works miracles in Acts to promote allegiance to Christ. Babylon, the harlot, is a counterfeit of the church, the bride of Christ.

The Beast counterfeits Christ in a striking number of ways. He has a counterfeit resurrection in the form of a mortal wound that has been healed (13:3). The miraculous character of his healing creates astonishment and a following for the Beast, just as the miracle of the Resurrection creates a following for Christ. The Beast has ten crowns (13:1), parallel to Christ's many crowns (19:12). The Dragon (Satan) gives the Beast "his power and his throne and great authority" (13:2), just as the Father gives the Son his authority (John 5:22–27). Worship of the Dragon and the Beast go together (Rev. 13:4), just as worship of the Father and the Son go together (John 5:23). The Beast claims universal allegiance from all nations (Rev. 13:7), just as Christ is the Lord over all nations (7:9–10).

Moreover, the first verse of chapter 13, which introduces the Beast, sets forth a parody of creation. Satan stands "on the shore of the sea" and calls up from the sea a Beast in his own image, with seven heads and ten horns, corresponding to the seven heads and ten horns of the Dragon (12:3). Just as the Son is the image of the Father, so the Beast is the image of the Dragon. In addition, the imagery of the sea alludes to the time when God called forth an ordered creation from the water (Gen. 1:2). Thus, the Dragon is a counterfeit creator, aping the creative activity of God the Father.

In this counterfeiting work lies both danger and hope. The danger is that the counterfeit will be mistaken for the true. Idolatry, as a counterfeit of true worship, is close enough to the truth to attract people and ensnare them. On the other hand, hope comes from the fact that counterfeiting expresses the dependence and failure of evil. Satan is not a second creator, but only a counterfeiter. And he is a poor one at that, because his imitations are hideous! Can anyone in his right mind, with eyes open to the true nature of Satan's imitations, still honestly want to follow him?

The Root Issue: Idolatry

According to Revelation, the root issue of life in this world is the issue of true and false worship. Do we worship God or Satan? Do we serve Christ or the Beast? Do we belong to the bride of Christ or to Babylon, the harlot?

But in drawing these conclusions we are moving rather fast. Let us first consider what the book of Revelation was saying to its original audience, the Christians in the seven churches of Asia (1:4).

What focal issues confronted the seven churches? How did Revelation instruct them on these issues? In the original first-century context,[3] the Beast represented the Roman Empire in its godlessness and idolatrous claims. The worship of the Beast was an issue because the Roman government expected all the subjects of the Empire to participate in the cult of emperor worship. By doing so, people demonstrated their allegiance and their political submission. For a polytheist, such an expression of allegiance was no problem. Jews were a recognized exception because of their monotheism. But as it became harder to view Christianity as a sect within Judaism, Christians were in danger of intense persecution, because they appeared to be politically disloyal.

The False Prophet most likely represented the priests of the imperial cult and perhaps others who supported it. Babylon, the harlot, represented the city of the world in its economic might as well as its luxury and debauchery. Babylon was preeminently Rome. But the seductions of Rome were reflected also in the seductions of each of the seven cities where the seven churches were located.

In effect, the temptations to idolatry took two complementary forms: brutality and seduction. On the one hand, the Beast threatened death to those who did not worship him. Worshiping the emperor involved a threat: do it or die. On the other hand, Babylon, the harlot, promised pleasures and ease to those who joined with her. Joining with the pagan life of the city involved an enticement. Social and economic well-being seemed to demand participation in the idol-saturated social life of the city, and literal harlots offered their physical pleasures as well. The options were power or powerlessness, pleasure or suffering, riches or poverty.

The first century offered a particular instantiation of a larger principial pattern. Spiritual war was in progress. There was no neutrality. People either served God or a counterfeit. They engaged in true worship or idolatry.

It should be no surprise that we can generalize the pattern beyond the first century. After all, Satan is always a counterfeiter. "For Satan himself masquerades as an angel of light" (2 Cor. 11:14). He has no other choice. He is not the Creator. Hence, he can only be an imitator, a counterfeiter of God's majesty, glory, and power. Since God is always the same, the ways of Satan are fundamentally always the same. Hence, in harmony with the idealist approach to Revelation, it is possible to generalize and apply the book today. Indeed, Revelation asks for such application: "He who has an ear, let him hear what the Spirit says to the churches" (Rev. 2:7).

In our day, the most obvious or direct manifestations of the Beast are found in oppressive governments. Strong-arm governments make quasi-idolatrous claims. In their heyday, Communist governments around the world demanded total obedience from their subjects. They offered a counterfeit ideology with its own philosophy of history (dialectical materialism), its version of sin (economic wrongs), its version of final hope (the utopian communist society of the future), its authoritative writings (in China, above all, Mao's Red Book), its quasi-ecclesiastical vanguard (the Communist Party).

Strong-arm governments of the right may also be oppressive. Saudi Arabia prescribes the death penalty for anyone who converts from Islam to Christianity.

Babylon also has her manifestations in our day. Big cities in the West offer a host of illicit pleasures in anonymity. No one asks questions about absolute right and wrong. In addition, consumerism threatens to make the pursuit of money into an idol. We worship not only money, but things and pleasures that money can provide. To crown the parallelism with the harlot imagery of Revelation, sexual pleasure has become the chief pursuit of a hedonistic society.

The lessons here parallel what sociologists could tell us. Idolatry can be and is institutionalized. Idolatry is of course a practice or temptation for individuals. But it involves more than individuals. Idolatry pervaded the social structures, the atmosphere, and the assumptions of first-century Asia Minor in a way that is difficult for a modern, secularized Westerner to conceive.

Secularization has supposedly freed us from the power of religions and therefore from idolatry. But, as Jacques Ellul and Herbert Schlossberg perceive, the truth is that secularization dispenses with gross physical idols in order to make way for more subtle idols.[4] We give whole-souled commitment and blind trust to scientific technique, state power, progress, revolution, sex, or money. The more recent demons may be worse than the earlier ones (Matt.

12:43–45). And the new idolatry travels in its subtlety through institutions. The institutions of power include civil government, industry, and financial institutions. But the "knowledge industry" has also more than ever developed institutions of power: the mass media, advertising, political propaganda, and educational institutions. The False Prophet is at work. These large-scale institutions give out a message that is reinforced by the voices of friends and neighbors. Too often one's friends and neighbors advocate and obey the same view of the world that the large institutions represent.

Subtle Idolatry

The most blatant forms of idolatry include literal worship of the emperor or head of state, or literal worship of sexual union, as was the case in ancient temple prostitution. But, as we have already hinted, more subtle forms exist. Communism is officially atheistic, but nevertheless requires a total commitment to the state. Such commitment is ultimately religious in character. The modern city is officially secular, but seduces us into giving an ultimate commitment to pleasure and self-fulfillment.

Once Revelation has attuned us to the character of idolatry, we can detect still more subtle forms of it. Modern democratic states officially eschew the totalitarian claims and practices of Communism. But state power still has idolatrous attraction. If problems are severe, people feel that state power must be the answer, the deliverer. Despite the repeated failures of government bureaucracies to manage adequately the multitudinous cares of citizens, people still look to the state as if it were their messiah. If problems arise with the economy, with physical health, with guaranteeing comfort in old age, with poverty, with racial discrimination and prejudice, let the state take care of it. Look at the immensity of its power. Where can we better invest our hopes than in this concentration of power? "Who is like the beast? Who can make war against him?" (Rev. 13:4).

Likewise, advertisers saturate the modern marketplace with sexual themes. The visual pictures of advertising not so subtly promise that if you use their product, you will be more attractive to persons of the opposite sex.

In fact, the Beast and Babylon in Revelation are universal symbols. They speak of the allure of power, riches, and pleasure. Who has not been snared? Subtle forms of idolatry worm their way into the lives of Christians. We thought that we surrendered the lust for power when we gave our lives to Christ. Perhaps only much later do we become aware of the way in which we enjoy a thoughtless and sometimes brutal exercise of power over our family members or our colleagues. Or we find ways of gaining power through emotional manipulation rather than direct confrontation.

We thought that we surrendered the lust for riches when we committed ourselves to tithing. But we only later become aware that we greedily claim the remaining nine-tenths as fully ours. We thought that we surrendered the lust for pleasure when we agreed in our heart to follow the Ten Commandments and live by Christian standards. Only later did we become aware that in subtle ways we still selfishly grasp for pleasures at the expense of others, always within the framework of obeying "the letter of the law."

Sin has deep roots within us. It subtly and alluringly entangles our hearts. Who will deliver us from it?

The monks tried a radical solution to these idolatries: total renunciation. The vow of obedience solves the problem of power, the vow of poverty solves the problem of riches, and the vow of celibacy solves the problem of pleasure. Or does it? No, sin and idolatry are more subtle than that. If one cuts them off at one level, they reappear in concealed form further down. Christ's death, not self-imposed rules, is our sanctification.

> Since you died with Christ to the basic principles of this world, why, as though you still belonged to it, do you submit to its rules: "Do not handle! Do not taste! Do not touch!"? These are all destined to perish with use, because they are based on human commands and teachings. Such regulations indeed have an appearance of wisdom, with their self-imposed worship, their false humility and their harsh treatment of the body, but they lack any value in restraining sensual indulgence. (Col. 2:20–23)

Actually, we should neither totally condemn nor totally approve of monks. To their credit, many of the monks through the ages did trust in Christ. In some ways, their vows expressed genuine devotion to Christ. Their labors contributed to piety, learning, and charitable service for the benefit of the larger society and for the glory of God. Yet the vows and the service alike were inevitably contaminated with the problems indicated in Colossians 2:20–23. Their motives were mixed, as are all our motives in all our striving today.

We may think that the monk's solution is too extreme, but we invent for ourselves a more subtle form of it: a pacifism or withdrawal that renounces power and confrontation, or a legalistically imposed "simple lifestyle," or disdain for sex within marriage.

But most of us in the modern West are more likely to be attracted to false compromises than to false renunciations. We join the religious dance on Sunday for the sake of our psychological well-being and in order to get some instructions about how to minimize our sufferings. The rest of the week we live like everyone else, with enough superficial Christian distinctives and restraints to salve our conscience and give us a sense of superiority.

Christians as well as non-Christians can be attracted not only by false promises of self-centered pleasure, but also by false promises of salvation. Ideologies can offer their own forms of counterfeit salvation. Marxism promises to save us from economic sin and the worship of money by taking charge of the means of production and distributing everything fairly. We cannot master our own lust for riches, so (we falsely hope) the Marxist system will step in and do it for us.

Feminism promises to save us from the agonies of sexual confusion and lust. We cannot master our own sexual lust or shame or confusion, so feminism will produce a renovation of society that will tell us how to treat one another. In one form of feminism, sexuality is mere plumbing. If we would overcome the distortions of our past, we would find that we are really all identical. Then there is no problem. In another form of feminism, if we only allow everyone to do his or her own thing, with no stereotypes or false moralisms, we will be all right.

We are searching for liberation. Deep down we know, although we may be reluctant to admit it, that all is not well and that we are tangled, distorted, impoverished, and frustrated. We want relief. And if the Christian way is too painful, too humiliating, too incredible, or too slow, well, we will grasp for alternatives. The alternatives are thus alternative ways of salvation: they are idols.

Forms of the Beast and of Babylon meet us not only in institutions, but also in individualized, psychological fears and desires. We are driven negatively by fear and positively by lust. On the one hand, the Beast represents the temptation to worship idols through fear. We fear pain, humiliation, punishment, or the opinion of others. Fear turns us away from worshiping God and toward bowing down to whatever threatens us. On the other hand, Babylon represents the temptation to worship idols that seduce us and promise pleasure. Lust turns us away from worshiping God and toward bowing down to whatever entices us with the promise of intense thrill or satisfaction. For each person, the fears and the lusts may have a slightly different texture. So each person experiences idolatry in a slightly different form. But all of us struggle with variants of the twin idolatries of fear and lust, of the Beast and Babylon. God calls us to reject these idolatries in favor of the true fear, the fear of God, and the true desire, the desire for the satisfactions of God's presence (Rev. 22:1–5).

In short, the idolatries depicted in Revelation, as well as the true worship in Revelation, have dimensions that are both corporate and individual, blatant and subtle. In his commentary on Isaiah 13, Oecolampadius understands both sides. Corporately, "neither can Christians refrain from rejoicing with good hearts, if Rome [a corporate Babylon] should ever put an end to its tyranny." On the individual level, "through him [Christ] every day we conquer Babylon in ourselves."[5]

We should note also that idolatry has a historical dimension. Idolatries rise and fall within the nexus of historical development and judgment. Apostate Jerusalem was destroyed in A.D. 70. Rome, in its official commitment to paganism, passed away with Constantine's conversion; its corruptions were destroyed in other senses with the removal of the imperial capital to Byzantium in 330 and the sack of Rome in 410. We could look at still other events that broke the hold of idolatry.

The greatest events are Christ's death and resurrection, taken together, and his second coming.[6] But between them we can find many other judgments that are shadows of the two great judgments. Through these two great events, God also breaks the power of idolatry on a smaller scale, day by day: the Holy Spirit brings Christ to us and applies his work to us. We die and receive Christ's resurrection (Col. 2:20–3:4; 2 Cor. 4:10–12; Phil. 3:10–11). Through fellowship with Christ, God transforms us, in our individuality, our families, our churches, our communities, and our institutions.

Deceit and Blindness

To return to the main point: idolatry corrupts our understanding of God, sometimes blatantly, sometimes subtly. But whether blatant or subtle, idolatry blinds and deceives those who practice it. Idolaters fool themselves into thinking that, yes, they are worshiping God, or at least worshiping some god. They worship that which seems to them to deserve their worship. Idolaters develop a blindness to what they are really doing and the foolishness of it. As Psalm 115:4–8 points out, idols have mouths that cannot speak and eyes that cannot see. But, in addition, idols promote blindness and dumbness in their worshipers: "Those who make them will be like them, and so will all who trust in them" (v. 8).

But this blindness never amounts to a mere vacuum, an innocent absence of knowledge. We grasp the counterfeit, we grasp the substitute, only because it is a counterfeit of the true God. The counterfeit is attractive only because it imitates God. We love the counterfeit only because we cannot escape God and our dependence on him. The alternative to worshiping God is not worshiping nothing, but worshiping a substitute, worshiping a counterfeit. And the counterfeit must be sufficiently successful to give the illusion of satisfying our needs and longings for God.

Moreover, the counterfeit shows its dependence in the very act of counterfeiting. The Beast is who he is only as a counterfeiter of Christ's power and Christ's resurrection (Rev. 13:3). But his bestial character also proclaims his inferiority to Christ. As creatures, people instinctively know that they should worship Christ. They show it when they worship the Beast, who is a counterfeit of Christ. But being sinners, people prefer the counterfeit to the truth. Hence, we do not escape God even in the act of idolatry; rather, we show that we still ought to worship the original Creator. We know God and simultaneously distort and suppress our knowledge of him (Rom. 1:18–32).

In this situation, it is important to note that idolatry is not a wholly self-conscious, clearheaded, deliberate act of worship. In fact, idolatry always involves deceit and therefore confusion. We confuse God with idols. Our thinking and acting become darkened. Hence, when we serve idols, we are not fully aware of every aspect of what we are doing. Particularly in the modern secular world, where the idols are more subtle and less visible, idol worship may be tacit in character.[7] Idolatry corrupts our thinking and action, and part of the corruption makes us unaware that it is corruption.

Idolatry of any kind inevitably has an effect on biblical interpretation. If we do not know God rightly, if we replace him with an idol, then we also distort his word into the word of an idol. Our interpretations shift because our conception of the author has changed. Yet our interpretations do not necessarily shift so as to become totally absurd or nonsensical. The idol closely imitates the true God. Analogously, the false interpretation of the Bible closely imitates true interpretation. In actual practice, the true and the counterfeit subtly intertwine with one another, so that only God can accurately separate them.

Thus, the blindness of idolatry includes interpretive blindness. But as we grow spiritually, we are better able to interpret the Bible correctly.

ENDNOTES

1. Holy war is not in fact confined to chapters 6–20. Chapters 2–3 present the issues of spiritual warfare in less symbolic form. Chapters 4–5 present God, who controls

the battle. Rev. 21:1–22:5 presents the final triumph of God, the termination of the war in victory. The final exhortations in 22:6–21 reinforce the call to battle. Hence, in a broad sense, all of Revelation deals with holy war.

2. See, e.g., G. R. Beasley-Murray, *The Book of Revelation* (London: Marshall, Morgan & Scott, 1974), 207.

3. See, e.g., Beasley-Murray, *The Book of Revelation;* Leon Morris, *Revelation* (London: Tyndale, 1969); and many other commentaries.

4. Jacques Ellul, *The New Demons* (New York: Seabury, 1975); Herbert Schlossberg, *Idols for Destruction: Christian Faith and Its Confrontation with American Society* (Nashville: Nelson, 1983).

5. Johannes Oecolampadius, *In Iesaiam Prophetam HUPOMNEMATON, hoc est, Commentariorum, Ioannis Oecolampadii Libri VI* (Basel: Andreas Cratander, 1525), 105a.

6. Oecolampadius rightly points to these two greatest historical events: "Again, how greatly it pertains to faith and hope, that once Babylon was devastated by Christ, and all liberty was restored, for he says: Be of good cheer, for I have overcome the world [John 16:33]." "However, a full and true overthrow of the world will take place at the end of the ages of this world" (ibid.).

7. The work of Michael Polanyi distinguishes helpfully between explicit and tacit knowing, between focal and subsidiary awareness. See Polanyi, *Personal Knowledge* (Chicago: University of Chicago Press, 1958); Polanyi, *The Tacit Dimension* (London: Routledge & K. Paul, 1967).

CHAPTER 14

.

THE GLOBAL DISTORTION
OF INTERPRETATION

*Dottie Doctrinalist: If we get one doctrine wrong, it is likely to cor-
rupt our thinking in a lot of other areas of doctrine. Look at the Roman
Catholic idea of the authority of tradition. It is only one point of doctrine.
But error at this one point prevented them from thoroughly breaking with
doctrinal corruption and confusion in a lot of other areas.*

*Peter Pietist: I can see a parallel pattern in my devotional life. If I
allow greed or pride to grow within me, it soon corrupts my devotional
life. I no longer pray as much, and my prayers start being shallow and
perfunctory. My joy dries up. It spreads like cancer.*

*Curt Cultural-Transformationist: If a major social institution goes
bad, it can frequently have corrupting effects on almost every sector of
society. Look at what happened in the former Soviet Union. Bad government and economic failure put strains on the family, on education,
and on the environment.*

*Herman Hermeneut: Do you think that the same thing could hap-
pen in hermeneutics, in the way in which we interpret the Bible?*

We have seen that God in his triunity is the archetype for the key distinctions and structures involved in biblical interpretation. When our knowledge of God is corrupted, we may expect our interpretation to be corrupted
also. At the same time, according to Romans 1:19–21, even idolaters know
God. They worship idols against the background of a knowledge of God that
they suppress in unrighteousness. Hence, corrupt interpretation is not as bad
as it could be. Insofar as interpreters tacitly retain a knowledge of God, their
interpretive results may be better than their explicit theory of interpretation
deserves.

But our knowledge of God inextricably influences our interpretation. The following examples illustrate some of the influences.

Perspectives on Communication

As we saw in considering communication, the speaker, the discourse, and the audience are inextricably related to one another. Understanding communication involves all three as coinherent perspectives—the expressive, informational, and productive perspectives. The three perspectives coinhere by analogy with Trinitarian coinherence. But suppose an interpreter worships a counterfeit instead of the true God. Then he is likely to counterfeit the relationships between the speaker, the discourse, and the audience.

The simplest type of counterfeit is a simple monism that assigns primacy to one of the three, while trying to suppress coinherence. The speaker, the discourse, or the audience is transformed into a kind of god that becomes the supposed source of all meaning. Thus, in modern interpretive theories, we find author-centered approaches, text-centered approaches, and reader-centered approaches, all distorted by their idolatry. Yet each is a plausible counterfeit. Because God is God, coinherence still functions beneath the surface. Hence, any of the three approaches can retain some of the insights found most forcefully in the other approaches.

Our knowledge of God influences interpretation in an even more obvious way, because he is present in our consideration of speakers, discourses, and audiences. Let us consider these one at a time.

Knowing God, the Author of the Bible

First, consider the authors of the Bible. How does knowledge of God influence our understanding of the authors? There are, of course, many human authors for the various books of the Bible. But when we confess that the Bible is the word of God, we acknowledge that God is the divine author, who superintended and prepared the human authors so that they wrote just what he intended them to say. The human authors in their instrumental role should not be left out of account. But we know that they should not be left out of account only because God shows it to us in the Bible. God himself, speaking to us in the Bible, assures us that he took these people into his counsel, and gave them understanding of his ways (Num. 12:6–8; Ex. 33:13; 1 Cor. 2:16; John 16:13). Hence, God, the divine author, is right at the center of this communicating activity. To know the author is to know him. If we are darkened in our understanding of God, our knowledge of the Bible will inevitably suffer, sometimes subtly, sometimes radically. Thus, in John 8, Jesus says,

> Why is my language not clear to you? Because you are unable to hear what I say. You belong to your father, the devil, and you want to carry out your father's desire. (v. 44)

> He who belongs to God hears what God says. The reason you do not hear is that you do not belong to God. (v. 47)

> Though you do not know him [the true God], I know him. (v. 55)

Knowing God in His Connection with the Central Subject Matter of the Bible

Second, in the process of understanding, we must also know something about the subject matter of the communication. Foreigners listening to a conversation about American football might find it very confusing and understand little, unless they knew something about the rules of football and had seen a game. Likewise, to understand the Bible we must have some acquaintance with the topics that it discusses. We are bound to misunderstand some things, and to understand others poorly, unless we have some familiarity with the subject being discussed.

Of course, much of the Bible speaks about events, experiences, institutions, thoughts, and emotions that are similar to our own. Such things are, to some degree, accessible to almost any human reader. But this accessibility is still a matter of degree. For example, indignation over lying and injustice, as in Psalm 5:8–10 and other psalms, is to some extent a common experience. But, on the average, it is better understood by those who have had keen and intense encounters with injustice in their own life. Birth pangs and widowhood occur in all societies, but comparisons based on them (e.g., Isa. 13:8; 54:4) are again best understood by people who have had more direct and intense experiences with them.

In the Bible, all the details in various areas of knowledge are there to promote our salvation. The Bible focuses above all on telling us about God, who he is, what he has done, and how we are to respond. It discusses salvation:

our sin and rebellion against God, his promises, his saving works in history, his justification and reconciliation in Christ, his gift of new life in the Spirit, and so on. We cannot expect to understand and interpret such matters accurately without some knowledge of the subject matter. That is, we must have experienced salvation ourselves. We must know God, know our own sin, appropriate and trust his promises, experience justification and reconciliation in Christ, and so on. Now, to be sure, in a mysterious sense all human beings have some knowledge of these things. All human beings (except Christ himself) are sinners, and all know God (Rom. 1:20–21). All people experience in some form the pressures of guilt and alienation from God, and from these needs they might theoretically infer something about the nature of the remedy. Indeed, the religions of the world bear testimony even in their most distorted and deceitful forms that people long for salvation. All non-Christian religions offer distorted counterfeits of Christian salvation.

Without saving knowledge of God and communion with him, people stumble in the darkness of their own imaginations and desires, which they then impose on Scripture. God sends his light in order to give us saving knowledge of him (2 Cor. 4:6). His light illumines everything at once. Only when we know the holiness of God do we know the seriousness of our sin. Only when we know the grace and forgiveness of God are we freed to admit the full extent of our guilt and to refuse to shift blame. Only when we know the power and wisdom of God do we see the deeper riches of his gift of salvation. Hence, only people who know God deeply, and are themselves saved, know the subject matter of the Bible with the necessary thoroughness. And even they are, in this life, only in the process of learning these things (Phil. 3:10–14; 1 Cor. 13:9–12).

The Bible itself gives some examples of the effects of knowing God poorly. Paul describes the Gentiles as "darkened in their understanding and separated from the life of God because of the ignorance that is in them due to the hardening of their hearts" (Eph. 4:18). Peter speaks of the fact that "ignorant and unstable people distort" Paul's writings, "as they do the other Scriptures, to their own destruction" (2 Peter 3:16).

Or consider the Sadducees. They were among the religious experts of their day, and certainly knew many facts about the Bible. But Jesus indicted them "because you do not know the Scriptures or the power of God" (Matt. 22:29). Among their failings was that they did not know the power of God. Their knowledge of God was spiritually defective. Moreover, Jesus concluded his argument with them by stating that God "is not the God of the dead but of the living" (v. 32), another pointer to the centrality of knowing God.

Knowing God in Order to Know the Addressees

Third, accurate interpretation requires knowledge of the addressees of communication. In many cases such knowledge overlaps with, or is included in, knowledge of the subject matter of communication. For example, baptism "for the dead" at Corinth (1 Cor. 15:29) could be analyzed either as a question of subject matter (what issue or practice is Paul talking about?) or as a question of addressees (what were the Corinthians doing?). If we knew the answer to one question, we would simultaneously know the answer to the other.

In general, the entire set of the addressees' historical circumstances is potentially relevant to interpretation. But not all aspects of historical context are equally relevant to all types of communication. A theological treatise may have very little direct connection with immediate events, whereas a report of current events will have many connections. Particular circumstances prove to be more significant only when the text alludes to or presupposes some aspect of the circumstances. Hence, the relevant historical circumstances are in fact simultaneously part of the necessary knowledge of the addressees and part of our knowledge of the subject matter. The addressees, who understand the circumstances, take them into account as they receive the text, and we must also do the same in order to understand the impact of the text on the addressees. Likewise, textual allusions to historical circumstances have the effect of including the relevant aspects of the circumstances within the area of subject matter addressed by the text.

In short, understanding the addressees and understanding the subject matter are highly correlated. Everything that we have said about understanding the subject matter also applies to understanding the addressees.

But there are still some particular respects in which the knowledge of God affects our understanding of the addressees. First, our knowledge of God influences our discernment of the text's purposes and goals for the addressees. In writing texts, authors aim at changing the addressees in certain ways. They aim at persuading people of certain truths, or encouraging certain attitudes, or commanding certain courses of action, or the like. In the case of biblical texts, God is the primary author. Thus, knowing him is important in assessing the purpose of the texts for their addressees.

Next, knowing God influences our understanding of the addressees themselves, and how they undertake to understand. All human addressees are made in the image of God. Just as we cannot understand ourselves deeply apart from knowing God, so we cannot understand others well without that same knowledge.[1] In particular, we are likely to accuse or excuse people falsely if we are not schooled in a proper sense of God's righteousness and mercy. God's wisdom illumines the subtlety of sin.

> But should we once begin to raise our thoughts to God, and reflect what kind of Being he is, and how absolute the perfection of that righteousness, and wisdom, and virtue, to which, as a standard, we are bound to be conformed, what formerly delighted us by its false show of righteousness, will become polluted with the greatest iniquity; what strangely imposed upon us under the name of wisdom, will disgust by its extreme folly; and what presented the appearance of virtuous energy, will be condemned as the most miserable impotence. So far are those qualities in us, which seem most perfect, from corresponding to the divine purity.[2]

Knowing the addressees more deeply enables us to see how God works through the text to overcome and rebuke sin, and to provide words of healing for his redeemed people.

Next, knowing God influences our perception of how the addressees' knowledge of God affects their reception of the text. We see ways in which they may have been tempted to distort its meaning, and ways in which God provides redemptive means for overcoming such distortion.

Knowing God in Interpreting Jesus' Parables

Some of the parables of Jesus clearly exhibit this process at work. Let us consider the parable of the sower in Mark 4:2–20. This parable is, among other things, a parable about parables. It is a parable about hearing the word (4:9, 14–20, 23), and, in the immediate context, the word in question is preeminently the word of Jesus' own preaching. The comments in 4:10–12 confirm this impression by indicating that the disciples want to know about the function of Jesus' parables in general.

Now consider the interpretation of the parable, as recorded in Mark 4:13–20.[3] This passage shows that the word is received in a variety of ways. Likewise in verse 11, Jesus distinguishes two groups, "you" and "those on the outside," only one of which understands the message of his parables. The difference in effect is obviously due to the difference in the audience. One part of the audience is spiritually healthy, while the other is not. The same point is confirmed by the mysterious saying in verses 24–25. The disciples, who already "have," through their relationship to Jesus, will be "given more." Others, who have not, will experience further blindness. The hardening in 4:12, like that in Isaiah 6:9–10, represents not an arbitrary act on God's part, but a judgment on the sinfulness of the people.

The central axis in the process of understanding the parable is Jesus himself. When the disciples were alone with him (v. 10), they received his explanation of the parable. The disciples' relationship to Jesus, together with their willingness to come to him to ask questions, led to further understanding. Without this relationship to Jesus, they would not have had as much understanding.

The process through which the disciples went illustrates the more general process involved in anyone's understanding of any parable. The ministry of Jesus as a whole provides a decisive context, orientation, and illustration for his parables. Hence, those who were sympathetic with Jesus' ministry, and who already perceived in it the dawning of the saving work of God, could begin to associate the character of his ministry with the pictures from the parables, and thus provide themselves with guidelines for further reflection. However, those who were hostile to Jesus' ministry may have heard some of his parables and departed tantalized but confused. Even when they finally saw the thrust of a very pointed parable, they refused to take it to heart, but rather further hardened themselves (Mark 12:1–12).

Thus, the parables illustrate that knowledge of Jesus and his purposes exerted a telling influence on understanding. Understanding a parable was not a matter that could be approached in a safe, antiseptic, neutral objectivity. The addressees were already committed. They found themselves already in process, already belonging to some kind of soil, already being questioned about the quality of their hearing. They were already for Jesus or against him (Matt. 12:30). Moreover, their perception of Jesus' ministry cannot be separated from their spiritual knowledge of God and communion with him. Knowing God and knowing Jesus go together. To be for Jesus involved seeing that God was working salvation through him. This knowledge would only gradually blossom into the knowledge that Jesus was himself God (John 20:28). But even at the beginning, knowledge of Jesus, incomplete though it was, was intertwined with knowledge of God. Conversely, to be against Jesus was to be alienated from God himself.

All of these matters regarding the addressees affect us more directly than we might suppose. As we listen to the Bible, we also become numbered among the addressees to whom God speaks. Our relationship to God then radically influences how we relate ourselves to the text. Do we see ourselves as actually being addressed by God, or are we simply looking at an ancient text? If we remain onlookers, we may think that we escape the obligation to apply the demands of the text to ourselves. But by doing so, we show that we have misconstrued the purpose of God. God calls us, no less than others, to repentance (Acts 17:30), and he writes the text for us also (note Rom. 15:4; 4:23–25; 1 Cor. 10:11).

Thus, the quality of our knowledge of God and of our communion with him affects all three major areas involved in interpretation: it affects our understanding of the author, our understanding of the subject matter, and our understanding of the audience. The effects are often subtle in nature. But sometimes they are radical, as when the Sadducees misjudged the question of the resurrection of the dead (Matt. 22:23–32).

Many people who are in rebellion against God and whose knowledge of God is impoverished do still understand various facts from the Bible. They understand after a fashion. But what types of things they understand, how they understand them, and the extent to which they understand them are all inevitably and foundationally conditioned by the character of their knowledge of God.

Knowledge Even of "Basic" Meaning Is Affected

Jesus' parables illustrate in a particularly vivid manner the importance of our spiritual state, our relationship to God. Mark 4:11–12 asserts that "the secret of the kingdom of God" is not accessible to all. Rather, "to those on the outside everything is said in parables." The obvious implication is that Jesus spoke in parables in order to veil the truth from those outside.[4]

Contrary to Adolf Jülicher, some of the parables were mysterious.[5] They did not have a meaning that was immediately transparent to everyone. The disciples, by hearing the explanation in verses 13–20, understood a meaning that many others did not (Mark 4:34; Matt. 13:51). We cannot escape this awkward fact merely by distinguishing between meaning and application, or between technical exegesis and personal appropriation. In any ordinary sense, "meaning" as well as application is at stake here. Sinful rebels did not perceive either the meaning or the application. People were not likely to understand even a first-order meaning of some parables unless they were committed to Jesus. And the more they were committed, the more they understood (Mark 4:24–25).

Surely part of the point of the parable of the sower is that sin can have a variety of baneful effects on our reception of the word of God. For some, it can mean that they stop their ears to the word virtually as soon as they hear it, and so they never know its meaning on even a minimal level. For others, it can mean hypocrisy. They formally confess a truth, but deny it in action.

What distinguishes the insiders is that they are good soil, in fellowship with Jesus, the Master. The difference is holistic, a difference between two kingdoms. The Holy Spirit, present in Jesus' ministry, must work comprehensive change, not merely step in at the last stage to supervise the final harvesting of the fruit.

The Quest for Scientific, Neutral Objectivity in Interpretation

We may now turn to some other examples of modern theories of interpretation, asking again how knowledge of God affects these theories. We take as our first example a particularly influential form of thinking about interpretation, namely, the Enlightenment ideal. The Enlightenment developed an ideal of religiously neutral interpretation. According to this ideal, scholars should follow only the dictates of reason, not religious commitment. Scholarship should examine the Bible as a historical text, and determine its origins and meanings by rational canons of research on which persons of all religious backgrounds can agree. Scholarly interpretation ought not to be influenced by religious commitment.

This form of interpretation has proved attractive for several reasons. First, it recognized the problems and abuses that are possible with interpretation that is dominated by a long tradition (medieval interpretation) or by a theological system (as in postreformational confessional interpretation). Second, it promised a way to move beyond the theological disagreements caused by tradition and theological systems. People hoped that reason would be a source of unity where religion had become a source of contention. Third, giving a key role to reason harmonized with philosophical and cultural trends along the same lines.

In all these respects, the Enlightenment grasped some fragments of the truth. In all three areas just mentioned, it touched on truth and yet also produced a counterfeit.

Consider the abuse of tradition. Commitments to tradition or theological systems do create a potential for abuse. The tradition or theological system can become an idol. The Enlightenment saw the enslavement to idols. God was bigger and more rational that what tradition or theological systems sometimes represented him to be. The Enlightenment conception of neutral reason was a shadow of the rationality, wisdom, and self-consistency of God. Hence, it contained a fragment of the truth, and that made it attractive. But it also subtly counterfeited the rationality of God. Supposedly, people could judge the contents of revelation independently of any commitment to God. And that idea repeated Satan's distortion of the truth in Genesis 3. Rationality became an abstract, impersonal principle of consistency, a projection into the sky from sinful human ideas of rationality.

In certain respects, we may even say that the Enlightenment error concerns the Trinity. God's self-consistent rationality is his faithfulness to himself and is therefore personal. It is the Father's faithfulness to the Son and the Son's faithfulness to the Father, through the Spirit. Moreover, the wisdom of God is his Word, in whom all things hold together (Col. 1:17). But since the Trinity is incomprehensible, this sort of rationality is not acceptable to rebellious human beings. They project a unitarian abstract principle, whether this bears the name of God or Reason or Logic.

Second, the Enlightenment promised unity. What fragment of truth is represented in this promise? According to John 17:20–27 and Ephesians 4:1–16, unity in the truth is indeed God's goal for renewed humanity. But counterfeiting mixes itself with this fragment of truth. According to the Enlightenment ideal, unity among human beings comes not from greater fellowship with Christ through the Spirit, but by scholarly independence from religious commitment. The Enlightenment at this point postulated reason as a savior more promising than Christ. Reason is supposedly better at overcoming human contention and alienation. But this new savior is still close enough to the truth to be attractive; reason is a counterfeit for Christ, the wisdom of God.

Third, in the Enlightenment, the primacy of reason harmonized with certain philosophical and cultural trends. Because God is one, all truth is in harmony. Thus, here also there is a fragment of truth. But here also the truth is distorted, in that the philosophical and cultural trends of the day did not undergo redemptive transformation through Christ.

The effects of Enlightenment principles on biblical interpretation show a mixture of truth and its counterfeit distortions, just as we would expect. Consider, for example, the issue of historical research. The Enlightenment's suspicion of tradition resulted in a pronounced emphasis on recovering the original events as they actually happened, before tradition reworked them. This emphasis had a fragment of truth: God's authority implies an irreducible importance for the origin of his speech in a particular historical setting. At the same time, the Enlightenment counterfeited God's rule over history by assuming that miracles were incompatible with the idolized reason that it projected.

Or consider the issue of meaning. In accordance with the principle of rationality, the Enlightenment postulated an original unity of meaning. We should assume that rational speakers have proclaimed things that make sense. Given a reasonable amount of background information, one should be able to recover the sense, and even if the background information is insufficient, one should be able to weigh the alternatives rationally.

Here again there is counterfeiting. On the one hand, this unity of sense is close to the truth. There is indeed stability of sense according to the intention of the Father. But in accordance with the rationalistic, unitarian idolatry of the Enlightenment ideal of reason, this unity tended to be conceived as self-sufficient, independent of the knowledge of the triune God. Unity of sense was regarded as isolatable from coinherent perspectives involving application and import. Thus, the Enlightenment distorted and counterfeited the truth about God's meaning.

Idols inevitably fail. God breaks them and shows them to be worthless. Because they are counterfeits, they are derivative in character. Like Satan himself, they can never match God. Hence, those who serve them cannot find satisfaction.

So it is with the Enlightenment ideal. Abstract reason is part of an ongoing tradition, a tradition that grew and developed in human philosophical systems. As such, it fails to free us definitively from tradition. Rather, it simply subjects us to a different tradition, that of rationalism. But in the long run, this tradition fails to deliver the unity and stability for which people hope. The abstractions projected by different people are subtly different, according to the selfishness of their sin. Hence, people cannot agree even about what reason itself is. Biblical interpretation fragments. Historical reconstruction becomes problematic, and rationalistic interpreters cannot agree with one another about the meaning of a text.

By contrast, within a Trinitarian context, meaning coinheres with import. The sense of a particular text coinheres with the senses of all other biblical texts. The senses of the particulars are never understood apart from the import of the whole plan of God. Hence, differences about the sense of a particular text reside within a larger framework, in which the differences are often more like nuances within a larger whole. In agreement with Augustine, we regard as secondary the question concerning which truth is taught in a particular text, provided that we acknowledge truth as a whole. If my brother finds a different meaning than I do in a particular text, it is often nevertheless a meaning that I find in another text. On the other hand, if we are committed to a unitarian ideal of rational truth in isolated meanings, the failure to agree is catastrophic, because the perspectives of import and application are not available to maintain practical unity in the midst of disagreement in detail.

We may find similar problems in dealing with the relationships among speaker, speech, and hearer, or among the expressive, informational, and productive aspects of communication. Enlightenment rationality most easily conceives of communication as informational. And indeed it is. Thus, there is a fragment of truth in this viewpoint. At the same time, there is counterfeiting: the expressive and productive aspects tend to be either overlooked entirely or reduced to (and absorbed into) the informational aspect.

Over time, the unsatisfactory character of the reduction tends to produce reactions. Romanticism exalted the feelings and expressions of the artistic genius. Not information, but expression, was primary. Modern reader-response theories react to the boring claim of unitarian meaning by multiplying meanings through the different interpretations of different readers. Liberationist interpretation reacts to the now boring claim of neutral objectivity in scholarship by pointing to the personal, social, and economic commitments that drive scholarly activity in certain directions.

Liberationist Interpretation

As a second example, therefore, let us consider liberationist interpretation. Liberationist interpretation reacts to some of the deficiencies of the Enlightenment. In doing so, it affirms some of the truths that the Enlightenment eclipsed. Over against the Enlightenment's preoccupation with information, liberationists emphasize the productive aspect of communication. Communication, they say, is in the service of a goal, whether of oppression or liberation. Over against the individualistic tendency of the Enlightenment, liberationists stress the corporate, cultural influences on all interpretation. Over against the Enlightenment's preference for the rational interpretation of the educated, privileged intellectual, we find an emphasis on the interpretation of the poor.

Often God raises up a prophetic voice within the church to warn people of sin. But he can use pagans as well. At times, non-Christians may see Christians' sins more clearly than Christians do (in a manner parallel to the perception of Jewish sin by pagans in Romans 2:24). Surely God has used non-Christian Marxists in this very way.

Thus, one may find fragments of truth in liberationist analyses of the sins of the powerful. Among these sins we must include the sins of Christians in power and Christians who try to preserve the privileges of power and wealth. In all this analysis, liberationists are but imitating the analysis of the idolatries of power, wealth, and pleasure contained in the book of Revelation. They are longing for the liberation that God brought in the Exodus and supremely in Christ.

But liberationists, like everyone else, can be snared by counterfeits of the truth. How then shall we separate the counterfeit from the true original within liberationist theory and praxis? Again we are confronted with a subtle combination, as subtle as the subtlety of sin and the devil. The task is immense, which is why whole books can be devoted to it. It is a worthy task. But for the moment I must confine myself to a few simple observations based on Scripture.

Revelation offers an analysis, a critique, and a remedy for the sins of the powerful and the wealthy (Rev. 18). It equally offers a remedy for counterfeiting idolatries. The powerful invoke counterfeit ideologies to protect their status (Rev. 13:11–18). This critique applies to liberationist ideologies as well as others! Liberationists as well as others construct counterfeit idolatries that nourish their social and political needs. Both suggestive and disturbing are Karl Mannheim's and Michael Polanyi's analyses of why Marxism attracts alienated intellectuals by satisfying some of their unique longings.[6]

Revelation's hermeneutic of suspicion applies also to our own interpretation of Revelation! The book of Revelation cannot simply be equated at every point with our human interpretation of it. Even in the interpretation of Revelation, we are in the midst of spiritual warfare. We encounter the God of Revelation, but we also fall prey in subtle ways to the idolatries that Revelation depicts. These idolatries have corporate as well as individual dimensions. Social, economic, political, and satanic realities penetrate our existence. Hence, sinful interpreters can transform the Bible, and Revelation in particular, into an ideological weapon to promote pride, hatred, and oppression. Such perversion, sinful as it is, is yet a further confirmation of the truth of Revelation.

Despite the difficulties in faithfully interpreting Revelation, it remains the primary tool for reforming society for at least one fundamental reason: it is the pure and reliable word of God, even when we do not receive it as such. God sits on his throne, and the Lamb reigns in his presence. Through God and the Lamb, whom we meet in Revelation, we receive definitive purification, yes, resurrection, from the ways of the world. The ongoing liberation in the presence of the God of Revelation surpasses all the counterfeit liberations of this world, and ultimately encompasses whatever fragmentary insights and freeing actions the liberation movements of this world have claimed for themselves.

Reader-Response Interpretation

In reader-response interpretation, we see another reaction to the deficiencies in the Enlightenment ideal. There are a variety of reader-response theories, and we can here discuss the whole area only in a simplified way. In general, reader-response theories emphasize hearers and readers, over against the tendency from the Enlightenment to reduce everything to information. The reader makes an irreducible difference.

We also find variations on liberationist concerns in reader-response circles. The Enlightenment postulated a single, abstract meaning that is always the same. This sameness is a distortion of the stability of God and his word. Over against this distortion, reader-response approaches champion divine creativity. We can become creative in our response to texts, rather than being tyrannized, oppressed, and straitjacketed by the demand that we reiterate one meaning and nothing more. In this view, we see both an element of truth and a counterfeiting of the truth. The truth is that God is creative and that he invites readers to respond creatively in applying his word to their particular circumstances. The counterfeiting occurs if we then pretend that this creativity eliminates the stability of God and our obligation to submit to his fixed demands. God, with his unchangeable standards, is present in the realm of interpretation as well as elsewhere.

Deconstructionist interpretation also counterfeits. It utilizes the truth of the coinherence of perspectives. Odd perspectives and starting points may yet be perspectives on the whole of truth and an entire text. Deconstruction constantly uses the coinherence of language, truth, and persons. It then throws light on us and on texts, and it may show the creativity of God that is reflected in us. But it also appears to denounce all stability and "logocentrism." It wants to destroy the idols of which it is sick, and in this respect it shows truth. But it fails to detect the most fundamental idol of all: man-centeredness in contrast to biblical God-centeredness and Christ (logo)-centeredness. And thus it is only a counterfeit of Christ, who alone is able truly to destroy our idols.

Orthodox Reactions

As we have already mentioned, we who consider ourselves orthodox Christians are not entirely free from the snares of idolatry. We can see the effects of idolatry even in the way that we react to contemporary trends in interpretation. Typically, we orthodox scholars have absorbed some of the older idolatries of the Enlightenment. But these idolatries have become so thoroughly and subtly diffused throughout the world of scholarship that we are no longer aware of them. We repudiate the new idolatries in liberationist, reader-response, and deconstructionist interpretation. But we do so for mixed motives. We repudiate the counterfeit and the idolatry, to be sure. But we do so partly because the new movement threatens the old idol to which we are attached, the idol of the Enlightenment.

Or, if we are more sophisticated, we may concede that there is some fragment of truth in the new approaches. But we still fail to see the full radicalness of the new. The new approaches do not call for mere tinkering with the old. They do not say, "Add decorations, peripheral modifications, and cosmetic improvements." Rather they say, "Destroy the idol that you followed." And they offer a fundamentally new perspective on the whole process of interpretation. (Even though the new approaches are counterfeits, they are plausible, because coinherence makes it possible for one starting point to offer a vision of the whole.)

Tinkering with the old Enlightenment approach does not move beyond the unitarian idol that it represents. That is, the old rationalism of the Enlightenment demanded that one epistemology and one hermeneutical theory must provide unity without diversity. This idea of hermeneutics, with unity of structure but not diversity, is still unitarian at bottom. There is still an idol here, and tinkering does not overthrow it.

At the same time, other people, even among Christians, adopt the new approaches too uncritically. We become acutely aware of the idolatry present in the old ways, but we are not yet aware of the idolatry in the new ways. Or we may modify the new ways to eliminate the most blatant manifestations of idolatry. But here too we are content with peripheral changes, changes that still leave the root of idolatry untouched.

Social critics can warn us that it is easy to be content with the status quo from impure motives. We want to protect our personal comfort, not the truth. The ideal of reducing interpretation to technique is partly a product of Enlightenment rationalism and partly a product of the twentieth-century fascination with technique (because of the power of technique in applied science). There is some truth here. Our abilities to accomplish tasks through technique display the faithfulness of God and the skill of human beings made in his image. But this sort of ability gets counterfeited. And then we look to technique as a god. From technique we want a guarantee of success. We use technique as a counterfeit for God's promises. And we want this guarantee to bypass suffering. It must bypass crucifixion.

The same truths hold in the area of biblical interpretation. The growth of technique and of technical detail in interpretation may snare us into idolatry. We want interpretation without crucifixion. We trust in technical expertise and in method, in order to free ourselves from the fear of the agony of hermeneutical crucifixion. That is, we do not want to crucify what we think we already know and have achieved. We want painless, straightforward progress toward understanding, rather than having to abandon a whole route already constructed.

But the way of Christ involves bearing the cross. Christ offers us resurrection power, and hence the hope of renewing rather than losing the old. But the renewal always involves crucifixion. Many of us are too comfortable to be willing.

The Pervasiveness of Spiritual War

The book of Revelation, in its vision of spiritual war, may once again help us to see our situation rightly. God is present in the whole arena of earthly life. The issue of true worship is at stake at every point in life. True worship is at stake also in every area of biblical interpretation. The Trinitarian nature of God is at stake, since over and over again the basic structures of interpretation derive from who he is. Each chapter in this book may be considered as a chapter about spiritual warfare, since each chapter traces out ways in which God's character is at issue. And thus the counterfeiting of idolatry is bound to affect all aspects of interpretation.

ENDNOTES

1. John Calvin, *Institutes of the Christian Religion* (reprint, Grand Rapids: Eerdmans, 1970), 1.1.2.

2. Ibid.

3. For various reasons, not to be discussed at this point, I believe that the interpretation given in Mark 4:13–20 is not a later addition at variance with Jesus' own purposes, but supplies Jesus' own private interpretation to the disciples. The mainstream of biblical scholarship has enveloped itself in unnecessary confusion at this point. There are several contributing reasons. For one thing, the mainstream has lost confidence in the divine authority of some aspects of the Gospels' message. Second, it

does not recognize the signs of its own spiritual unbelief in relation to the personality and consciousness of the real Jesus of Nazareth (see Geerhardus Vos, *The Self-Disclosure of Jesus* [Grand Rapids: Eerdmans, 1954]). Third, it has fallen into erroneous methodologies in analyzing the transmission of gospel tradition.

4. In particular, the word *hina* ("so that") at the beginning of verse 12 is to be interpreted as an expression of purpose (Robert H. Gundry, *Mark: A Commentary on His Apology for the Cross* [Grand Rapids: Eerdmans, 1993], 202; C. A. Evans, *To See and Not Perceive* [Sheffield: JSOT, 1989], 92–99). Yet even if this part of the interpretation is not correct, the general thrust of 4:11–29 points in the same direction.

Some scholars argue against these conclusions on technical grounds and offer alternative interpretations of the key verses. (For example, see the discussion in Gundry, *Mark*, 195–204.) But note that parallel ideas occur in Isaiah 6:9–10, Mark 4, and elsewhere, all authored by the Holy Spirit, who is not in tension with Jesus. In view of the other evidence, we can see that Jesus could well have intended his parables to have a veiling function. This interpretation best fits the context of Mark 4.

I would suggest that scholars themselves are not neutral in this matter. Some may be attracted to alternative interpretations because this "veiling" interpretation does not match their idea of Jesus. Defective ideas about God, and therefore about what may be expected of Jesus, have contaminated scholarship at this point as well. In fact, at times when scholars err out of tendentiousness, they are themselves one more illustration of the principle of the parable!

5. On Jülicher's role in parable interpretation, see Madeleine Boucher, *The Mysterious Parable: A Literary Study* (Washington: Catholic Biblical Association of America, 1977), 3–10; also Craig Blomberg, *Interpreting the Parables* (Downers Grove, Ill.: InterVarsity, 1990); Leland Ryken, *How to Read the Bible as Literature* (Grand Rapids: Zondervan, 1984), 99–154.

6. See Karl Mannheim, *Ideology and Utopia: An Introduction to the Sociology of Knowledge* (New York: Harcourt, Brace & World, 1968), 136–46, 215–22; Michael Polanyi and Harry Prosch, *Meaning* (Chicago: University of Chicago Press, 1975), 3–21; Michael Polanyi, *Personal Knowledge* (Chicago: University of Chicago Press, 1958), 226–43.

■

CHAPTER 15

DISTORTIONS IN TERMS

Oliver Objectivist: I can agree with a good bit of what we have been saying. But surely now, in matters of interpretation, some things just are what they are. Everyone with sufficient technical competence can agree.

Missy Missiologist: But a cultural setting can limit who has access to technical competence. So what is the average person supposed to do?

Peter Pietist: Even if people agree on technical matters, don't their attitudes and their service to God still differ? They agree only in outward form.

Herman Hermeneut: And is the agreement so thoroughgoing as it may sometimes appear?

Objectivist: Well, take the area of word meanings. Dog means "dog." What more is there to say?

Because God is present in all interpretation, our view of him affects everything. Hence, counterfeiting and deceit, by distorting our view of God, can have an influence on details as well as on global frameworks. In fact, they affect how we deal with the very words of language. Let us see some of the ways in which this occurs.

The Destruction of Would-be Autonomous Categories

Recall from our earlier discussion that every term in language enjoys classificational, instantiational, and associational aspects, reflecting the Trinitarian character of God. If terms reflect the character of God, then idolatrous distortion can affect our treatment of them. Thus, we expect our understanding of terms to be influenced by idolatry.[1]

To begin with, what implications do we draw in considering the fundamental categories that we use in thinking, reasoning, and communicating? Consider the medieval controversy between realism and nominalism. Realism maintained that universals had a "real" existence, whereas nominalism contended that universals were simply convenient names for collections of individuals. Realism tended to exalt the unity of the universal (the class) at the expense of diversity. Nominalism tended to exalt the diversity of particulars (the individual things) at the expense of unity (the universal).

This dichotomy is in fact a false one. Unity and diversity are equally ultimate. The unity of the universal, that is, of the class or "kind," is an expression of the classificational aspect, while the diversity of the particulars is an expression of the instantiational aspect. Both presuppose each other, and neither is more fundamental than the other. There is no such thing as a pure universal that one could grasp apart from particulars. There is no such thing as a pure particular apart from the (universal-like) features that it possesses in accordance with the plan of God. The unity of class and the diversity of particularity both rest on the ontologically ultimate unity and diversity of God, as expressed in the classificational and instantiational aspects, respectively.

Our analysis has still broader implications, applicable to Western philosophy as a whole. Since before the days of Plato and Aristotle, Western philosophy has concerned itself with fundamental ontology (the theory of what exists). What is the fundamental ontological character of things? Philosophy has endeavored to explore this ontology through human thought and human language. Philosophers produce systems of categories. These categories supposedly enable us to obtain insight into the systematic character and structure of the world. For example, in Plato, the categories of "form," "good," and "idea" play a key role. In other philosophies, the categories may be different. But some particular categories always play a key role. The philosopher sets forth these categories as particularly promising for understanding the world.

In the time of Descartes and Kant, philosophy came to focus largely on epistemology (the theory of knowledge), rather than simply on ontology. In the twentieth century, it has focused on language. Through all these variations, fundamental categories have played an important role.

Now what do these categories look like under close inspection? We have to deal with words. These words belong to human language. And, as we have seen, human language is not autonomous or self-sufficient. Every single term or category of human language is dependent on divine language.

Classificational, instantiational, and associational aspects belong together—they enjoy a mysterious coinherence testifying to God's Trinitarian character. Yet pagan philosophers do not want to acknowledge that dependence. They prefer to walk in darkness, rather than light (John 3:19–20).

Characteristically, within the system of rationalistic philosophers, philosophical categories claim self-sufficiency. The categories simply are what they are. They identify themselves not in the mystery of the Trinity, but in the supposedly exhaustive clarity of self-sufficiency.[2]

Typically, philosophers exalt the classificational aspect of categories at the expense of the associational and instantiational aspects. The categories of classical philosophy supposedly need no associations or instantiation in order to be understood. In fact, if they were needed, association and instantiation would potentially introduce "impurities." The categories are grasped by pure reason or pure insight, independent of ordinary life and personal idiosyncrasies.

To be sure, the categories may typically apply to various instances, but the instances are not necessary for the existence of the categories. That is, no instantiation is really needed. The essence of a category remains completely independent of the grubby instantiations through which, in actual life, the categories may have been learned by real people. In Plato, the instantiations of the forms actually contaminate the forms and confuse knowledge by bringing in matter. In other cases, with more debt to Aristotle, the forms may exist only "in" their instantiations, but human reason still suffices in principle to distinguish the form from the particularity of its instantiations. The self-identity of what is really common to the instances is still considered unproblematic.

The rationalistic philosopher claims deity by being able to master language in one divine vision. If not all language can be mastered, at least the philosopher masters that crucial piece of language that he needs in order to make his systematic assertions and his universal claims. In his vision, the philosopher triumphs over the mystery of coinherence by reducing everything to the pure identity of a class (the identity of the category). Thus, philosophers think that they can manipulate their categories without reference to an associational aspect or an instantiational aspect. The categories are supposedly association-free and instance-free.

Philosophers are in fact human beings. Hence, they have themselves learned language from associations and instances. Their present knowledge is not in fact free from the "contamination" of their past learning, nor from their present bodily existence. They themselves are instantiations of humanity. Their own thoughts and words are instantiations of human thoughts and words. They themselves live within social and historical associations, in the context of their own bodies.

But philosophical reflection is idealized. Philosophers project their reflection out toward an ideal that is association-free and instance-free. If they are candid and alert, they may admit that this projection is somewhat idealized. But the idealization is useful, if not necessary, to provide the sort of results that they desire.

But we can now see that the particular type of idealization that characterizes rationalistic Western philosophy is intrinsically and irreducibly idolatrous. According to this approach, the ideal category is a self-identical classification, with no instantiational or associational aspect. Or, if it has instantiational or associational aspects, they are trivial and can safely be ignored in philosophical reflection. This view of categories is intrinsically monistic or unitarian.

Sometimes philosophers may admit that differentiation exists. But it still comes in at a subordinate level of application. Each category is intrinsically an undifferentiable, monadic, classificational universal, but it does somehow differentiate itself into instances when applied to the real world in practical terms.

This differentiation is analogous to the kind of differentiation postulated in a modalistic view of God. The modalistic heresy says that God in himself is one, in a pure undifferentiated manner. God reveals himself in three persons as three modes of revelation or three modes of action of the one original. God differentiates himself into Father, Son, and Holy Spirit in his contact with his creation, but not as he is in himself. Rationalistic philosophy presupposes a unitarian view or at best a modalistic view of God in its approach to fundamental categories.

If philosophical rationalism is a false trail, what about empiricism? For empiricists, the event, the datum, the percept, or the particular instance is fundamental. (Thus, modern empiricism is akin to medieval nominalism.) In essence, empiricists begin by exalting the instantiational aspect at the expense of the classificational and associational aspects. At its root, this approach is just as unitarian and just as idolatrous as the rationalistic approach. The main difference is that the instantiational aspect is deified, not the classificational aspect.

When empiricists express their views, they use categories that they consider unproblematic, universal, and self-identical. The categories of "sense data" or "physical objects" or "sense experience" function in the same deified role as the categories of rationalistic philosophy. Such a result is inevitable. If there is only one level of being and one level of knowledge, then one's own analysis, to be correct, must have virtually divine status. It must make universal assertions and at the same time be exhaustively grasped by the philosopher.

Philosophies oriented to relations have analogous difficulties. We have in mind both structuralism in its more philosophical forms and deconstruction. Here the ultimate starting point is with the associational aspect. Relational philosophies advocate unitarianism or modalism by collapsing the classificational and instantiational aspects into the associational aspect. The classificational aspect comes into being as nodes within a system of relations. The instantiational aspect comes into being as events within a system of language and culture.

Relational philosophy has the same difficulty that all pagan philosophy has when it attempts to state itself. The statements come out in language claiming universality, but without association or instantiation. Theoretical formulation falls victim to the same difficulties that beset rationalistic philosophy. Deconstruction, to its credit, sees the problem, and gives to its own discourses a paradoxical status.

Human language and human categories are in actual fact dependent on our Trinitarian God. They display God's "eternal power and divine nature" (Rom. 1:20). In fact, since God's nature is Trinitarian, human language reflects this Trinitarian nature. But non-Christians do not want to submit to the Trinitarian God. They substitute idols, whether made of wood or made of thought. They wish to be autonomous. So they make their idols, in order to govern them as well as to worship them. Their idolatry is manifest in their would-be autonomous approach to fundamental categories.

Idolatry cannot succeed. There is only one God, and he rules the world in righteousness (Ps. 97:1–2). Rationalism, empiricism, and relationalism falsify the very nature of the language that they use. Yet rationalism, empiricism, and relationalism remain plausible. They appear to give us powerful insights. Why?

They are plausible precisely because the classificational, instantiational, and associational aspects coinhere. Each is presupposed by the others, as we have seen. But each also involves the others. Each in a sense encompasses the others. The classificational aspect always involves the identification of instances in association. Properly understood, it tacitly includes the instantiational and the associational as inevitable aspects of its being.

Rationalism exploits the perspectival character of the classificational aspect in order to view all of reality through it. Similarly, empiricism uses an instantiational perspective, and relationalism uses an associational perspective. All three rely on coinherence. All three are close to the truth, as a good counterfeit must be. All three fail because they worship their own unitarian corruption rather than the Trinitarian God.

Applying the Expressive, Informational, and Productive Perspectives

We can also use a second triad of categories, namely, the communicative triad, consisting of the expressive, informational, and productive aspects. As we have seen, these three aspects belong to God's speech. By analogy, they characterize human speech. Because speech and knowledge are closely intertwined, we can also extend their application to human knowledge. By means of this triad, we can again see the deficiencies in pagan philosophical systems.

Rationalism projects the idea of absolute rationality or absolute truth. This projection utilizes the informational perspective. But the ideal is unitarian rather than Trinitarian. Rationalism denies that the truth of God is personal (the expressive aspect). And it denies that the truth of God is eternally productive (the productive aspect). Instead, it conceives of truth as a rational abstraction that is independent of practical effects. Hence, the truth so conceived is not ultimately God's truth, but the rationalist's own truth.

Pragmatism projects the idea of absolute data, that is, absolute effects. It thus utilizes the productive perspective. But again, the ideal is unitarian, denying the expressive and informational aspects. (The informational aspect is denied in that truth consists only in "effectiveness.") Note that the result idolizes an aspect of the creation (data), rather than recognizing the Creator.

Finally, subjectivism projects the idea of absolute personality, that is, absolute personal expression. It twists the expressive perspective into a unitarian counterfeit. It idolizes human personality, instead of recognizing the Creator.[3]

ENDNOTES

1. The following discussion appears in expanded form in Vern S. Poythress, "Reforming Ontology and Logic in the Light of the Trinity: An Application of Van Til's Idea of Analogy," *Westminster Theological Journal* 57 (1995): 187–219.

2. For a similar dissatisfaction with the use of formal modal logic in metaphysics, see James F. Ross, "The Crash of Modal Metaphysics," *Review of Metaphysics* 43 (1989): 251–79. From a Thomistic point of view, Ross raises many objections to the attempt to have abstract universals or predicates that are independent of instantiations (actual individuals to which they may apply). But insofar as Thomism conforms to an Aristotelian view of categories, it is still deficient.

3. John M. Frame has already arrived at the same conclusion, using his triad of perspectives—the normative, situational, and existential perspectives. See John M. Frame, *The Doctrine of the Knowledge of God* (Phillipsburg, N.J.: Presbyterian and Reformed, 1987), 73–75, 89–90, 109–22.

Frame observes that rationalism tries to reduce everything to rules, thus deifying a normative perspective. Empiricism tries to reduce everything to data, thus deifying a situational perspective. Subjectivism tries to reduce everything to the personal subject, thus deifying the existential perspective. Non-Christian systems of categories are most often rationalistic, in that the categories have no necessary attachment to the data that instantiate them (the situational perspective) or to the persons who formulate and understand them in a personal context (the existential perspective).

Alert readers will perceive that the expressive, informational, and productive perspectives are analogous to Frame's existential, normative, and situational perspectives, respectively. But the two sets of perspectives are not completely the same. My triad of perspectives applies archetypally to God and ectypally to creatures. By contrast, Frame's triad is asymmetric (as he himself recognizes, p. 63). The normative perspective is focused on the law, which is divine (p. 63). The existential and situational perspectives are oriented toward creatures, namely, people and the world.

Frame's triad is then an analogical image of mine. I believe that Frame's approach remains useful in emphasizing the interrelatedness of norm, world, and self in people's practical, concrete reception of the word of God.

·

CHAPTER 16

REFORMING THE
OGDEN-RICHARDS
TRIANGLE FOR MEANING

Oliver Objectivist: Dictionary makers don't have to go into all the things that philosophers fight about. They just do their job. So in a dictionary we have information that doesn't depend either on philosophy or on religious conviction, but merely on technical competence.

Herman Hermeneut: But don't dictionary makers, either tacitly or explicitly, have a certain framework for their understanding of what they are doing? Don't they make some key assumptions about how language operates, what words are, what meanings are, and so on?

Objectivist: Yes, but they can agree. Years ago, Ogden and Richards set out the basic theoretical framework, and it has proved serviceable ever since.

Herman Hermeneut: Let's look at it.

Both true worship and idolatry affect the details of interpretation as well as its global structure. As one example of these effects, let us consider the Ogden-Richards triangle.

The Ogden-Richards Triangle

The Ogden-Richards triangle offers a model for the nature of linguistic symbols.[1] The original diagram is reproduced below.

The three principal elements are "symbol," "thought or reference," and "referent." The symbol is a particular phonological or graphical form, such as *e-l-e-p-h-a-n-t*. The thought or reference is the meaning-content of the form, such as the idea of an elephant. The referent is the thing in the world being

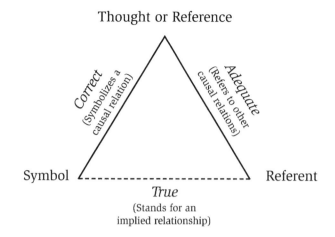

Figure 16.1. Ogden and Richards's triangle

talked about, such as an actual elephant. Stephen Ullmann prefers to relabel the vertices of the triangle as "name," "sense," and "thing," respectively.[2] Moisés Silva labels the vertices "symbol," "sense," and "referent."[3]

Our own framework can account for this natural division. But for that purpose we need to make several distinctions. First, recall that God's purposes toward us involve control, meaning, and presence (as previously defined). He controls what happens in the world, that is, he creates and controls referents. He does so through his word, which expresses meaning. The meaning includes both thought and symbol. Thus, we may correlate the referent with God's control. We correlate thought and symbol with the meaning aspect. So far, from the triad of control, meaning, and presence, we have used two aspects, control and meaning. The Ogden-Richards triangle has completely left out the third indispensable aspect, namely, the person of the language user. A careful description would then reemphasize this excluded aspect.

Now thought and symbol both belong to the meaning aspect. So what is the difference between them? Thought has to do with the things about which we think and speak. Symbol has to do with the things by means of which we speak, that is, sounds or letters, or perhaps other symbols such as Morse code or sign language.

Symbol, then, depends on the media within the created world that people use in communication. But these media, though created, have a divine archetype. Starting from John 1:1, we affirm that God the Father is the original speaker, while God the Son is the original word spoken. The Holy Spirit is the original breath carrying that word to his destination (Ps. 33:6; cf. Ezek. 37). Within the created sphere, the analogue of the Spirit is the created breath of human speakers. The word goes forth as sound in the air. We therefore claim that the sound aspect, or graphical aspect, is built by analogy on the Spirit. The thought aspect is built by analogy on God the Father, whose thought is then expressed in the Word. The lingual expression as opposed to the thought is analogous to God the Son, the Word. In sum, we have three aspects, thought, lingual expression, and sound, where the Ogden-Richards triangle has only two, thought and sound.

Ullmann and Silva, unlike Ogden and Richards, label the top vertex as "sense" rather than "thought or reference." By doing so, they focus on the lingual expression; they leave the mental activity, the thought, in the background. This alteration of terminology is useful, in that it more clearly accomplishes what Ogden and Richards probably wanted, namely, to put the focus and emphasis on the linguistic aspect. Whichever label we use, within a Christian framework we recognize a coinherent relation among thought, discourse, and sound.

To understand the triangle more precisely, we need one further distinction. Ogden and Richards did not intend that the triangle should represent merely the function of one particular utterance, but rather the systematic function of sense, symbol, and referent throughout a particular language. They wanted to describe the internal structure of a language system. Rather than dealing with one particular utterance, they were concerned with the general pattern of usage summarized in a dictionary or a grammar. The dictionary records that *elephant* means an animal of the family *Elephantidae* in all its various occurrences. Speakers of English must know the meaning of the word in general in order to understand it in particular occurrences. That is, they already know a language, including the facts reported in a dictionary.

As we might expect, the particularities of utterances and the generalities of a language are correlative to one another. The particularities show the instantiational aspect, while the generalities show the classificational aspect. Both the particularities and the generalities enjoy a system of relations with all other particularities and generalities, thus forming a system of relations. The relations manifest the associational aspect. Since the instantiational, classificational, and associational aspects image the Trinity, the distinctions among utterances, generalities, and systematic relations also image the Trinity.

It follows, then, that just as the persons of the Trinity coinhere, language generalities, utterances, and systemic relations coinhere. Thought, linguistic expression, and sound realization coinhere. Referents, meanings, and speaking persons coinhere.

Since God is one God, there is unity in language. A linguistic symbol is what it is in a unity through the joint presence of symbol, thought, and referent. Since God is triune, there exists also the possibility of distinguishing between symbol, thought, and referent.

Hence, the triangle can aid in identifying certain fallacies. The dotted baseline connecting symbol and referent, plus the additional vertex labeled "thought," remind us that the relationship between symbol and referent is indirect. Errors can arise if we ignore this complexity. In a word-and-thing approach, we may naively equate a symbol with its referent. For example, when we deal with abstract theological words like *righteousness*, the referent is similar to what we might call a theological "concept." Hence, we equate word and concept. We then fall into confusions like the "historico-conceptual method typified by *TDNT*."[4] For example, we might reason that because the Hebrew word *dabar* may *refer* to a dynamic historical event, it must *mean* "dynamic historical event." But it actually means "word, thing, matter," a quite colorless designation.[5]

Hence, the triangle is a useful summary of some distinctions that need to be borne in mind in interpretation. But we must also recognize that the triangle is a simplification in several respects.

1. It does not address the mysteries residing in the relationships between communicators and their utterances. The aspect of presence, and with it the participation of speakers, is left out.

2. It does not explicitly explore the mysteries involved in the relationship of thought to language and sense. It can give the illusion that sense and thought could in principle be isolated from one another.

3. It does not distinguish explicitly between particular utterances, linguistic generalities, and the relations of these to other linguistic regularities. It thereby runs some danger of confusion. For example, the label *symbol* could suggest focusing on a particular occurrence of *steal* in a particular copy of a particular English version of Ephesians 4:28. It would thus focus on a particular discourse. Or the same label could cover all occurrences of *steal* in all actual or even possible contexts. It would thus focus on the language generalities. Or it could examine the relation of *steal* to other words in the same semantic domain.

4. The triangle places in the background the contextual dimensions of communication. But in fact, meaning exists only in close connection with the operation of a larger context, as we have seen in our reflection on the coinherent relationship between "sense" and application and import. The

diagram proposes to analyze the function of meaning that attaches to a unit, whether a word, a morpheme, or a longer expression. But units are perspectivally related to contexts and hierarchies, producing an import.

5. The triangle can easily suggest that the symbol and the sense are neatly separable from one another. But remember that symbol focuses on the aspect of utterance, while sense focuses on the aspect of meaning. In any particular case, these are two aspects of the same communication. The two poles are not neatly separable. All meaning comes in "form-meaning composites," as Pike has argued.[6]

Hence, symbol and sense are perspectivally related. Each irreducibly involves the other, by virtue of coinherence. A symbol is not a symbol unless it symbolizes, that is, unless it already has sense that is inseparable from its identification as a symbol. Conversely, any particular sense is recognizable and identifiable as the same only through media, that is, through symbol.

When Ullmann and Silva try to define the upper vertex of the triangle more closely, the involvement of symbol with sense becomes even more apparent. Ullmann says that sense is "the information which the name conveys to the hearer."[7] This definition certainly invites us to focus on truth content or thought content. But in a broad sense a symbol "conveys information" about its own phonological form. Such information is not merely trivial, but must be utilized by any language learner or interpreter. Hence, the shape of the symbol as symbol is also part of the information conveyed. Silva defines sense as "the mental content called up by the symbol," where the words "mental" and "content" once again zero in on speakers and their thoughts. But in fact our "mental contents" in a broad sense include the loose associations between dogs and the sound of the word *dog*. Thus, the distinctions in this area do not really succeed in distinguishing in some absolutely definitive way between symbol and sense.

6. Since the referent is "non-linguistic," it is tempting to exclude the referent from linguistic analysis and to retain only the symbol and the sense.[8] This exclusion rests on the valid intuition that the situation and the understanding by persons in the situation are perspectivally distinguishable. Ullmann provides an example.

> The atom [the referent] is the same as it was fifty years ago, but since it has been split we know that it is not the smallest constituent of matter, as etymology suggests; moreover, it [the sense] has been enriched with new connotations, some fascinating, others terrifying, since the advent of the atomic age—and the atomic bomb.[9]

But again, distinguishable aspects are not separable. Meaning depends on persons who communicate, and persons depend on a situation and norms about which to talk. Hence, the referent cannot be eliminated from the analysis.

These last two points are especially important. In point 5 we assert that symbol and sense (form and meaning) are perspectivally distinguishable, but not separable. Similarly, in point 6 we assert that sense and referent are perspectivally distinguishable, but not separable. Point 6 can be made even more strongly by considering God's speech, in contrast to human speech. God governs all the facts, that is, all the referents. All the referents are what they are in response to God's words of decree. God's word governs the facts. The facts obey the word. To have facts outside God's word would be impossible and meaningless. Thus, having meaningful referents for human beings depends on having referents whose every aspect is subjected to God's word, to his "sense." All referents are, ultimately, completely comprehended by sense. Of course, the finite understanding of sense by human beings does not exhaustively grasp referents. But language as a vehicle for divine communication is not exhausted by the human understanding of it.

The Roots of Linguistic Distinctions

Another major limitation of the Ogden-Richards diagram or of any analogous diagram is that it cannot ultimately explain its distinctions. For example, the diagram expresses the fact that symbol and sense are distinguishable as form and content. Well and good. But how do we so distinguish them? Semanticists can bring forward any number of illustrations to help us grasp the distinction. They say, "The spelling of *dog* as *d-o-g* is the symbol, and the sense is the marking out of an area of meaning, such as 'an animal of the species *Canis familiaris.'*" But what makes it possible to see the general pattern from the illustrations? We intuitively know that form and content are distinct, because we already have the capacity to distinguish them. Illustrations and explanations always presuppose prior capacity to "see the point." Ultimately we have this capacity because of some unanalyzed commonness in human nature. But human nature itself does not exist in a vacuum. We know what content is because we know God's truthfulness, that is, the thought of the Father and the expression in the Son. We know what linguistic form is because we know God's articulate discourse through the Spirit.

Similarly, the distinction between sense and referent is valid, but what are its roots? This distinction in human communication images the distinction in divine communication between God's decree (sense) and the created things obeying his decree (referent).

These two distinctions thus ultimately go back to distinctions about God and the nature of his interaction with the world. The ways in which these two distinctions refer back to God is typical. We cannot understand a single distinction introduced by semanticists without the personal presence of God in his triunity.

There is still an additional complexity. Since the persons of the Trinity coinhere, the three vertices of the Ogden-Richards triangle coinhere by analogy. Most semanticists have not really admitted this fact to themselves, but continue to act to some extent as if ideally the vertices were perfectly separable. We may suspect that idolatry is a factor in this distortion. In unitarian idolatry, to have knowledge we must have knowledge of unities with no remaining diversity; that is, we must have isolatable unities.[10] The isolation of unities then also reflects a kind of polytheism, because there are still many unities. Because we live in God's world and continue to know God in spite of ourselves, these implications never become as destructive of knowledge as they could be. But counterfeiting still produces mixtures of truth and error throughout the analysis of language. Counterfeiting distorts our knowledge of the Trinitarian God. This distortion affects our knowledge of the Ogden-Richards triangle, and this distortion, in turn, affects our knowledge of the sense of every word in our language. The effects are subtle, but pervasive.

Thus, the differences in our knowledge of God affect all aspects of interpretation, including even the more technical aspects, such as the study of the sense of a particular word. Christians and non-Christians differ radically in their knowledge of God (Eph. 4:17–24). Hence, they differ radically and inevitably in interpretation. The differences affect biblical interpretation first of all and most obviously. But the same arguments lead to the conclusion that differences in knowing God affect the interpretation of any document or any created thing.

ENDNOTES

1. Charles K. Ogden and I. A. Richards, *The Meaning of Meaning: A Study of the Influence of Language upon Thought and of the Science of Symbolism,* 8th ed. (New York: Harcourt, Brace & World, 1946), 11.

2. Stephen Ullmann, *Semantics: An Introduction to the Science of Meaning* (Oxford: Blackwell, 1964), 57.

3. Moisés Silva, *Biblical Words and Their Meaning: An Introduction to Lexical Semantics* (Grand Rapids: Zondervan, 1983), 103.

4. Ibid., 107. See in particular Silva's discussion on pp. 105–7. The extensive work by James Barr, *The Semantics of Biblical Language* (London: Oxford University Press, 1961), makes the same points at length. Barr's "illegitimate identity transfer" and "illegitimate totality transfer" (p. 218) are mistakes naturally made by people who equate symbol and referent.

5. The example comes from Barr, *Semantics*, 131.

6. Kenneth L. Pike, *Language in Relation to a Unified Theory of the Structure of Human Behavior*, 2d rev. ed. (The Hague: Mouton, 1967), 62–63; Pike, *Linguistic Concepts: An Introduction to Tagmemics* (Lincoln: University of Nebraska Press, 1982), 111.

7. Ullmann, *Semantics*, 57.

8. So ibid., 56.

9. Ibid.

10. Jacques Derrida inveighs tirelessly against the illusion that we can separate the signified from the signifier, that is, the sense from the symbol. And he is right! Virtually the entire Western metaphysical tradition insists on signifying an absolute, free in principle from any concrete act of signification using a particular signifier. This tradition is contaminated with unitarian idolatry. Neither Derrida nor the metaphysical tradition has adequately reckoned with the triune God, who can be both signified and signifier in himself, and who can differentiate himself from himself within himself, in coinherence.

■

CHAPTER 17

DIFFERENCES IN THE DOCTRINE OF GOD AMONG CHRISTIANS

Oliver Objectivist: *I will admit that we run into tremendous problems if we start looking at non-Christians who interpret the Bible. They bring to the Bible all kinds of biases. But among evangelical Christians, at least, we have agreement about matters of basic worldview. So couldn't we eliminate the remaining biases among ourselves?*

Peter Pietist: *We still have to deal with the hidden sins of our hearts.*

Curt Cultural-Transformationist: *We still have to deal with the baleful influence of corrupt modern institutions. These subtly affect Christians as well, as long as we are living in the world.*

Missy Missiologist: *We still have to deal with enormous cultural differences that Christians confront in different parts of the world.*

Dottie Doctrinalist: *We still have to deal with doctrinal differences among Christians.*

Objectivist: *Let's take the case of doctrinal differences. Sure, we have minor differences about issues like baptism, church government, and eschatology. It is easy to see how a bias might enter if we come to a text that addresses one of these disputed issues. Each person will secretly hope that the text supports his position.*

But the disagreements are limited. We can become aware of what the disputed doctrines are. In our minds, we can mark the texts where bias enters. We exercise special caution with those texts. But we are still on safe ground with the great majority of texts.

Doctrinalist: *But among evangelicals some doctrinal differences are more serious. What about the differences between Calvinists and Arminians?*

Objectivist: *Yes, I can see that that is more serious. I guess there are more texts involved. But still, couldn't we limit the effects to those texts that talk about the issues dividing Calvinists and Arminians?*

Laura Liturgist: But don't doctrinal differences affect our perceptions of who it is that we worship? Who is God?

Pietist: Are you saying, Laura, that Calvinists and Arminians may differ in their doctrine of God? Both sides believe in the God of the Bible, don't they?

Doctrinalist: Yes, but we can't ignore the differences in how they understand God's foreknowledge and omnipotence.

Herman Hermeneut: But haven't we already seen that the doctrine of God affects everything else? So we seem to have a difference that would affect the interpretation of all biblical passages.

Objectivist: That's absurd. People do agree sometimes, you know. You can't say that differences in one area necessarily affect another.

We have seen that Christians differ from non-Christians. This difference is most fundamental. But, in more subtle ways, Christians also differ among themselves.

In this life, sin still contaminates even those who are born again, those whose lives belong to Christ. We know God, but our knowing is still tacitly contaminated by sin. Hence, it is no surprise that Christians differ in their knowledge of God. And those differences have effects on interpretation.

Tacit and Explicit Knowledge of God

What we state and teach we make explicit. But we also live with a tacit background of additional knowledge that we have not yet made explicit.[1] Moreover, especially when the knowledge of God is involved, we may fail to live up to our own teaching and our own explicit knowledge. Perhaps we *say* that we believe, but our works do not show it (James 2:14–26). In that case, our tacit knowledge is corrupt, while our explicit knowledge may seem to all appearances to be orthodox. Conversely, sometimes our tacit knowledge may be in better shape than our explicit teaching. James I. Packer describes one important instance of this phenomenon in regard to God's sovereignty in salvation:

> There is a long-standing controversy in the Church as to whether God is really Lord in relation to human conduct and saving faith or not. What has been said shows us how we should regard this controversy. The situation is not what it seems to be. For it is not true that some Christians believe in divine sovereignty while others hold

an opposite view. What is true is that all Christians believe in divine sovereignty, but some are not aware that they do, and mistakenly imagine and insist that they reject it.[2]

In our terminology, all Christians *tacitly* hold to divine sovereignty, but some *explicitly* deny that they do.

The recognition of tacit knowledge is especially important when we consider how our knowledge of God affects biblical interpretation. The effects of our knowledge of God are pervasive, as we have seen. But the effects are usually tacit. We are usually not consciously aware of the effects. For example, we do not usually say consciously, "Because I hold a unitarian view of God, I must hold that, in accordance with Ogden and Richards's triangle, the symbol *dog* is isolatable from the thought 'dog.'" Or, we do not often say, "Because I hold a Trinitarian view of God, I must hold that the symbol *dog* coheres with the thought and meaning of *dog*." Effects of this kind are for the most part tacit.

Consequently, the effects of our knowledge of God are complex. In one sense, in accordance with Romans 1:18–21, even atheists know God, in spite of their protestations to the contrary. Only by virtue of their knowledge of God can they use language and function in the world. Yet distortions and corruptions in our knowledge of God have destructive effects. Hence, even among Christians we cannot simply ignore differences in our knowledge of God.

An Example with Regard to Divine Sovereignty

We may take as an example the differences among Christians over the security of the believer. Some Christians, including me, think that anyone who is once saved remains saved to the end. Others think that people can be genuinely saved and yet later lose their salvation. The first view is sometimes called "eternal security," but I prefer the usual description in Reformed theology, "perseverance of the saints." We do not mean that a person is saved on the basis of an isolated, ill-defined event of "commitment" in the past, regardless of apostasy or unrepentant continuation in gross sin (cf. 1 Cor. 6:9–10; Gal. 6:7–8). Rather, we mean that God so upholds those who are savingly united to Christ, that all of them persevere in genuine faith in him until the end. God keeps us in his love, so that we continue believing in Christ. Romans 8:29, 38–39, John 6:39, 54, and Philippians 1:6 are some of the classic texts supporting this position.[3]

In this, as in other doctrinal disputes, J. I. Packer's observations apply. Some Christians in their explicit statements deny the doctrine of perseverance. But if they trust in Christ for salvation, they must at bottom trust in him comprehensively. Hence, they are in fact trusting in him to hold them fast and cause them to persevere. They believe tacitly the doctrine that they deny explicitly.

But the explicit differences in doctrine do make a difference. And this difference touches on the doctrine of God. At least in many cases, people on the two sides of this controversy hold different views concerning the relation of God's will to man's will. We who believe in perseverance believe that God can work his will through human wills. We know that saints continue to sin. And they can harden themselves. They can refuse to repent for a time. The human will is thus an active reality. But God works in and through human willing, and can turn the heart as he wishes (Prov. 21:1; cf. Phil. 2:12–13).

On the other hand, those who deny perseverance often think of the human will as "inviolable" and ultimate in the sense that God either cannot or will not "interfere" with human decision-making. God is doing his part, but it is largely up to us to decide whether we will apostatize.

We find, then, two conceptions of the human will in relation to God's will. And behind them are different conceptions of God's will and plan with respect to mankind in general.

Hence, the larger doctrinal differences between theological systems are at work here. There are many dimensions to the issues here, as the multifaceted controversies among Arminians, Calvinists, Lutherans, and Roman Catholics demonstrate. Not one doctrine but many are at stake. When we consider the effects of whole systems of doctrine, it is not merely a few verses, but a great many verses, whose interpretation is affected.

But the effects may extend even beyond those verses that speak explicitly about the human will or the divine will. Suppose that we hold corrupt conceptions in this matter. These corruptions may easily affect our interpretation of language and history. Human speaking involves responsibility and creativity before God, the speaker. Human action involves responsibility and creativity before God, the actor. Hence, differences on this issue have subtle effects on our judgments about human speaking and acting. If we wrongly see human action as independent of God's control, won't our belief affect our view of the men who wrote Scripture? Did they act "independently," or were their actions so controlled by God that the result is also fully God's word, as the Bible teaches (2 Peter 1:21)?

Moreover, our understanding of the human will inevitably affects our understanding of God's will. People make genuine decisions in accordance with their desires. They have a kind of earthly "creativity" in action. This creativity is a finite image of God's original, infinite creativity. What then is the relationship between human creativity and the stability of our union with Christ? The ultimate background to these questions is the relationship between the stability and the creativity of God. These are perspectivally related aspects of a triune God. Our knowledge of the harmony between human willing and the stability and constancy of God's plan ultimately derives from our knowledge of God in his triunity. When our knowledge is corrupted at this point, it corrupts our knowledge at all other points at which God's triunity is important; that is, it affects all the topics that we have discussed in this book. This one doctrinal difference thus threatens to contaminate biblical interpretation in a pervasive fashion.

Conclusions About Differences in Biblical Interpretation

What do we conclude? The fact is that Christians disagree with respect to the doctrine of God. As long as such differences exist, we cannot expect to have generically "Christian" biblical interpretation. Rather, we will have Arminian, Calvinistic, and other kinds of biblical interpretation. The differences do not merely impinge, as one might think, on a few hotly disputed texts that speak directly about the sovereignty of God in salvation. Rather, the effects impinge in principle on every passage in the Bible, and on every single event described in the Bible.

Fortunately, there is only one God. And we do not escape his presence or his grace in spite of our sin. Even to the degree that interpretations of biblical texts are counterfeit in nature, they are still counterfeits of the truth. The truth is the word of God that never passes away and that will triumph for all eternity (Matt. 24:35). Full unity among Christians in their interpretation is an eschatological goal rather than a present possession (Eph. 4:13–15). Yet unity is real even today, by virtue of the gift of God and our union with Christ (Eph. 4:3–6). God has given us a Bible that speaks clearly about the major issues of salvation. He has given us the Spirit and renewed our minds so that we are willing to receive his teaching. We can rejoice in what he has given us, even as we realize that we can still grow (1 Cor. 13:12).

ENDNOTES

1. See, e.g., the discussion of tacit knowledge in Michael Polanyi, *The Tacit Dimension* (London: Routledge & K. Paul, 1967); Polanyi, *Personal Knowledge* (Chicago: University of Chicago Press, 1958).

2. J. I. Packer, *Evangelism and the Sovereignty of God* (Chicago: Inter-Varsity, 1961), 16.

3. For fuller discussion, see, e.g., Louis Berkhof, *Systematic Theology,* 4th ed. (Grand Rapids: Eerdmans, 1968), 545–49; Loraine Boettner, *The Reformed Doctrine of Predestination* (Philadelphia: Presbyterian and Reformed, 1963), 182–201; G. C. Berkouwer, *Faith and Perseverance* (Grand Rapids: Eerdmans, 1958).

CHAPTER 18

•

THE REDEMPTION OF INTERPRETATION

Fatima Factualist: It seems that sin contaminates our vision of God. And from there it can contaminate everything. It seems we are in a desperate situation. What can we do about it?

Peter Pietist: We can repent, that's what! God has redeemed us, and he will continue to redeem us. We have to trust that he will remove all the contamination.

Oliver Objectivist: Sin is a problem, all right. But is subjective sin the only thing that matters? People could easily believe that objectivity is only for the next world, for the time when we are finally made perfect. What's to prevent our giving up Bible study for now and letting everyone run wild?

Curt Cultural-Transformationist: One thing to prevent it is our practical needs. We can't waste time making excuses or putting forward crazy interpretations when the world out there needs transforming.

Laura Liturgist: And God prevents our straying. Don't forget the role of worship in our transformation and purification. Meeting God is at the heart of redemption.

Missy Missiologist: And let's not forget the role that exposure to other cultures can play.

God is present in all of his creation. He is present in all of our knowing. Our knowledge of God and our communion with him affect our interpretation of the Bible in every area. We have looked at a few of these areas: our conception of the Bible, truth, meaning, communication, interpretive theory, history, global hermeneutical frameworks, semantics, and lexicography (through the Ogden-Richards triangle).

But we are blinded by sin (2 Cor. 4:3–4). We need to grow "in the knowledge of God" (Col. 1:10), corporately as well as individually (Eph. 4:11–16). At the heart of interpretive growth and growth in biblical understanding is continued redemptive growth through union with Christ. We join with Paul in saying, "I want to know Christ and the power of his resurrection and the fellowship of sharing in his sufferings, becoming like him in his death, and so, somehow, to attain to the resurrection from the dead" (Phil. 3:10–11). We participate in Christ's triumph.

In the Bible, God speaks his word to us, not to achieve the triumph of autonomous human subjectivity or the meaninglessness of infinite chaotic plurality, but the triumph of his grace. He forgives us. He justifies us. He heals us.

He does these things in the realm of biblical interpretation as in every other realm. As the Lover, he now issues his invitation to come and dine at his table. "Blessed are those who are invited to the wedding supper of the Lamb!" (Rev. 19:9). "Whoever is thirsty, let him come; and whoever wishes, let him take the free gift of the water of life" (Rev. 22:17). "You will fill me with joy in your presence, with eternal pleasures at your right hand" (Ps. 16:11). In his word, God even now gives us eternal communion with himself: "The words I have spoken to you are spirit and they are life" (John 6:63).

Jesus Christ has opened the door to heaven (Heb. 10:19–20). He has given the Holy Spirit to guide us to himself (Acts 2:33; John 16:12–16). The church, led by the Spirit, feeds on the truth of Christ.

Rejecting Worldly Irrationalism

It would be easy to misunderstand this invitation of God in either of two ways: from the point of view of irrationalism, or from the point of view of rationalism. Let us consider irrationalism first. Our age is highly addicted to the drugs of boundless irrationalism, egoism, hedonism, and subjectivism. We want to go our own way, to do what we want, to be our own gods. If we can use religious language and even the Bible itself to justify our ways, we will gladly take this foolish route. We inject our own ideas into the biblical text. We lazily content ourselves with the views with which we are already comfortable.

But at root we are rebelling. God condemns it. God, the warrior, will cut us down and destroy us by his word for so doing. But in Christ he comes not only to destroy the old man, but to bring to life the transformed new man in the image of Christ (Col. 3:9–10). God the Father chastises his children, in order that we may share his holiness (Heb. 12:4–11).

What I am saying is that the Bible is not a wax nose that we can twist into whatever shape suits our fancy. Rather, the word of God is an unchangeable standard that governs us. The word of God is more destructive than fire and harder than rock (Jer. 23:29). The person who humbly listens soon enough discovers plenty of hard, upsetting teachings and demands. He finds plenty of things at odds with what he would like to believe. No matter where he may have started, he finds himself more and more at odds with his native culture. Look at what the modern West does not welcome, but which the Bible clearly sets forth: the reality of God, the exclusive claims of the gospel, the destruction of human pride in the cross, the reality of hell, the practice of identifying and excommunicating heretics, the reality of demons and demon possession, the denunciation of Mammon, and the obligation to honor authority in the church, the family, marriage, government, and business.

Autonomous irrationalists want control. They want control of their lives independent of what God says. So they aspire to control even what God says by putting their own words into God's mouth. God's word controls them too, by locking them into their self-chosen prison of the echo chamber of their would-be autonomous voice. God calls upon us to humble ourselves. Let us admit that our prison is pure misery, open the prison door, and hear his voice.

Rejecting Worldly Rationalism

On the other hand, our age is equally addicted to the drugs of boundless rationalism, scientism, and objectivism. The addict is likely to see in my words only another, more dangerous drug of subjectivism. The addict does not recognize the distinctive qualities of real food. I may seem to rationalists to be talking about the utter destruction of scholarship and rationality, whereas in fact I am talking about taking off the old man in order to put on the new (Col. 3:9–10), about dying to an autonomous conception of rationality in order to put on true rationality through fellowship with the sanity and rationality of God himself.

The rationalist then says, "How? Specify the way. Lay it out clearly, and specify the limits and controls." In a sense, I have done so, particularly using the transmission perspective on interpretation and laying out three steps. In a sense I have dealt with the same issue by discussing the truth and its counterfeits. We could add more to these chapters. We could say much more about what characterizes proper and improper interpretation.

But people who are addicted to rationalism will never find themselves satisfied with an approach that is as open-ended as mine. We are tempted to want to reduce everything to mechanical technique, to pin everything down. We fear that the only alternative to nailing down every aspect of interpretation is a boundless, irrational subjectivity. To those who are addicted in this way, I must point out that the only remedy is spiritual, and that it cannot be fathomed or reduced to technique. Nicodemus asks "how," and Jesus replies,

> I tell you the truth, no one can enter the kingdom of God unless he is born of water and the Spirit. Flesh gives birth to flesh, but the Spirit gives birth to spirit. You should not be surprised at my saying, "You must be born again." The wind blows wherever it pleases. You hear its sound, but you cannot tell where it comes from or where it is going. So it is with everyone born of the Spirit. (John 3:5–8)

Thomas also asks Jesus a "how" question: "Lord, we don't know where you are going, so how can we know the way?" And Jesus has the answer: "I am the way and the truth and the life. No one comes to the Father except through me" (John 14:5–6).

Autonomous rationalists want perfect control and transparency that is reducible to technique. But only God controls transcendently. God's word controls us, our every thought, and our every move in interpretation. God calls us to humble ourselves and admit that we are but weak, emotion-laden creatures.

Redemption

So what do we do?

The twentieth-century West can be a very distracting place. The sheer volume of activity and the size of the marketplace of ideas tempt us to be "worried and upset about many things" (Luke 10:41). We are rushing about like Martha in Luke 10:38–42. But "only one thing is needed" (v. 42). That one thing can be expressed in a variety of ways, but they all boil down to this: standing in awe of God. The Scriptures put it in various ways:

> Mary . . . sat at the Lord's feet listening to what he said. (Luke 10:39)

> Now this is eternal life: that they may know you, the only true God, and Jesus Christ, whom you have sent. (John 17:3)

The fear of the LORD is the beginning of knowledge, but fools despise wisdom and discipline. (Prov. 1:7)

Hear, O Israel: The LORD our God, the LORD is one. Love the LORD your God with all your heart and with all your soul and with all your strength. (Deut. 6:4–5)

Johannes Oecolampadius, in expounding Isaiah's vision in Isaiah 6, explains at greater length:

Whoever acts as a preacher, observe in Isaiah 6 the nature of your office. The task is this, that with Isaiah you may first be a disciple rather than a teacher, and may be among those who have seen God, those whom Scripture calls "taught by God" [1 Thess. 4:9]. May you also be called by God, as was Aaron [Heb. 5:4], and not like Nadab and Abihu [Lev. 10:1–3], and Korah, and others [Num. 16:1–35].

Uzziah intruded into sacred things from his own audacity [2 Chron. 26:16–21]. May the desire of Uzziah die in you first. Such desire dies if you do not receive glory from people [John 5:41]. For from arrogance is born in the mind the contagious disease of leprosy, which is a symbol of heresy.

That you also may see, with Moses, that great vision in the burning bush, take off your shoes [Ex. 3:1–10]. Throw off the garment made of skins and from the earth, filthiness and dirtiness of passions. With them you will not be fitting. Having put them off, you may be sent or may teach. That you may be sure that you are called, you must be prostrated Saul, and rise up Paul [Acts 9:3–19]; you may no longer seek the things which are of the flesh, the things which belong to pharisaical righteousness [Phil. 3:4–6], the things which are yours, but those of Jesus Christ, and those of others who are in Jesus [Phil. 2:21, 4].

Withdraw, you also, with Ezekiel to the river Chebar [Ezek. 1:1], lest you seek to be praised by people and to be called rabbi [Matt. 23:7–8].

And when you know God and see how great is his majesty, beyond profound and inscrutable judgment, and how great is his goodness [Ex. 34:6], then, if the vision be a call to teach, teach. Otherwise, you will be among those who run but are not sent [Jer. 23:21–22], and instead of the word of God you offer the trash of your dreams.

If you search the Scriptures, in them you will see God. And when Uzziah has died, you may declare God fullest and best.[1]

Hermeneutical salvation, like all other aspects of salvation, is by grace alone. We act with hermeneutical responsibility only because God has acted on us, through the Spirit of Christ, the Redeemer (John 15:16; 6:37–40, 65). The beginning of the Christian life comes through God's grace, but progress after that beginning also comes through God's grace (Gal. 3:3). Far from eliminating work and excusing laziness, grace is the basis for vigorous and fruitful work, the work of scholarship, the work of meditation, the work of loving God, and the work of painful obedience in the world:

> If anyone would come after me, he must deny himself and take up his cross daily and follow me. For whoever wants to save his life will lose it, but whoever loses his life for me will save it. (Luke 9:23–24)

> Continue to work out your salvation with fear and trembling, for it is God who works in you to will and to act according to his good purpose. (Phil. 2:12–13)

> Therefore, my dear brothers, stand firm. Let nothing move you. Always give yourselves fully to the work of the Lord, because you know that your labor in the Lord is not in vain. (1 Cor. 15:58)

People who want to make hermeneutical progress through autonomous control cut themselves off from the living water. Those who grow in union with Christ go from strength to strength (Ps. 84:7), "until we all reach unity in the faith and in the knowledge of the Son of God and become mature, attaining to the whole measure of the fullness of Christ" (Eph. 4:13).

ENDNOTE

1. Johannes Oecolampadius, *In Iesaiam Prophetam HUPOMNEMATON, hoc est, Commentariorum, Ioannis Oecolampadii Libri VI* (Basel: Andreas Cratander, 1525), 57a–57b. The translation and the scriptural references are mine. I have reworded some sentences for smoothness.

BIBLIOGRAPHY

Augustine. *Confessions.* In *A Select Library of the Nicene and Post-Nicene Fathers of the Christian Church,* edited by Philip Schaff. Reprint. Grand Rapids: Eerdmans, 1979.

Barr, James. *The Semantics of Biblical Language.* London: Oxford University Press, 1961.

Beasley-Murray, G. R. *The Book of Revelation.* London: Marshall, Morgan & Scott, 1974.

Beckwith, Roger T. *The Old Testament Canon of the New Testament Church and Its Background in Early Judaism.* Grand Rapids: Eerdmans, 1985.

Berkhof, Louis. *Principles of Biblical Interpretation.* Grand Rapids: Baker, 1950.

———. *Systematic Theology.* 4th ed. Grand Rapids: Eerdmans, 1968.

Berkouwer, G. C. *Faith and Perseverance.* Grand Rapids: Eerdmans, 1958.

———. *Holy Scripture.* Grand Rapids: Eerdmans, 1975.

Blomberg, Craig. *Interpreting the Parables.* Downers Grove, Ill.: InterVarsity, 1990.

Boettner, Loraine. *The Reformed Doctrine of Predestination.* Philadelphia: Presbyterian and Reformed, 1963.

Boucher, Madeleine. *The Mysterious Parable: A Literary Study.* Washington: Catholic Biblical Association of America, 1977.

Calvin, John. *Institutes of the Christian Religion.* Reprint. Grand Rapids: Eerdmans, 1970.

Carson, D. A., and John D. Woodbridge, eds. *Hermeneutics, Authority, and Canon.* Grand Rapids: Zondervan, 1986.

———, eds. *Scripture and Truth.* Grand Rapids: Zondervan, 1983.

Clowney, Edmund P. *Preaching and Biblical Theology.* Grand Rapids: Eerdmans, 1961.

———. *The Unfolding Mystery: Discovering Christ in the Old Testament.* Colorado Springs: Navpress, 1988.

Eddy, Mary Baker. *Science and Health with Key to the Scriptures.* Boston: Trustees under the Will of Mary Baker G. Eddy, 1934.

Ellul, Jacques. *The New Demons.* New York: Seabury, 1975.

Evans, C. A. *To See and Not Perceive.* Sheffield: JSOT, 1989.

Fairbairn, Patrick. *The Typology of Scripture.* Reprint. Grand Rapids: Baker, 1975.

Frame, John M. "The Doctrine of the Christian Life." Unpublished classroom syllabus, Westminster Theological Seminary in California, Escondido, California, n.d.

———. *The Doctrine of the Knowledge of God.* Phillipsburg, N.J.: Presbyterian and Reformed, 1987.

———. *Perspectives on the Word of God: An Introduction to Christian Ethics.* Phillipsburg, N.J.: Presbyterian and Reformed, 1990.

———. "Scripture Speaks for Itself." In *God's Inerrant Word,* edited by John W. Montgomery, 178–200. Minneapolis: Bethany Fellowship, 1974.

Gaffin, Richard B., Jr. *The Centrality of the Resurrection: A Study in Paul's Soteriology.* Grand Rapids: Baker, 1978.

Gaussen, Louis. *Theopneustia: The Bible, Its Divine Origin and Entire Inspiration.* Reprinted as *The Divine Inspiration of the Bible.* Grand Rapids: Kregel, 1971.

Gruenler, Royce G. *Meaning and Understanding: The Philosophical Framework for Biblical Interpretation.* Grand Rapids: Zondervan, 1991.

Gundry, Robert H. *Mark: A Commentary on His Apology for the Cross.* Grand Rapids: Eerdmans, 1993.

Hirsch, E. D. *Validity in Interpretation.* New Haven: Yale University Press, 1967.

Hodge, Charles. *Systematic Theology.* Reprint. Grand Rapids: Eerdmans, 1970.

Jaki, Stanley L. *The Road of Science and the Ways to God.* Chicago: University of Chicago Press, 1980.

Kline, Meredith G. *The Structure of Biblical Authority.* Grand Rapids: Eerdmans, 1972.

———. *Treaty of the Great King: The Covenant Structure of Deuteronomy: Studies and Commentary.* Grand Rapids: Eerdmans, 1963.

Kline, Meredith M. "The Holy Spirit as Covenant Witness." Th.M. thesis, Westminster Theological Seminary, 1972.

Kuhn, Thomas S. *The Structure of Scientific Revolutions.* 2d ed. Chicago: University of Chicago Press, 1970.

Ladd, George E. *A Theology of the New Testament.* Grand Rapids: Eerdmans, 1974.

Lovelace, Richard F. *Dynamics of Spiritual Life: An Evangelical Theology of Renewal.* Downers Grove, Ill.: Inter-Varsity, 1979.

McCartney, Dan, and Charles Clayton. *Let the Reader Understand: A Guide to Interpreting and Applying the Bible.* Wheaton, Ill.: Victor Books, 1994.

McKim, Donald K., ed. *The Authoritative Word: Essays on the Nature of Scripture.* Grand Rapids: Eerdmans, 1983.

Mannheim, Karl. *Ideology and Utopia: An Introduction to the Sociology of Knowledge.* New York: Harcourt, Brace & World, 1968.

Montgomery, John W., ed. *God's Inerrant Word.* Minneapolis: Bethany Fellowship, 1974.

Morris, Leon. *Revelation.* London: Tyndale, 1969.

Nyquist, James F., and Jack Kuhatschek. *Leading Bible Discussions.* Rev. ed. Downers Grove, Ill.: InterVarsity, 1985.

Oecolampadius, Johannes. *In Iesaiam Prophetam HUPOMNEMATON, hoc est, Commentariorum, Ioannis Oecolampadii Libri VI.* Basel: Andreas Cratander, 1525.

Ogden, Charles K., and I. A. Richards. *The Meaning of Meaning: A Study of the Influence of Language upon Thought and of the Science of Symbolism.* 8th ed. New York: Harcourt, Brace & World, 1946.

Packer, James I. *Evangelism and the Sovereignty of God.* Chicago: Inter-Varsity, 1961.

——. *"Fundamentalism" and the Word of God.* Grand Rapids: Eerdmans, 1958.

Pike, Kenneth L. *Language in Relation to a Unified Theory of the Structure of Human Behavior.* 2d ed. The Hague: Mouton, 1967.

——. *Linguistic Concepts: An Introduction to Tagmemics.* Lincoln: University of Nebraska Press, 1982.

Pike, Kenneth L., and Evelyn G. Pike. *Grammatical Analysis.* Dallas, Tex.: Summer Institute of Linguistics, 1977.

Polanyi, Michael. *Personal Knowledge.* Chicago: University of Chicago Press, 1958.

——. *The Tacit Dimension.* London: Routledge & K. Paul, 1967.

Polanyi, Michael, and Harry Prosch. *Meaning.* Chicago: University of Chicago Press, 1975.

Poythress, Vern S. "Christ the Only Savior of Interpretation." *Westminster Theological Journal* 50 (1988): 305–321.

——. "Divine Meaning of Scripture." *Westminster Theological Journal* 48 (1986): 241–79.

———. "A Framework for Discourse Analysis: The Components of a Discourse, from a Tagmemic Viewpoint." *Semiotica* 38, no. 3/4 (1982): 277–98.

———. "God's Lordship in Interpretation." *Westminster Theological Journal* 50 (1988): 27–64.

———. *Philosophy, Science and the Sovereignty of God.* Nutley, N.J.: Presbyterian and Reformed, 1976.

———. "Reforming Ontology and Logic in the Light of the Trinity: An Application of Van Til's Idea of Analogy." *Westminster Theological Journal* 57 (1995): 187–219.

———. "Science as Allegory." *Journal of the American Scientific Affiliation* 35 (1983): 65–71.

———. *The Shadow of Christ in the Law of Moses.* Reprint. Phillipsburg, N.J.: Presbyterian and Reformed, 1995.

———. *Symphonic Theology: The Validity of Multiple Perspectives in Theology.* Grand Rapids: Zondervan, 1987.

Ridderbos, Herman. *The Coming of the Kingdom.* Philadelphia: Presbyterian and Reformed, 1969.

———. *Redemptive History and the New Testament Scriptures.* Revised. Phillipsburg, N.J.: Presbyterian and Reformed, 1988.

Robertson, O. Palmer. *The Christ of the Covenants.* Grand Rapids: Baker, 1980.

Rogers, Jack, and Donald McKim. *The Authority and Interpretation of the Bible: An Historical Approach.* New York: Harper & Row, 1979.

Ross, James F. "The Crash of Modal Metaphysics." *Review of Metaphysics* 43 (1989): 251–79.

Ryken, Leland. *How to Read the Bible as Literature.* Grand Rapids: Zondervan, 1984.

Schaeffer, Francis A. *Escape from Reason.* Downers Grove, Ill.: InterVarsity, 1968.

———. *The God Who Is There.* Chicago: InterVarsity, 1968.

Schlossberg, Herbert. *Idols for Destruction: Christian Faith and Its Confrontation with American Society.* Nashville: Nelson, 1983.

Selwyn, Edward G. *The First Epistle of St. Peter.* 2d ed. London: Macmillan, 1947.

Silva, Moisés. *Biblical Words and Their Meaning: An Introduction to Lexical Semantics.* Grand Rapids: Zondervan, 1983.

———. "Ned B. Stonehouse and Redaction Criticism." *Westminster Theological Journal* 40 (1977–78): 77–88, 281–303.

Sterrett, T. Norton. *How to Understand Your Bible.* Rev. ed. Downers Grove, Ill.: InterVarsity, 1974.

Stonehouse, Ned B., and Paul Woolley, eds. *The Infallible Word.* Reprint. Grand Rapids: Eerdmans, 1953.

Strom, Mark R. *Days Are Coming: Exploring Biblical Patterns.* Sydney: Hodder and Stoughton, 1989.

Thiselton, Anthony C. *New Horizons in Hermeneutics: The Theory and Practice of Transforming Biblical Reading.* Grand Rapids: Zondervan, 1992.

Ullmann, Stephen. *Semantics: An Introduction to the Science of Meaning.* Oxford: Blackwell, 1964.

Van Der Laan, Harry. *A Christian Appreciation of Physical Science.* Hamilton, Ont.: Association for Reformed Scientific Studies, 1966.

Van Til, Cornelius. *Christian-Theistic Evidences.* Nutley, N.J.: Presbyterian and Reformed, 1976.

Vos, Geerhardus. *Biblical Theology: Old and New Testaments.* Grand Rapids: Eerdmans, 1966.

———. *The Self-Disclosure of Jesus.* Grand Rapids: Eerdmans, 1954.

Wald, Oletta. *The Joy of Discovery in Bible Study.* Rev. ed. Minneapolis: Augsburg, 1975.

Warfield, Benjamin B. *The Inspiration and Authority of the Bible.* Reprint. Philadelphia: Presbyterian and Reformed, 1967.

Wolterstorff, Nicholas. "The AACS in the CRC." *Reformed Journal* 24, no. 10 (December 1974): 9–16.

———. *Divine Discourse: Philosophical Reflections on the Claim That God Speaks.* Cambridge: Cambridge University Press, 1995.

Woodbridge, John D. *Biblical Authority: A Critique of the Rogers/McKim Proposal.* Grand Rapids: Zondervan, 1982.

INDEX OF SCRIPTURE